THE AESTHETICS OF DESIGN

THE AESTHETICS OF DESIGN

Jane Forsey

OXFORD
UNIVERSITY PRESS

OXFORD
UNIVERSITY PRESS

Oxford University Press is a department of the University of Oxford.
It furthers the University's objective of excellence in research, scholarship,
and education by publishing worldwide.

Oxford New York
Auckland Cape Town Dar es Salaam Hong Kong Karachi
Kuala Lumpur Madrid Melbourne Mexico City Nairobi
New Delhi Shanghai Taipei Toronto

With offices in
Argentina Austria Brazil Chile Czech Republic France Greece
Guatemala Hungary Italy Japan Poland Portugal Singapore
South Korea Switzerland Thailand Turkey Ukraine Vietnam

Published in the United States of America by
Oxford University Press
198 Madison Avenue, New York, NY 10016

Library of Congress Cataloging-in-Publication Data
Forsey, Jane.
The aesthetics of design / Jane Forsey.
pages cm
Includes bibliographical references.
ISBN 978-0-19-996436-9 (hardcover : alk. paper) 1. Aesthetics.
2. Design—Philosophy. I. Title.
BH39.F659 2013
111'.85—dc23
2012026324
ISBN-13: 978-0-19-996436-9

3 5 7 9 8 6 4
Printed in the United States of America
on acid-free paper

For Bill,

who has a very nice, if slightly inferior, coffee-pot.

CONTENTS

ACKNOWLEDGMENTS

I would like to thank Bonnie Penfold, for her enthusiastic support for, and contributions to, the early stages of the project; and Beth Savickey, for the right advice, at the right time, in the right way. I am particularly grateful to Lars Aagard-Mogensen and Else Mogensen for their generosity, kindness, and friendship, and for providing me with a tranquil place to think about philosophy.

This project has been assisted by funding from the University of Winnipeg's Research Office.

Introduction

> The aspects of things that are most important for us are hidden because of their simplicity and familiarity (One is unable to notice something because it is always before one's eyes).
>
> Wittgenstein, *Philosophical Investigations* §129.[1]

Wittgenstein's words perhaps best capture the underlying motivation that drives this project: a comprehensive study of design is an attempt to make visible the apparently mundane and familiar, an attempt to uncover the significance of what is so ordinary as to pass beneath notice. From the teapot to the shoe, from the dustpan to the bicycle, there is almost no part of our daily lives that has not been designed, manipulated, and manufactured, and few of our daily activities that do not interact with design in some direct way. Design, it has been suggested, "is one of the basic characteristics of what it is to be human, and an essential determinant of the quality of human life."[2] Its power and ubiquity are not to be underestimated: designed objects save our lives (the portable defibrillator), ease our

1 I am grateful to Beth Savickey for bringing this passage, and the philosophical import of making visible the everyday, to my attention. Any misrepresentation of Wittgenstein's remark is entirely my own.

2 John Heskett, *Toothpicks and Logos: Design in Everyday Life* (New York: Oxford University Press, 2002), 4.

labours (the automatic washing machine), entertain us (the television), shape our homes and workspaces (the condominium, the cubicle), as much as they can kill us (the automatic weapon). Yet for all this, design itself largely passes beneath our direct notice.

Uncovering the significance of what is "always before one's eyes" is, fundamentally, a philosophical labour, as Wittgenstein saw, but in the case of design it is also an aesthetic one: beautiful or classic designs are lauded in annual competitions and in permanent museum collections, such as MOMA in New York, the Design Museum in London, and the Pinakothek der Moderne in Munich. These are designs made aesthetically visible in a particularly public and institutionalized way. More specifically, however, the way we shape our environments, furnish our homes, and choose our dress involves aesthetic choices and judgements as much as it does practical and moral considerations. We opt for that particular sofa, when any one would really do; we paint, repair, and renovate our homes beyond the requirements of strict comfort and function; we agonize over the colour and style of the cars we drive and we take great care in how we lay the dinner table before our guests appear. These more personal and quotidian choices and experiences are no less aesthetic, and form, I wish to suggest, a central part of our interactions with design. Yet for all this, design has been virtually ignored by philosophical aesthetics. Aesthetic theory has traditionally occupied itself with fine art in all its forms, with notions of beauty and sublimity in art and nature, and sometimes with the phenomena of craft and popular culture. And aesthetics, too, has concerned itself with the significance of these phenomena for human life. But there has not yet been a systematic analysis of design itself by the discipline. The present work is a preliminary attempt to rectify this imbalance, and to argue for a place for design within philosophical aesthetics.

Three main challenges confront a fledgling theory of design. The first asks how we can define design as distinct from the traditional categories of art and craft; this is a question of ontology, and I provide an analysis of design that distinguishes it as a class of objects and practices that merit separate philosophical attention. The second asks how our experiences and judgements of design are specifically aesthetic, and how these differ from our interactions with art, craft, and natural beauty. Here I develop a theory of aesthetic judgement that singles out the distinctive form our approbations of design take, which nevertheless places them on a continuum with aesthetic judgements of other kinds of phenomena. Finally, of course, is the question of the import of design, for aesthetics and for philosophy as a whole. I am not interested so much in the separate moral, social, or political judgements we make about design, of the sort we make about other types of things, but rather in the way that design is deeply implicated in what it means to be human. Design, I argue, is one of the things "most important to us" because it is so deeply embedded in the lives of contemporary individuals. By beginning with our aesthetic interactions with design, I am also claiming a more central place for aesthetic experience in understanding human life as a whole. Aesthetics as a discipline has become marginalized from the general concerns of philosophy in part because of its preoccupation with the fine arts. An aesthetics of design functions as a corrective to this trend, and offers an avenue both for broadening the scope of aesthetic inquiry and for re-integrating aesthetic theory into philosophy as a whole. My overarching goal in this project is to make design visible to philosophy as an important part of our lives, through the lens of our aesthetic interactions with it. Design, I contend, is of great philosophical interest, yet has until now been unaccountably overlooked.

This is an ambitious project, that is, one that cannot be completed by simply inserting design into the current practices and methodologies of philosophical aesthetics, to be analyzed and appraised on the model of the fine arts or of natural beauty. Because design has distinctive features—it involves, for example, primarily functional objects—and because our interactions with design largely take place in the course of our familiar and quotidian activities, a focus on design perforce requires an expansion of the traditional categories of the discipline. But because I wish to claim that design is, first, an aesthetic phenomenon, my theory of design cannot emerge ex nihilo as utterly unrelated to the history and tradition of aesthetics as a new form of philosophical inquiry. It needs to remain related to the discipline. In this regard, to demonstrate that design is a legitimate object of aesthetic attention, I critically engage with the tradition, and argue that design can be defined and evaluated in ways that are not wholly unlike the other, more familiar aesthetic subjects. Thus I consider—and take a stand on—some of the major debates in the area: between formalism and expression theory in aesthetic ontology, and between realism and subjectivism in theories of beauty or aesthetic appreciation. But once I have demonstrated that design can be analyzed in these traditional ways, I then also argue that a complete understanding of design cannot be achieved by merely *adding* it to the growing list of phenomena of current aesthetic interest: art, nature, music, popular culture, food, architecture, and the like. In fact, a focus on design enriches aesthetic theory. It poses a challenge to its methodological model, exposes weaknesses in that model, and forces an expansion of the way we philosophers have generally gone about our aesthetic business.

I thus proceed in the following way: first, I presuppose that we *do* have aesthetic experiences of design, and make aesthetic judgements about designed objects. The question I seek to answer is *how* we do, and how these experiences and judgements differ from those of other aesthetic objects. Chapter 1 provides an ontology of design that distinguishes it from art and craft (as a specific kind of object with unique characteristics). This helps us to establish the boundaries of what delineates the aesthetic focus of this study. Design, I argue, is primarily functional, meant to be used rather than contemplated, and is distinct from art in particular because of its lack of profundity and originality, or because of its familiarity and quiddity. The properties that characterize design as a unique kind of phenomenon also indicate that as a candidate for aesthetic appraisal it merits separate attention.

Chapters 2 and 3 turn to the question of what constitutes aesthetic experience, one of the most complex in the discipline. A consideration (and rejection) of two historically predominant schools of thought about the nature of beauty or taste—as residing in the properties of objects on the one hand, or in our pleasurable responses to them on the other—leads me to argue for a theory of aesthetic experience that situates it within the activity of judgement itself. To make good this claim, I defend a Kantian account of aesthetic judgement as the most fully developed and closely scrutinized theory that philosophical aesthetics has to offer. Because Kant's work is difficult, and requires an assessment of the place of aesthetic judgement within philosophical psychology as a whole, I dwell on his work at some length. Readers already familiar with his *Critique of Judgement* may wish to simply pass over the exegesis in the second half of chapter 2. For those without such familiarity, a grounding in Kantian theory is essential for the claims I make in chapter 3 about the judgements of beauty that are specific to design. The Kantian notion of dependent beauty, as a unique form of judgement, provides the most cogent model for understanding design excellence. And it is with this notion that we can best understand our particular aesthetic experiences of design.

The first three chapters of this work, then, locate design within the tradition of philosophical aesthetics and seek to provide a contribution to the discipline (rather than a radical departure from it). Chapter 4, however, signals a change of direction, for while design can be singled out as an object of aesthetic appraisal that should be included among others that the discipline has embraced, still it differs from other aesthetic phenomena in the way that it intersects with our daily lives. To fully understand design, we must consider it within the context of our quotidian activities and immanent concerns. In chapter 4, I turn to a recent movement in philosophical aesthetics that focuses on the aesthetic import of the everyday.

Everyday Aesthetics seeks to make visible the beauty and significance of the mundane and the familiar. I consider the relevance of its claims for a theory of design. Everyday Aesthetics attempts to broaden the traditional categories and methodologies of the discipline to better suit the peculiarities of quotidian objects and experiences, but it also functions as a critique of the narrowness of scope of aesthetics (as primarily art-centred, and as thus alienated from important ways in which the aesthetic directly touches our lives). Despite a similarity in overarching goals, however, I demonstrate that Everyday Aesthetics fails to live up to its promise on two fronts. First, its directly aesthetic claims are often inconsistent and lack philosophical rigour. This is due, in large part, to its dismissal of a great deal of the aesthetic tradition. Second, this dismissal forces the movement to seek support for its claims of the significance of the everyday outside of aesthetics itself, in moral, or broadly ethical, theory. I argue that these moves fail to grasp the import of design—and the everyday more generally—because the aesthetic takes second place to either a prior set of moral commitments or to an ethical-existential theory of self-understanding. Everyday Aesthetics errs in suggesting that the only way to establish the legitimacy and value of our aesthetic experiences is to ground them in these more "serious" normative aspects of our lives, lest they be considered frivolous because of their connection to pleasure. By contrast, I show that the theory of design, as I have developed it, provides a model for a rich aesthetics of the everyday, one that has direct significance for human lives that need not be mediated by way of moral or existential theory. And it is here that design provides its strongest challenges to the discipline.

This returns me to the lesson of Wittgenstein's words, and their meaning for this project. We fail to grasp the aspects of things that are most important for us when we fail to notice them. Design has heretofore been hidden from our theoretical gaze because of its very simplicity and familiarity, and this project seeks to make it visible. The aesthetic value of design is further overlooked if it is treated merely as another object (on the model of the fine arts), to be appraised in similar ways. Resisting this move has been the achievement of Everyday Aesthetics. But the particular significance of our aesthetic interactions with design remains occluded when superimposed by other normative structures. Wittgenstein's remark ends: "We fail to be struck by what, once seen, is most striking and powerful." And this is where Everyday Aesthetics fails: it sees the aesthetic import of the quotidian and the familiar but fails to be struck by it, and instead turns away. I conclude this project by attempting to bring this importance to the fore.

Finally, a caveat: this work seeks to provide a cogent theory of design more than merely a general exploration of the phenomenon. But, as with any foray into uncharted philosophical territory, there are a number of pressing questions about design that are not addressed. Design's historical development in relation to industrialized manufacture; its dependence upon market forces; and the ways in which these forces may determine our aesthetic responses are not examined. No full treatment of design will be complete without these considerations, and while I could claim that a complete account of art likewise requires a response to such questions, this merely dodges the issue. Design, more than art or craft, is the child of twentieth-century modes of production, and a philosophy of design ought rightly to take its particular history into account. In my defense I can only claim that the conceptual problems I focus on in this work are prior to—and foundational for—the more material, historical, and sociological concerns of professional design theorists and historians. I hope that by making design visible to philosophy I will initiate a long and fruitful exploration of the topic.

Chapter 1

The Ontology of Design

1. SOME METHODOLOGICAL CONSIDERATIONS

The first task of an aesthetics of design is to delineate the scope of its concern. To do this, we might begin by asking, "What are the objects or practices that comprise the category of design"? Or, we might ask, "What do we mean by 'design' in particular, as opposed to, for instance, 'art', 'craft', and so on"? These two questions, while related, are not equivalent and lend themselves to different methodological approaches. In both cases, we can say that we seek a working *definition* of design adequate to our theoretical purposes, but in the first case we seek to identify a group of objects or practices by their similarities such that we can know them to be the same kind of thing; in the second case, we are analyzing the meaning of a concept or word in an effort to explain and perhaps prescribe its use. Nick Zangwill has described the different strategies in these terms:

> [In the first case we] want to know about a range of objects and events, not about the words or concepts that we use to talk about those things. We are interested in objects, not concepts—the world, not words. We are doing metaphysics, not linguistic or conceptual analysis.[1]

1 Nick Zangwill, "Are There Counterexamples to Aesthetic Theories of Art?" *Journal of Aesthetics and Art Criticism* 60, no. 2 (2002): 116.

While my concern in this chapter lies with metaphysics—with the nature of the objects and practices that accumulate (or should be collected) under the term "design," and so with the first question more than the second, I do not agree that a metaphysics of objects can be so neatly separated from an analysis of our language and concepts or so directly pursued. Before we begin trying to define design, then, we need to consider what this task entails, and some of the challenges faced by an ontological theory, particularly in aesthetics.

The metaphysical project in general has historically been fuelled by the desire to uncover the essential nature of things, whether they be material, mental, mathematical, or cultural entities. And what I will call the metaphysical approach—pre-Kantian and again more recent—has attempted to provide an a priori argument that delineates the necessary and sufficient conditions for something to be an entity of a certain kind. However, while such phenomena as mathematical objects, substances, or minds presumably do not change (and that is arguable), artistic practices and works of art and craft (and design) certainly do. A triangle can with confidence be defined a priori as a three-sided closed figure whose interior angles equal 180 degrees, but what counts as art or design has not remained stable, and the unreflective adoption of a methodology from one area of philosophical enquiry to another more often exposes its weaknesses than its strengths. The benefit of focusing on the metaphysics of things rather than on the analysis of concepts or linguistic practices (and I think this is Zangwill's point) is that we can allow for the possibility that the "world" is broader than our words to describe it, or that while there may be a range of things that are designed, there may also be no universally shared concept of "design" or consensus about its use. That is, we may err in our linguistic practices, or simply not sufficiently reflect about them, and attending to them alone may not adequately capture the range of objects that are of theoretical interest here. Particularly insofar as the present project seeks to bring to the attention of philosophical aesthetics a category of objects and practices that has heretofore been neglected by the discipline, there is good reason to look beyond the phenomenology of linguistic usage in an effort to get to the things themselves and make a case for their consideration. But the very idea that design differs from craft and art is itself grounded in the phenomenology of our concepts and our linguistic and creative practices. We would have no object of inquiry at all if we did not begin with what we think and talk about when we use the term "design" as opposed to "art," "fine art," or "craft." And what we talk about, with art especially, has undergone dramatic historical change that provides an important methodological lesson here.

While ancient philosophers may have been interested in poetry, tragedy, painting, and music, the term "art" as *technē* for the Greeks or *ars* for the Romans referred to a broad range of skills that included rhetoric, the martial arts, and what we today consider the "crafts" of blacksmithing, shoemaking, and carpentry, among others. A relatively more stable cluster of the so-called "fine arts" was not recognized until the eighteenth century with the twin rise of connoisseurship and aesthetic theory.[2] The fine arts then became associated with what Kristeller called the "Modern System of the Arts," which canonized certain forms, specifically architecture, sculpture, painting, music, and poetry, and the study of these formed the core of the developing field

2 See M. H. Abrams, "Art-as-Such: The Sociology of Modern Aesthetics," in *Doing Things with Texts: Essays in Criticism and Critical Theory* (New York: Norton, 1991) and "Kant and the Theology of Art," *Notre Dame English Journal* 13 (1981) for a thorough treatment of the development of the notion of fine art in the eighteenth century.

of philosophical aesthetics.[3] As new creative practices arose, some of these too were included in the category of fine art and so were also of aesthetic interest: narrative forms such as the novel, dance, and in the twentieth century, film and photography. The categories of craft and popular or mass art, for instance, did not arise until they were needed to identify those forms and practices that were excluded from the class of objects called the fine arts. And until relatively recently, these categories were then also overlooked by aesthetic theory as being outside the scope of its concerns.

These historical changes point in the first place to the overlap between conceptual analysis and metaphysical theory, and in the second to the particularly historical nature of the aesthetic enterprise. Zangwill, in an understatement, concurs that "it seems that what counts as the target for explanation in the theory of art is somewhat shifting," but this does not concern him overmuch: "so long as the aesthetic theory succeeds in giving the essence of a great many artforms, I do not think that we should worry too neurotically about whether it covers every item in the Modern System of the Arts."[4] For Zangwill, the theory comes first as an a priori undertaking that is then applied to objects in the world. The fact that his particular theory of art somewhat surprisingly includes "industrial design . . . weaving, whistling . . . and fireworks displays" that do not coincide with our current practices or commonplace understanding

3 Paul Oskar Kristeller notes, in "The Modern System of the Arts: A Study in the History of Aesthetics (I)," *Journal of the History of Ideas* 12, no. 4 (1951) that "this system of the five major arts, which underlies all modern aesthetics and is so familiar to us all, is of comparatively recent origin and did not assume definite shape before the 18th century" (498). See also his "The Modern System of the Arts: A Study in the History of Aesthetics (II)," *Journal of the History of Ideas* 13, no. 1 (1952). Peter Kivy, in his *Philosophies of the Arts: An Essay in Differences* (Cambridge: Cambridge University Press, 1997), makes reference to Kristeller's claims in chapter 1.

4 Zangwill, "Are There Counterexamples," 117.

of the notion of fine art is, for him, "of little consequence."[5] To some extent, he claims, "we must set up the target and then shoot at it,"[6] and indeed setting up the target is what I propose to do in this chapter. But the theory must explain the phenomena, and *which* phenomena are to be explained depends to a large extent on current practice, concepts, and linguistic use. A definition of art that excludes works from its scope that are nevertheless commonly considered to be art—the prolonged "performances" of Christo or the street art of Basquiat, for instance—or that includes things that are not normally deemed art (whistling, fireworks)—will fail as a metaphysical theory either because it is narrowly counter-intuitive, or because it is so broad that it lacks explanatory power. Zangwill's is but one example of the metaphysical approach in aesthetics that seeks an ahistorical, essentialist definition of a historically situated, unstable, and diverse group of objects. Zangwill claims that he is focusing on the things themselves in his metaphysics, but at the end of the day his approach is more conceptual than he may wish to think: he has, in fact, stipulated a definition of the term "art" and then prescribed its use, unconcerned with the objects that may then fall by the wayside of his theoretical ambition. In fact, most essentialist ontologies of art fail, largely because they run aground on counter-examples: either works that lack one of the necessary criteria laid out by the theory (but which are nevertheless commonly considered to be art), or works that have emerged after the articulation of a given definition of art that cannot be subsumed under it, because of historical changes in artistic and linguistic practices themselves. Cultural entities are more vulnerable in the face of the totalizing demands of a priori metaphysics, and aesthetic objects

5 Ibid., 116.
6 Ibid., 117.

especially so: art does not seem to have an ahistorical essence that can be pinned down sufficiently to avoid the regular emergence of counter-examples to a theory's definitional criteria.

In what sense, then, am I employing a metaphysical approach in my definition of design? I am seeking here to distinguish design as a set of practices and objects from other categories common to aesthetic theory—notably art and craft—because the particular characteristics of design, I wish to claim, merit separate treatment, especially in our approach to their aesthetic evaluation, as we will see in subsequent chapters. So my goal *is* to provide some kind of ontology of design. But when I suggested at the outset that I would seek a "working" definition, I meant this quite strongly: I will not offer a definition of design in terms of its necessary and sufficient conditions because I think this approach is too constrictive. The perceived need for *definitions*, particularly of art, has tied us in philosophical knots for too long and has constrained aestheticians from exploring some of the truly interesting things to be said about our subject. If we look at the history of aesthetics, too much of our time has been spent trying to "set up the target," as it were, and too little in "shooting at it."[7] What I will do here is point to a number of characteristics that design seems to have that set it apart from art and craft and make it theoretically interesting if not metaphysically unique, as part of my larger goal of arguing for its inclusion in the scope of philosophical aesthetics. That is, I will claim that design is *not* art and *not* craft, although it surely shares some of the characteristics of each. But I will not claim that a certain group of objects or practices contains an essence that can be delineated in terms both necessary

7 Roger Scruton would concur. He has remarked, in "In Search of the Aesthetic," *British Journal of Aesthetics* 47, no. 3 (2007) that "[m]uch of aesthetics has really been rather futile," in particular its "constant wrangling over the definition of art," which he claims is full of "arbitrary questions and nonsensical boundary disputes" (238).

and sufficient, nor will I provide an a priori argument for what design must be as an aesthetic phenomenon. Indeed design, like the novel and film before it, is an emerging category of practices and works whose definition must be understood in tandem with both its own development and changes in the way that we talk about it. For this reason, we must consider design together with its history and the history of our treatment of it. This is a tall order, one that requires for its completion a sociology and a history of design along with its philosophical analysis, and I have no conceit that I can fulfill these requirements here.[8] What I will provide is the philosophical framework that I believe an adequate theory of design needs, and I will proceed like this: beginning with some intuitions about what we mean when we talk about design, and what we can learn from a consideration of our linguistic practices, I will move to contrasting design with certain metaphysical definitions of art and craft. Against this backdrop we will learn what design is *not*, but I anticipate that what will emerge is a developing picture of what makes design unique, and aesthetically interesting. In the final section, I will pull together these various strands into a fuller depiction of our target: a working definition of design as an apt object of philosophical attention.

2. INTUITIONS ABOUT DESIGN

And so, let me begin again: the first task in an aesthetics of design is to delineate the scope of its concern: just what objects or practices

8 As I noted at the end of the introduction, the emergence of design runs in tandem with developments in industry and the possibility of mass manufacture as well as the growth of market capitalism. A full treatment of the proliferation of design in our lives cannot ignore these factors: the creation of markets and the ways in which our choices can be, and are, coerced are equally relevant to understanding the complexities of the phenomenon that is contemporary design. It exceeds my brief to undertake this aspect of the study here.

do I wish to consider here? When we talk about design in its simplest terms, "design" is set against nature, "designed" against the natural, suggesting that it involves the intentional or the consciously planned. Design seems to be "artificial" in some sense of the word. If we look at the environments we inhabit, almost every aspect of them is designed at least in the sense that they have all been planned or manufactured rather than being naturally occurring, like a cave in a cliff-side might be. Indeed, the ideal of "getting back to nature" is that of the escape from human intervention and the human "footprint" in favour of the untouched, the untrammeled and the unexploited. But even with the environments in which we live, the artificial or manufactured runs deeper than we may like to think, and what we call natural is less and less the case. Of course our houses, our furniture, our clothes, and our tools are designed, but so too are the many natural elements in our lives, especially now. The plants in our gardens and houses are largely hybrids (I discovered on a houseplant I recently bought a tag instructing me that it had been "designed" by a subsidiary of Monsanto and that any reproduction of it was forbidden by copyright law). Our pets, likewise, if they are purebreds, have been engineered to have certain features and characteristics. The food we eat, even that which is not processed, such as fruits and vegetables, has been engineered and often genetically modified. And our own bodies, even, can no longer be said to be purely "natural," if any of us have had orthodontic work, plastic surgery, transplants, piercings, tattoos, and so on.

Design, as opposed to the natural, seems to be a category that contains everything touched or altered by human beings, one that would then have to encompass art and craft too. And clearly this is too broad for my purposes: I am not after a theory of *everything* here, and I want to distinguish design from art and craft in particular as an aesthetic phenomenon. Further, I do not want to suggest that we single out genetically modified corn or frozen pizzas as apt objects of our aesthetic appreciation. Yet why not? (There has been recent work in the aesthetics of food, for example.)[9] Why not indeed. The designed-versus-natural distinction does capture a couple of intuitions about the subject that may help us move forward, or at least indicate the direction in which we must go.

First, we learn that design encompasses the quotidian, the immanent (as opposed to the transcendent or the profound), the everyday, and that I am indeed interested in the aesthetic choices we make when we construct and inhabit our environments. Perhaps it is because we do not consciously *choose* GM vegetables over natural ones (in fact, the opposite is more often the case, when we do have the choice), that foods are not an obvious choice for inclusion in design as an aesthetic category. Here Zangwill's distinction between the "world" and the words we use to describe it is useful: many of us would not count corn, say, among the things we call "designed," perhaps because we do not know it has been so manipulated, or because we do not want to admit it, or even because, once aware of the fact, we consider this manipulation invidious rather than the source of approval or aesthetic appreciation. That our conceptual and linguistic practice excludes food and plants, and in most instances our own bodies, leads me not to conclude that we are therefore *wrong* in our designation of what is designed, but instead to pay greater attention to what in fact we do say and why.

9 See, for instance, the wide-ranging anthology edited by Carolyn Korsmeyer, *The Taste Culture Reader: Experiencing Food and Drink* (New York: Palgrave MacMillan, 2005), which has readings on "Food and/vs. Art" and the cultivation of taste; and Glenn Kuehn, "How Can Food be Art?" in *The Aesthetics of Everyday Life*, ed. Andrew Light and Jonathan M. Smith (New York: Columbia University Press, 2005).

Of course, in one sense we *are* wrong to exclude food and plants; on the designed-versus-natural distinction, everything that has been planned or manufactured by human beings has been designed. This includes frozen pizzas as much as it does pipe wrenches, anti-retroviral drugs, automatic weapons, and the ubiquitous dripping metal teapot found in restaurants across North America, all of which should then be at least candidates for aesthetic appreciation. What is interesting here is that the things we exclude in practice tell us less about the way we define them as designed or not, than about the way we evaluate and appreciate them. We may give our approbation to a new anti-retroviral drug, exclaim that this is a damned fine pipe wrench, or respond with dismay to the tasteless and soggy pizza, but are these *aesthetic* evaluations, or appraisals of a different kind? We must be careful here: an ontology of design simply seeks to describe the phenomenon; how we evaluate it is another matter, which I will turn to in due course. And we must keep these separate. Defining art, by contrast, is simpler in this one regard: art by definition is an aesthetic object, a candidate for aesthetic appraisal. We may also make other judgements about art—moral or economic or political—but primarily art stands as an object or practice that expects to be evaluated aesthetically. Design is more complex in that it is not always or only an aesthetic object, and our responses to design are, rightly, more varied because of the many different ways design intersects with our lives. Craft, I think, also shares in this complexity. This does not mean that we cannot offer an aesthetic *treatment* of design, or that design is not, in part, an interesting aesthetic phenomenon. Clearly, it is also more than this. In this chapter, I want to get on the table simply what design *is*, absent discussion of its evaluation, and this may mean the inclusion of some objects and practices that we would not normally accord our aesthetic approbation. On the designed-versus-natural distinction, this may include vegetables and guns as much as it does laptop computers and shoes. If the distinction is too broad to stand as a working definition of design, it cannot be because we do not appreciate these items aesthetically, but must be for some other reason that it is my intention to discover.

The second intuition that the designed-versus-natural distinction calls up is that to be designed is to be intentionally planned or created by some*one*. This seems to suggest that the designer is of some importance in our theory but of how much importance is not immediately clear. And this also seems to suggest that design is an *object* that is the product of an act of creation. For instance, perhaps we do not make aesthetic judgements about leaky teapots or anti-retroviral drugs because they have no acknowledged authors and so are not "works" of design in the way that *La Danse* is a work by Matisse, or a set of wine goblets is a work by Philippe Stark. And corn, while its genetic makeup may have been modified in a laboratory, is not the work of an author either, because it in fact can grow naturally like any other plant species, and is not conspicuously made by the hands of one individual.

Using the model of art as a guide, we can see that a work of art is usually considered to be a unique original, made by a particular—known—artist. Art is "handmade," if you will (as is craft), and its having actually been produced by a given artist is important—otherwise it is a forgery, a reproduction, a copy, and so on. This of course cannot be a necessary condition of art: late Matisse cut-outs like his *Blue Nude* series were not actually *made* by him—he directed assistants to assemble his collages once he became bedridden—and other acknowledged works of art are more explicitly collaborative, such as opera and film, where the "author" of the finished product is not solely the composer or the director. Literature poses a different sort of problem because while there may be a sole author, there is not a single text, but many, none of which are original in the way that a painting may be. But that a work of art must be made by an artist—have an author—and somehow be the unique original product of his or her creative work—is a persistent notion in aesthetic theory, even if it is not ontologically unproblematic.

With design, this strong link between art and artist breaks down in a number of interesting ways. While we may say we own a set of wine-glasses by Stark, those glasses are not his *work* in the sense of having actually been *made* by him, for instance. While we commonly acknowledge that a Rolex watch or a Volkswagen Jetta is a designed object, and while we give awards to the new iPhone, their makers, Rolex, Volkswagen, and Apple, are not individuals at all, but corporations employing large numbers of designers whose names we often do not know, none of whom actually constructed the cars we drive or the watches and phones we use, and whose individual roles in their production are often unclear. More broadly still, we speak approvingly of "Swedish design" when we refer to some furniture, or "Italian design" when we point to our cooking pots and espresso machines without acknowledging either an individual or a corporate collaboration, yet remaining clear that we consider these objects to be works of design, worthy of our appraisal. Does the designer not matter at all, then? In what way, if any, is the product we use the "work" of a designer? And what exactly does a designer produce if it is not an object that is a unique original that we can then assess?

These questions suggest that the relation of designer to designed is murkier than that between artist and art, and that it poses some interesting philosophical problems. The fundamental ambiguity at the heart of the notion of design has been well captured by John Heskett in his book *Toothpicks and Logos: Design in Everyday Life* with the grammatically correct but nonsensical phrase, "design is to design a design to produce a design,"[10] which is nonetheless illuminating. In the first instance, we have the definiendum, the general concept of design that we seek to understand. In the second, we have the activity of designing, presumably carried out by an individual or a collective. The third place is filled by an intermediary product, what Heskett calls a "proposal," and in the final place we have the finished product, "the concept made actual."[11]

To what do we refer when we commonly speak of design, and which of these elements comprises the candidate for our appraisal or the object of our aesthetic judgement? The third element I think we can exclude, in part because we do not normally see or have access to a designer's proposals. An artist may make preliminary sketches of a painting—and we may in some cases collect them when they are available, as with Michelangelo's sketches for the Sistine Chapel, or da Vinci's many diagrams and anatomical studies—but we do not normally consider these to be finished "works" in themselves. In many if not most cases studies and sketches are discarded once the work is complete. With design, moreover, a sketch of a wine-glass is not the glass that we can hold and appreciate—Heskett's use of the term "proposal" indicates the tentative and unfinished nature of this third element. That Heskett includes an intermediary step between the activity of the designer and the finished product indicates how unclear and distant the relation between the two actually is. In fact, I will claim that this intermediary step or "gap" is itself one of design's distinctive features that sets it apart from art and craft.

But before we come to that, let us first consider our other two options: that design refers primarily to the activity of an individual author (or collective) on the one hand, or that it refers to a finished

10 John Heskett, *Toothpicks and Logos: Design in Everyday Life* (Oxford: Oxford University Press, 2002), 5.
11 Ibid., 5–6.

product or some unique original on the other. In fact, theories of art are divided as to their focus along these same two lines; equally they emphasize either the creative act of the artist in the making of a work, and identify art with this activity, or they define art as an object on the grounds of some quality or feature it has that sets it apart as a special kind of thing, such as Zangwill has done. Which aspect is emphasized leads to noticeable differences in definitions of art, and attending to only one at the expense of the other has never been completely successful. Nevertheless, in the following sections I will consider both of these emphases separately and look to what we can learn about design if we do the same. If we cannot define design solely in terms of one of these elements—activity or object—we will at least see how each contributes in important ways to our understanding of what design is.

If we gather together these intuitions here, the focus of my work on design in this chapter begins to take rudimentary shape. First, it will be a descriptive project that attempts to bracket out our normative judgements of design to get at what simply identifies it as a historically contextualized phenomenon; second, we can see that my particular focus is with the immanent and the quotidian—design is a ubiquitous element of our everyday lives and not a stand-alone object of aesthetic contemplation. Thus I do not intend to stake my definition of design on examples of the famous, like Max Stam and Bauhaus, or the "branded" like Chanel and Nike, to the neglect of the merely workmanlike or common. Design as we refer to it is something that is meant to be *used* rather than merely appreciated, and when it is appreciated, it is for reasons other than its fame, as we will see in later chapters. This focus on use, I will suggest, brings design closer to craft than art, because it permeates our daily lives in a way that fine art usually does not, and its ubiquity forms part of its philosophical interest in this study. Finally the ambiguity of our talk about design shows that the notion must be understood as somehow situated within the relation of designer to designed product in a way that distinguishes it from art and craft but that does not emphasize one relata at the expense of the other. Design is an emergent twentieth-century phenomenon that depends on the means of mass production in a way that art and craft do not. These intuitions will be developed in the following sections as I contrast design with art and craft, first as a kind of object with distinctive features, and then as a particular form of practice, as each element will play an important role in the development of our final picture.

3. DESIGN AND ART, DESIGN AND CRAFT

i. *Formalism and Art as an Object*

Theories of art that focus on the object include the formalism of Clive Bell and Roger Fry, and more recent work on aesthetic properties by Monroe Beardsley, Frank Sibley, and Nick Zangwill. What these theories have in common is that they seek to define art in terms of some property or quality that all artworks have in common, that differentiates them from other kinds of things. These properties are usually considered at least necessary, if not sufficient, for an object to be identified as art.

Bell's theory developed as a response to the demise of mimetic definitions of art—that art is the representation or imitation of reality, with verisimilitude as its goal—brought about in part by the advent of photography and later film.[12] Bell was writing, instead, against the backdrop of developments in post-impressionist and

12 See, for example, Arthur Danto, who makes this argument in "The End of Art," in *The Philosophical Disenfranchisement of Art* (New York: Columbia University Press, 1986).

modernist abstract painting and sculpture. For Bell, if art is not—or no longer—about representational content, it must instead be all about *form*. However—and provided that the form/content distinction can legitimately be made—every object has form of some kind, so Bell sought to identify the specific form artworks possess that makes them unique. He suggested that art can be identified by its "significant form": "lines and colours combined in a particular way, certain forms and relations of forms"[13] that together will produce a particular "aesthetic emotion" in the viewer. Any and all works that possess significant form will arouse this kind of "aesthetic ecstasy,"[14] while this emotion, in turn, is evidence that we stand before a bona fide work of art.

Bell's particular attempt to define art failed on a number of grounds. First, it was both too narrow and too broad, buckling under the sheer weight of counter-examples. While our appreciation of Cézanne, Mondrian, or Klee may well attend to the formal elements of composition in their works, Bell would have us exclude, presumably, Bosch, Breughel, most of the Renaissance, and all forms of narrative painting. He calls such works "Descriptive Painting" and includes in this non-art category "[p]ortraits of psychological and historical value, topographical works, pictures that tell stories and suggest situations, [and] illustrations of all sorts," none of which excite that particularly aesthetic emotion we are capable of feeling.[15] On the other hand, if

13 Clive Bell, *Art* (New York: Capricorn Books, 1958), 17.

14 Ibid., 34.

15 Ibid., 22. That is, Bosch et al. could still be considered art on Bell's definition but only on the basis of their formal elements, and irrespective of their (descriptive or narrative) content. Critics of Bell would suggest that these works stand as counter-examples to his theory because we do not ignore their content to appreciate their form alone. In fact, in many cases we prize works for their depth of content even if their formal properties do not arouse us in the way that Bell describes. For a discussion of such content, see section 3.ii below.

anything with the property of significant form is art, then a jug or a quilt, a fighter jet or a shoe could *also* be art, for there is no prima facie reason why other kinds of objects are unable to possess the combination of lines and colours Bell describes. This focus on a single feature as an a priori requirement for something to be art is precisely what led Zangwill much later to the counter-intuitive inclusion of whistling and fireworks in his theory. The problem with an emphasis on a single quality of an object is that anything at all that possesses that quality must perforce merit inclusion in the definition, and anything that lacks this quality must be excluded, whether or not this runs counter to linguistic practice or common aesthetic experience.

Bell's theory further fails in that it is circular. Because, I suspect, he could not give a solid analysis of what significant form actually amounts to in a given work (he does not describe it in much greater detail than what I have given), Bell was forced to tie this property to our reaction to it—an aesthetic emotion—and define one in terms of the other. Significant form is that which produces aesthetic emotion, which is produced only by significant form, and together they define art. "The objects that provoke this emotion we call works of art"; and again, "Significant Form is the one quality common to all works of art."[16] But because both of these terms have been coined by Bell himself, neither of them can be clearly or easily identified. With the emotion, we would need a way to distinguish it from other sorts of feelings (am I feeling it now? Is *this* it?), and with the specific feature, too, we would need to be able to pick it out. If it were empirically verifiable, like redness or squareness, or even proportion, Bell's task would have been easier. But the property he uses to identify art is, in fact, not an

16 Ibid., 17, 18.

empirical property at all in the way we would normally understand such a thing, but an *aesthetic* property, unique in that it must be *felt* rather than seen. "We have no other means of recognizing a work of art than our feeling for it"—and no other means of recognizing this emotion than by experiencing significant form.[17] Sibley's and Zangwill's theories escape this problem of circularity in that while they are also grounded in the idea of aesthetic properties, they provide deeper analysis of what these properties amount to, and claim that we can indeed pick them out. But these other theories are still open to the problem of counter-examples and charges of narrowness if they too closely circumscribe the aesthetic property or over-breadth if they do not.

But more importantly, in focusing on a so-called *aesthetic* property—whether of beauty or significant form or of some other kind—these sorts of theory run up against one of the intuitive problems I mentioned in the last section: they confuse definition with aesthetic evaluation, and are often reduced to tautologies. The definiendum is presumed in the definition: art (as a particularly aesthetic object) is defined by the properties that make it an aesthetic object—aesthetic properties, which gets us no further than saying design is to be designed. There is an additional burden on these theories to give an independent explanation, not only of what these properties are, but of what makes them *aesthetic* in the first place. With Bell in particular, we have a confusion of a definition of art with the evaluation of what makes an artwork any *good*. Significant form is an aesthetically valuable property—it affects the viewer with an appropriately aesthetic emotion that is the right response to art. There is no room in Bell's theory for *bad* art, for if a work lacks significant form it is not art at all. This is

17 Ibid., 18.

not to say that all theories of art that focus on the properties of the object encounter this problem or fail for this reason, but I do think they are vulnerable to it as soon as they claim that the properties of art are unique, or different in kind from the properties of any other things. I will return to this in chapter 2 when I consider aesthetic judgement and Zangwill's more sophisticated treatment of beauty. Here, what we can learn is not just that an ontology of design must avoid the confusion of definition and evaluation, but that it easily *does*, because of what this confusion tells us about the idea of art itself.

The presupposition that underlies object-centred theories that focus on aesthetic properties in particular is that what makes something a work of art is also what makes it significant or profound—art by definition is not *ordinary* but somehow transcendent, and whatever lacks, say, significant form is therefore from the beginning lesser, insignificant, quotidian. Bell writes,

> To appreciate a work of art we need bring with us nothing from life, no knowledge of its ideas and affairs, no familiarity with its emotions. Art transports us from the world of man's activity to a world of aesthetic exaltation. For a moment we are shut off from human interests . . . we are lifted above the stream of life.[18]

And again,

> Whatever the world of aesthetic contemplation may be, it is not the world of human business and passion; in it the chatter and

18 Ibid., 77.

> tumult of material existence is unheard, or heard only as the echo of some more ultimate harmony.[19]

Representational painting, craft, design, popular art, narratives, and so on, if they arouse our emotions at all, will arouse only the common or garden-variety emotions that are the stuff of everyday life because these works are unable to achieve the transcendence of art. These other objects, lacking such profundity, are "mere real things," to use Arthur Danto's phrase,[20] and their definition is often couched in negative terms, as lacking what the objects of the Modern System of the Arts have, and thus somehow failing to be of abiding aesthetic interest. We see this happening quite clearly in the aesthetics of craft, which labours under a cloud of sensed inferiority. Sally Markowitz, for instance, while she notes that craftworks "fare extremely well" on aesthetic accounts like Bell's (because they have line and colour themselves and thus may arouse our aesthetic emotions), nevertheless admits that art "has a positive evaluative connotation that craft lacks," a connotation that—rightly or wrongly—she attributes to an "elitism" in the arts themselves.[21] And Charles Fethe, noting that formalism identifies craft with "low-quality, hackneyed art," still accepts the presumption of art's profundity or transcendence: art "is indeed superior to craft."[22]

Rather than joining the defenders of craft to rail against this perceived exclusion from the rarified world of art, my ontology of design will instead embrace it. If design is anything, it is immanent rather than transcendent, quotidian rather than profound.

19 Ibid., 55.

20 Arthur Danto, *The Transfiguration of the Commonplace* (Cambridge: Harvard University Press, 1981). See especially chapter 1, "Works of Art and Mere Real Things."

21 Sally Markowitz, "The Distinction between Art and Craft," *Journal of Aesthetic Education* 28, no. 1 (1994): 55.

22 C. B. Fethe, "Craft and Art: A Phenomenological Distinction," *British Journal of Aesthetics* 17, no. 2 (1977): 131.

I am interested precisely in the "world of man's activity," the "stream of life," and the "chatter and tumult of material existence." Design is immune to certain problems in the metaphysics of art for just the reason that, whatever qualities designed objects possess, they will not be the ineffable features that appear to make art of such otherworldly importance. This is not to say that I wish to define design in negative terms, however. Fethe is correct when he claims that to "discover what makes art bad is not to learn what makes craft craft,"[23] and if we seek to learn what makes design design on the basis of some feature that designed objects possess, it will not be merely because they lack something that art has, but because they *have* something that art, perhaps, *does not*. The entire question of design's status vis-à-vis art is of little concern to me. If art is indeed transcendent, as many theorists would have us believe, this simply relieves me of having to try to describe design in similar terms, although the alleged profundity of art provides the reason, I have suggested, for the long-term neglect of other forms such as craft and design from the purview of philosophical aesthetics. But these presumptions about art leave me at least free to pursue the characteristics of design in this world, if not also in the next. The question, of course, is what these characteristics might be.

We may do well, at this point, to consider a range of examples of what the experts consider to be design. Two sources we can tap are, first, the National Design Awards (NDA) sponsored by the Cooper-Hewit Design Museum that is part of the Smithsonian Institute,[24] and the Annual Design Review (ADR), self-styled as "America's oldest and most prestigious juried design recognition program."[25] The ADR lists consumer products, graphics,

23 Ibid.
24 They can be found at www.cooperhewitt.org/NDA.
25 Please see their explanation of their awards at www.id-mag.com/annualdesignreview/.

packaging, environments, furniture, equipment, "concepts," and "interactive" (since 2005) as general areas of design. The NDA's categories are broader but perhaps more familiar, including interior design, landscape design, product design, communication, fashion, and "design mind," as well as awards for lifetime and corporate achievement. Examples from the NDA include such things as laptop computers, coffee tables, Birkenstock shoes, a soundwall at LAX (landscape design), airplanes, office chairs, magazine covers, and so on. With the exception of the "design mind" category, which refers to an individual, the NDA provides us with a wide variety of objects that, on this approach, ought to have some property in common that makes them "designed." I will consider one such feature and see how this aids us in our theory.

One quality all of these objects have in common seems to be the very immanent one of *function* or *functionality*. Each of these things is useful, or meant to be used in a specific way: the planes flown, the shoes worn, the office chairs sat in. If this is the case, we can claim that a thing is not a work of design unless it is also functional, or, on the metaphysical approach, we can say that function is a necessary condition of design. This will obviously require some teasing out. By function, I do not mean simply the use to which an object might be put. After all, almonds can nourish me, I can sit on a tree trunk or sleep in a cave, and in this sense almonds and caves are functional in that they can *serve* a function, or suit my purposes, or fulfill my needs for food and shelter. But we would be wrong to define these things in terms of their functions: except on some religious arguments from design, almonds and caves are simply part of nature, however useful they may be. Similarly, while a tire may function as—or be used as—a swing, its function is not to *be* a swing, and if we define it by its function, we call it a tire, not a swing.

The functional quality of designed objects lies in their being meant to be used in a given way, and this use is part of what it means to be that thing in the first place. But let us be careful here: by functional I clearly mean, first, that the designed object must serve a *human* function, and so be useful for, or suitable to, the very quotidian human purposes and needs that are part of Bell's "material existence" as such. Second, I mean that the object must have been intentionally *made* to serve those needs, rather than simply being found to be useful to us. Opposable thumbs are beyond question useful, and serve us extremely well, as do almonds and trees. But I would not define them as being *designed*, and the reason why points beyond their use to their maker (or lack of one). Obviously even the notion of function will involve the activity of designing, just as significant form is not an accident for Bell, but the product of an artist's creative activities. I will consider the activity of design in the next section. For the moment, we can say that the category of objects of interest here are those that have been manufactured or created by human beings—the non-natural, as our first distinction suggested—to have specific functions.

Within the vast range of human artifacts, however, we need to further distinguish design as those that can be *defined by* their function, in a sense that takes us as far back as Aristotle. What makes something a hammer is that it is meant to serve the function of—have the purpose of—hammering. While on occasion a rock or a pair of vice grips will also drive in a nail, neither is therefore a hammer: each object is being *used as* a hammer, which gives it, if you will, honourary "hammer-status" for the duration of its use. But with designed objects, their intentional functions are part of what define them as the kinds of things they are. An office chair *is* a thing meant to be sat on, and a shoe *is* a thing meant to be worn on the foot. This will prove important for the evaluation of design: a pair of vice grips, I will argue, cannot be acclaimed for being a well-designed hammer, for instance, whether or not they can be, or have been, used in this way, and despite the fact that they were designed with some (other) specific (human, quotidian) function in mind.

Designer David Pye would disagree with this proposed definition of design. In his book *The Nature and Aesthetics of Design*, he claims that the "purposes of things are the purposes of men and change according to who entertains them.... Any concept such as 'function' which includes the idea of purpose is bound to be an unsafe foundation" for design.[26] Instead, Pye would define function as "[w]hat someone has provisionally decided that a device may reasonably be expected to do at present,"[27] moving the notion of function from the object to what an individual uses it for. However, Pye fails to distinguish function from *use*. He notes that while his car has the purpose of taking his children to school, "the time has about come when its purpose should change to housing the chickens."[28] But a car is not a chicken coop, even while it may be used as one, and if we come across it, we would not claim that Pye's chicken coop was unusually car-shaped but that he was making an unusual use of an old car. Something else makes a car a car, and we can provisionally claim that it is the original or intended function of the thing *as designed* to be the thing it is.[29]

26 David Pye, *The Nature and Aesthetics of Design* (New York: Van Nostrand Reinhold, 1978), 16.

27 Ibid., 14.

28 Ibid., 16.

29 Glenn Parsons and Allen Carlson in their work *Functional Beauty* (Oxford University Press, 2008) argue against such intentionalist theories of function as Pye expresses, in favour of the notion of a "proper function" that "belongs to the object itself" (66). They note that "[w]e do not need a theory to tell us *that* propping up a garage door is not the 'right' function... of a particular shovel, but we do need a theory to tell us *why* this is the case" (85) and provide such a theory, adapted from the philosophy of biology (see chapter 3). They would no doubt argue that my definition of function here remains too intentionalist in its dependence on what a designer *intended* an object to be, but I find their reliance on marketplace success to determine the proper function of an object in

Pye further argues that things "simply are not 'fit for their purpose'"[30] because they rarely *work*. "Nothing we design or make ever really works"—airplanes "fall out of the sky," the car "ought to stop dead" with no one being thrown forward but doesn't[31]—and thus, presumably, the function of things cannot be that which defines them as objects of design. But here Pye is conflating what makes something a design with what makes it a good one: clearly some planes do not stay in the air (to horrible effect) and some cars are flops (like the Edsel and the Brickland), but because they did not serve their function well does not mean that they were not *functional objects* with a specific purpose from the outset. In fact, Pye cannot even claim that a thing does not *work* unless he first understands what it is that the object was meant to do, and this means that he must know what its function is, or is meant to be. The quality of functionality has similarities to the notions of purpose and use but is not reducible to these. I do not think that my olive pitter is particularly useful (a knife works just as well) but I do not deny that its function is to pit olives. And while I may find that an olive pitter fits the *purpose* of driving in nails (when the vice grips are not handy), in no way do I mistake it for a hammer. Function is part of how human-made objects are defined as being the kinds of things they are, and this, we can see, is a feature that designed objects all seem to have in common.

How far does this get us in our ontology? Does this *distinguish* design from other sorts of things? In the first place, function does have the effect of carving off natural phenomena from design. Even GM vegetables, while they may have been modified or "improved,"

fact confuses its definition with its merit, excludes designed objects that are not market successes, and lets natural objects like GM vegetables in by the back door, as it were, all of which I am trying to avoid doing here.

30 Pye, *Nature and Aesthetics of Design*, 14.

31 Ibid.

are not functional objects. The modification may make them more amenable to the aim of high yields in production, and we may use them for their nutritive value, but I would suggest that we do not define corn—whether modified or not—in terms of its immanent *function*.[32] More clearly, other natural phenomena such as volcanic rock, sea shells, and monarch butterflies are not functional objects on this view and hence not designed. But what of art and craft? Does this feature distinguish design from these other aesthetic phenomena? Let me address these separately. Does art have a function? The art-for-art's-sake movement, famously heralded by Oscar Wilde's dictum that "all art is quite useless," wished to elevate art from the baseness of mere human life and claim it as sui generis, being made for contemplation and nothing else.[33] Bell would have concurred: art is an *aesthetic* object, of purely *aesthetic* value. I could here trade on the presumption of art's transcendence and claim that the function of designed objects is immanent, quotidian, or more directly useful than art in that it is the stuff of human material existence.

32 It could be argued that just as GM corn is a designed *improvement* on some earlier strains, so too are Birkenstocks *improvements* on earlier models of sandals, and to admit the latter is also to admit the former as objects of design. However, even if we concede that Birkenstocks are modifications on an earlier or even original sandal, the first sandal was an intentional, functional, designed object, whereas the earlier strains of corn were not—they were simply part of nature. One could of course demand that I name the point at which the natural *becomes* the designed or "artificial," and this would indeed be difficult. Some flower hybrids, for instance, bear little or no resemblance to their naturally occurring relations. But rather than become mired in the metaphysics of identity here, I would point instead to two other features I will claim need be present in my definition of design: (*a*) the finished product must have apparent features we could attend to in our identification and evaluation of a given design, which will eliminate the DNA structure of corn as much as the molecular structure of, say, a new flu vaccine; and (*b*) the designed object must be *manufactured* if not mass-produced, rather than organic or naturally occurring. This will also omit hybrid plants but not perhaps gardens themselves.

33 Oscar Wilde, "Preface," *The Picture of Dorian Gray*, in *The Norton Anthology of English Literature* (2 vols., New York: Norton, 1968), II, 1403. For a fuller discussion of the goals of the art-for-art's-sake movement, see my "The Disenfranchisement of Philosophical Aesthetics," *Journal of the History of Ideas* 64, no. 4 (2003).

Design is meant to be used, art merely to be *looked at*. Wilde, and Bell, would interpret "useless" to mean "outside of human needs and purposes," or again, transcendent. And if art has no function in the sense of being useful, I have effectively distinguished design from it by my criterion. If I sought a definition of design in terms of the qualities or features of designed objects alone, I would provisionally try to make this argument work. But I have doubts about its success. First, my definition of design would be dependent upon Bell's (or someone else's) definition of art, and this weakens my ontology, making it good only so long as Bell's theory stands, which, we have seen, it is not likely to do. Second, I am concerned that going this route would make of immanence a normative rather than descriptive criterion, for art cannot *truly* be useless, else it would be discarded rather than prized. To be contemplated is still a *function* of some kind, and if art is created for this purpose, it is as functional an object as any other. We do not want to create a hierarchy of functions, with contemplation or exaltation being somehow more important or rarified than hammering or sitting; we must employ the notion of "immanence" carefully here. Nor can we say that the function of contemplation—as aesthetic—is different *in kind* from other functions that serve quotidian human needs, because art too must serve a human need or have a human use: who else's need could it serve? If we divide these needs into the material and, say, the intellectual or spiritual (the transcendent, in some sense), we will distinguish design from art on the grounds of serving immanent versus transcendent functions, and this *is* a normative distinction.[34] Unless we can somehow argue that art has no function at all (which I cannot see as being successful), we must

34 Would this also have us exclude from the notion of design other non-art but spiritual or transcendent objects such as Ouija boards or tarot cards or incense? This seems absurd.

conclude that the feature I claim of designed objects is not sufficient to distinguish them on metaphysical grounds from works of art. As aesthetic objects meant for mere contemplation, artworks are also defined by their functions. This is what makes them what they are too.[35]

Let us see if definitions of craft are of any help here. Initially, the quality of having a function seems to bring design much closer to craft. Craftworks are useful: teapots, quilts, ironwork, chests of drawers, and so on are all functional objects, and attempts to define craft reflect this. Markowitz, for instance, in considering ways to distinguish craft from formalist definitions of art, suggests that the aesthetic quality of craftworks is not purely formal, but rather a "functional aesthetic quality" that involves the "fitness of form" of an object "for its utilitarian purpose."[36] The presence of this added element of functionality to some aesthetic objects (but not others) shows up in our appreciation of them, which will involve "some sort of practical activity instead of mere contemplation": these objects in fact have to actually be used.[37]

Fethe seeks to define craft as functional objects that yet are "valued for more than their utility."[38] He writes,

> when we judge a craft object we base our judgements on the success of its "function"... on the power of its aesthetic qualities and on the way the two have been integrated. An object

35 Parsons and Carlson provide an interesting overview of attempts to define artworks according to their functions, in chapter 8 of their volume *Functional Beauty*.

36 Markowitz, "Distinction between Art and Craft," 58–59.

37 Ibid., 59. Markowitz is not defending this position: her goal is to consider the ways in which craft is considered inferior to art, and here, the physical activity of *using* the object she sees as "on most views irrelevant to or incompatible with aesthetic response" (59), and seeks to understand why this is so.

38 Fethe, "Craft and Art," 133.

> which retains either function or aesthetic qualities but not both loses the special complexity which gives craft its unique appeal.[39]

It is tempting here to form a tripartite division: artworks are those that have only aesthetic qualities, crafts have aesthetic *and* functional qualities, and designed objects are functional alone. An object-centred approach would seem to suggest this. But for the reasons that have been accumulating in our discussion this far, I think this division is simplistic, and indicates that attention to the qualities of an object alone is insufficient to distinguish design from art *or* craft. First there will be counter-examples: Markowitz mentions ceramicist Carl Borgeson, who "now makes deliberately non-functional teapots whose lids are glued on,"[40] and quilts in particular have in recent years migrated from the bed to the gallery wall.[41] Designed objects too, of course, are regularly placed in museums and galleries, where they are no longer used but merely admired, like the lighting fixture ("85 Lamps") by Rody Graumans and the "Paimio" chair by Alvar Aalto that are part of the MOMA's permanent collection.[42] Second, I maintain that the notion of an "aesthetic quality" is not unproblematically descriptive, carrying instead—often implicit—normative weight, and making this division more than strictly ontological. Third, I am not convinced we can consistently argue that artworks are without functions without, again, making a normative claim when we do this. If we categorize art as purely aesthetic, craft as quasi-aesthetic, and design as

39 Ibid., 134.

40 Markowitz, "Distinction between Art and Craft," 64.

41 We may say, and Zangwill would say, that this makes them works of art, but common linguistic practice militates against this move, as I have mentioned.

42 These can both be found online at http://www.moma.org/collection/depts/arch_design/index.html.

not aesthetic at all, we are still making reference to some normative criterion—whether a quality itself, or a type of (immanent or transcendent) function—and this impedes our definition. Finally, if we make this tripartite division, we will be perforce admitting that there is nothing about designed objects that is of aesthetic interest at all, which would fly in the face of all international design competitions, awards, and museums as well as our common practices and linguistic use. More importantly, this would quite clearly undermine my entire project. For if designs have no aesthetic qualities, why should my discipline spend any time on design at all?

Something like this division exists within the world of design itself. Design theorist Victor Margolin notes that design is often divided into three categories: the first, industrial (including product), graphic, stage, interior, and fashion design "tends to separate out more artistically oriented ways of designing" that can be contrasted with "engineering or computer science, which are technologically based" but which still yield material products. The third, "the design of immaterial products" like techniques and services, is the province of industrial engineering, urban planning, and so on.[43] Adopting Margolin's division would also have prima facie benefits: we could say, on an object-centred approach, that our philosophical interest lies with the first category—those quasi-aesthetic objects that are the result of "artistic" design—and then ignore the merely functional objects and the immaterial designs altogether. Our task would then be limited to distinguishing design from the quasi-aesthetic objects of craft, and we would be relieved of finding ways to eliminate, for instance, automatic weapons and software applications (as non-artistic) from the scope of our concerns.

43 Victor Margolin, "Introduction," in *Design Discourse: History, Theory, Criticism*, ed. Victor Margolin (Chicago: University of Chicago Press, 1984), 4.

Again, though, Margolin's distinction relies on a normative criterion—designs that are somehow artistic as opposed to those that are not—and this again confuses definition with aesthetic evaluation, which I have been trying to avoid. Further, all three categories claim to be functional, whether they yield material products or not, which indicates that my proposed criterion is again insufficient for an object-centred approach. The ADR's category of "interactive" has recognized an online photo editor and a 911 command centre radio application, and the NDA's award for "communication" in 2009 was the *New York Times* graphics department, all of which would equally be designs on the functional view, even if they do not yield a physical object as their products. And why not? The design of a web browser, while functional yet immaterial, seems to me equally a candidate for aesthetic appraisal, provided that there are apparent properties that can be appraised. All of this suggests that designs are not only objects and that "design" cannot be adequately understood on an object-centred approach focused on a single defining property.

I have been considering design from the point of view of function as its (only) salient property. Before we move on, we need to consider whether any other property would better serve our theory, and here I would like to return for a moment to the idea of form. We have seen that for Bell, art is distinguished by its formal properties only, and that for Fethe and Markowitz craft seems to be about form and function in equal measure, just as artistic design is for Margolin. What kind of role can form play in the identification of design as a category of objects? There are two opposing views to canvass here. First, if we attend to the rallying cry of the Bauhaus school (and much of modernism itself) that "form follows function," it seems to be of secondary importance at best. Dieter Rams, one-time president of the German Design Council and chief designer at Braun, claimed that "[p]eople do not buy a specific product just to look at it, rather because it performs certain functions. Its design must conform in the best possible way to the expectations that result from the function the product fulfills."[44] This suggests that the formal or apparent qualities of the designed object should play a minimal role in our understanding and appraisal of them. Rams continues,

> items should be designed in such a way that their function and attributes are directly understood.... The festival of colours and form and the entertainment of form sensations enlarges the world's chaos. To out-do each other with new design sensations leads nowhere.[45]

Rams—and the Bauhaus school—would concur with our suggested tripartite division, that designed objects are primarily, or purely, functional, and would clearly reject the idea that some design practices are, or should be, more "artistic" than others.

This strictly functional view leads to difficulties (apart from the immediate fact that it robs design of aesthetic interest entirely). First, as I have noted, all objects have form of some kind and to ignore the formal elements of design is as counter-intuitive as Bell's demand that we dismiss the representational content of art in our understanding of it. Further, Rams's injunction is normative rather than descriptive: for design to be any good, form *should* be superseded by function, which is clearly not the same as suggesting that designed objects have no form at all. The formal elements of design, in fact, appear to be necessary to our identification and differentiation of objects. Two wine-glasses, for example, may be functionally

44 Dieter Rams, "Omit the Unimportant," in Margolin, *Design Discourse*, 111.
45 Ibid., 112–113.

identical: designed for—and successful in—holding and airing wine and delivering it to the palate. What else is to distinguish a Philippe Stark goblet from a generic one purchased at Walmart if not its formal elements (and, perhaps, the quality of its materials)? Once we have got the function of the wine-glass right, what need would we have to continue designing new models but for alterations in their form? The distinctive form of a Stark goblet is, in part, how we identify it as a different design from countless others, and also in part, I will eventually argue, how we appraise it as being any good.[46] This suggests that design is not about function alone, and leads to the countervailing view, put forward by David Pye.

Pye defines design in terms of its formal properties, as that which "chooses that the things we use shall look as they do."[47] He argues that "whenever humans design and make a useful thing they invariably expend a good deal of unnecessary and easily avoidable work on it which contributes nothing to its usefulness," and this leads him to claim that design, primarily, is "doing useless work on useful things."[48] For Pye, design is all about form, or what he variously calls "decoration," "ornament," or "embellishment."[49] Nothing designers do, he claims, "is concerned with the requirements of use, economy, and access."[50] Pye's emphasis on form

46 Stephen Bayley and Terence Conran, in their book, *Design: Intelligence Made Visible* (Buffalo: Firefly Books, 2007), note that since 1950, "there have been no fundamental changes in the mechanism of the electric razor or, indeed, in the landscape of the human face, but the fact that the form of [Braun] razors has changed since then demonstrates that they . . . are sensitive to subtle aspects of appearance." Rams, they suggest, "has even admitted making last-minute adjustments to a razor design because the almost finished product did not achieve the effect he had in mind. He did not admit to having *styled* it, but that was what he meant" (53). And this makes the claims of strict functionalism more tenuous.

47 Pye, *Nature and Aesthetics of Design*, 11.

48 Ibid., 13.

49 Ibid.

50 Ibid., 77.

alone as a mark of design may in part be due to his dismissal of its function, as we noted earlier. And, while a formalist definition of design will be no more successful than that of art, Pye's view does offer a corrective to a strictly functionalist view. For one thing, Pye is right to remind us that not all elements of designed objects appear to directly contribute to their intended functions. The 1958 Studebakers, for example, especially the Golden Hawk and the Silver Hawk, had spectacularly non-functional fins designed by the Parisian industrial designer Raymond Loewy.[51] These fins in no way contributed to the ability of the cars to fulfill their functions, and in no way helped to identify them *as* cars instead of other kinds of things. Yet these fins marked the Studebaker as a unique design and aided in differentiating it from other cars of the same era. These fins also cannot be neglected in our aesthetic evaluation of the design of the Studebaker, as they are integral to what makes it the unique car that it was. Form, then, appears to play a necessary role in our ontology: it may not alone distinguish design from art and craft, given that all three kinds of objects have formal elements of some sort, just as all three appear to have a function. But form may be the element that allows us to tell designs apart from *each other*, and to mark them as original, other (functional) elements being equal. For while function allows us to define a hammer or car, it marks it out as a *kind* of thing, or a class of things. To distinguish two different hammers, function is not enough: we will have to differentiate them on the basis of their apparent or formal features—on how they look, or how they feel in our hands. I will return to this in the following section when I address the originality of art and design.

51 My thanks for this example to Steven Burns, who used it in a commentary he delivered on my paper "From Bauhaus to Birkenstocks: Towards an Aesthetics of Design" at the Canadian Philosophical Association's annual congress, Toronto, 2006.

What we can conclude for the moment is the following: if we consider design from the perspective of a class of objects, we can claim that function is a feature they all have in common, one by virtue of which they are defined as the kinds of things they are. This quality is clearly not enough to provide any kind of robust definition—even working definition—of design as a kind of object, nor does it adequately distinguish design from art or craft. All three types of products also have form, whether significant or not, and this notion of form also has some role to play in their definition. But that designed objects are all functional, or that they must have been made with specific functions in mind, does provide us with one piece of the puzzle that is design, as does the lingering notion of immanence, if we can only sort out how to properly deploy it. And while it may seem that we have done no more here than describe the quiddity of everyday things, this is not the case. We can now maintain that design, as a candidate for aesthetic appreciation, is a category that contains only intentional functional objects, and we can anticipate that our appraisal of them will be tied to this intended function rather than to whatever uses they might serve, or to only purely formal elements in their appearances.[52] We have also clarified our first intuition about the notion of design: what sets it apart from other sorts of things is not only that it is "artificial" rather than natural, nor even that it is manufactured, but that design refers to a category of objects that have been made to serve particular purposes. And this brings us inevitably to a consideration of the activity of design and its role in this emerging picture. If we return to the Annual Design Review and the National

52 Of course, I use the term "object" advisedly here, intending that it also capture the not strictly material designs of logos, websites, and the like, just as the notion of an "artwork" has expanded to include performance, sound, dance, and other forms that are not strictly material objects either.

Design Awards, while their categories name kinds of objects that are examples of (good) design, their awards honour the individuals behind the particular designs as much as the things themselves. Designers, then, are appraised in a way that is similar to artists, and it must be for something specific that they do. The next section focuses on design as an activity, and I will begin by contrasting this activity with that of art-making and craft.

ii. Expression and Art as an Activity

The primary emphasis in activity-centred views of art can be found in theories of expression: of the emotions, or ideas, or singular vision of an individual that distinguishes his or her work as fine art. Expression theories have garnered more attention, and have had more staying power, than formalist or object-centred theories, although the idea of expression around which they revolve has been interpreted quite widely. Simply put, these theories focus on expression as the particular activity that singles out art from other sorts of things. I'll look quickly at two different attempts to describe this activity as I introduce this section. For Tolstoy, art—as a work—embodies the expression of an artist's sincerely felt emotion and has the ability—indeed, is meant to—infect its audience in the same way. "Art is a human activity consisting in this, that one man, consciously, by means of certain external signs, hands on to others feelings he has lived through, and that others are infected by these feelings."[53] This condition is both necessary and sufficient to define art: a work's formal elements of style or composition, or its representative properties such as verisimilitude or narrative meaning, have no bearing on Tolstoy's definition. Nor, in

53 Leo Tolstoy, *What is Art?* In *Art and its Significance: An Anthology of Aesthetic Theory*, ed. Stephen David Ross (Albany: SUNY Press, 1994), 179.

fact, does Tolstoy explicitly distinguish between kinds of objects: anything, whether it be a novel, a painting, or a musical composition will be art if it displays the sincere emotion felt by the artist and transmits that emotion to its audience.

Tolstoy's theory is an early attempt to define art in terms of expression, and so exhibits its weaknesses most clearly. He does not explain how, by looking at a work, we can conclude that the artist felt a given emotion when she created it, for instance, or how we can judge her—or the work's—sincerity. Nor does he account for works that may move us but that were created by artists who perhaps did not feel the requisite emotion at the time of their creation. His "sincerity condition" is under-developed: we may find Beethoven's late string quartets to express sadness or *Guernica* to express horror, without thereby concluding that Beethoven or Picasso felt these emotions at the time of composition. In fact, the only way to verify the emotion felt by the artist—and so to identify a work *as* art—is to examine the circumstances of its production, or actually quiz the artist herself. From the work itself we can learn little: if we are moved by it, we could well have been manipulated, or could be reacting for purely personal reasons; if we fail to be moved by it, we could be merely obtuse, or the artist could have felt nothing, or perhaps the artist was sincere but just did not communicate her emotion effectively enough. From the point of view of the audience, we can know almost nothing about the artist's state of mind, and hence cannot identify a work as bona fide art. Even barring these particular problems with Tolstoy's formulation, expression theories tend to suffer from being under-determined: unless expression itself can be better described, there is no reason to limit this activity to the fine arts. A quilt, a tantrum, a letter, or a glance could all equally be examples of the expression of a sincere emotion, and have the ability to, in certain circumstances, likewise infect their audiences with the same, but none of these are commonly considered to be works of art.

R. G. Collingwood focused more explicitly on the activity of expression in his theory of art, so much so that in fact the art object almost completely disappears. Fine art, for Collingwood, as expression, is an activity in which the artist clarifies or realizes an inchoate emotion: "Until a man has expressed his emotion, he does not yet know what emotion it is. The act of expressing it is therefore an exploration of his own emotions."[54] Art as activity is thus a form of articulation and self-realization; more than mere discharge or display of, say, rage, "art proper" is a coming-to-know this rage *as* rage, through a candid internal and imaginative process whose "characteristic mark" is "lucidity or intelligibility."[55] "The artist proper is a person who, grappling with the problem of expressing a certain emotion, says 'I want to get this clear.'"[56] And this activity is primarily private or self-directed: the expression of emotion "is not addressed to any particular audience. It is addressed primarily to the speaker himself, and secondarily to anyone who can understand."[57] The artist's goal is not to produce a preconceived emotional effect on his audience, *pace* Tolstoy, but to discover and understand his own emotions and by doing so, perhaps permit the audience to undertake the same kind of process of self-discovery.[58]

For Collingwood, the art *object* is of secondary concern to this expressive activity, making his theory, as an ontology of art, hard to pin down. Collingwood claims that art "is an 'internal' or

54 R. G. Collingwood, *The Principles of Art* (Oxford: Oxford University Press, 1958), 111.
55 Ibid., 122.
56 Ibid., 114.
57 Ibid., 111.
58 Ibid., 122.

'mental' thing" and only secondarily is it a "bodily or perceptible thing." Of the two, he claims, the first "is the thing which the artist as such primarily produces," while the second is "only incidental to the first," a "subsidiary activity."[59] A work of art, he claims, "may be completely created when it has been created as a thing whose only place is in the artist's mind": there is no such thing as "an *objet d'art* in itself; if we call any bodily and perceptible thing by that name . . . we do so only because of the relation in which it stands" to the expressive activity that is art proper.[60] The manifestation of this activity in an object is by contrast an act of mere "fabrication."[61]

The problems that plague Collingwood's theory, and expression theory in general, are similar to those that faced formalism, and I will not belabour them: as essentialist, expression theory is again exposed to counter-examples—it is either too broad, allowing any suitably expressive act (and its product) to be considered art, or too narrow, omitting commonly accepted works on the grounds that they are not expressive enough or were not expressed in the right way. Its reliance on an activity that we do not witness makes it as difficult for us to pick out the evidence of expression in a work as it is to pick out significant form: in each case we must somehow *feel* its presence. Expression theories also have a new set of problems facing them, particularly those of explaining how an activity is transmuted into a work that we can appreciate. As with Tolstoy, we can ask how we can *see* the sincere emotion in the work itself, or know that the emotional content of the work was actually sincerely felt by the artist during its creation. And Collingwood's theory in particular has been charged with being idealist in its reliance on

59 Ibid., 37.
60 Ibid., 130, 37.
61 Ibid., 133.

a mental act as the primary locus of art proper. These problems have led some expression theorists to claim that "expressiveness" is actually a property of works themselves, one that we can reasonably experience, absent any knowledge of the activity used to produce it.[62] But this move makes expressiveness an aesthetic quality and shifts the focus of the theory from act to property, compounding rather than ameliorating its problems, for it returns us to the difficulties facing object-centred theories and brings us no closer to being able to identify expressiveness or pick it out.

Despite these problems, expression theory is the primary activity-centred approach to defining fine art. Throughout its many iterations (which are too numerous to canvass here) we can find certain common characteristics on which I would like to focus. First, art on this view is understood as original—the product of a unique expressive activity by a particular identifiable individual. Second, the shift from object to activity runs parallel to a shift in focus from form to content: what distinguishes fine art from other sorts of things is that is *says* something or *means* something, and it is primarily to this content that we should attend in our experience and evaluation of a work of art. Further, expression theory generally defends this content as being somehow deep, or profound, and as communicating an idea or vision of relevance or import for our lives and concerns. These two features—originality and profundity—amount to necessary conditions for a definition of art that runs through the activity-centred approach, and it is on the basis of these that I will consider both craft and design. The questions to be addressed here are whether originality and profundity are

62 This kind of position can be found, for example, in Nelson Goodman's *Languages of Art* (Indianapolis: Hackett Press, 1976); Suzanne Langer's *Feeling and Form* (London: Routledge, 1953); and Peter Kivy's, *The Corded Shell: Reflections on Musical Expression* (Princeton: Princeton University Press, 1980).

required for design, or are as relevant to our evaluation of design as they are to our evaluation of art. I will try to demonstrate that they are *not*.

Let me begin with art's claim of originality. For Collingwood, as for Tolstoy, sincerity is a prime factor in expression: an artist "is an artist only in so far as he is candid."[63] The originating activity that produces a work of art is one that is sincere, authentic, self-reflective, and emotional, and it is this activity that makes a work of art unique. If an artist expresses grief or rage, she—to be sincere—must be expressing her own particular feelings of grief rather than making a dispassionate claim about grief in general or trying to capture the grief someone else may have felt. And it is this personal emotional expression that differentiates works of art from each other as well as from other kinds of things, marking them as the original products of a given artist's expressive activity. This reflects a common intuition we have about art that I canvassed earlier: that it somehow embodies or expresses a meaning particular to it, one that cannot be transferred from one work or one artist to another because of the very particularity of the act of its creation. Two works may equally express grief, and so be similar, but they will not express grief in exactly the same way, because they reflect the emotional output of two different people. Our notions of forgery depend in part upon this view: a fake Picasso has not been made by his hand, but more, is not authentically the product of an activity the artist engaged in with all of the sincerity and personal feeling we expect. One of the reasons we feel defrauded when we discover a work is forged is because it is insincere: were I to faithfully reproduce *Guernica*, my work would fail to *be* the painting *Guernica* because I did not feel Picasso's emotions and

63 Collingwood, *The Principles of Art*, 115.

thus did not express or articulate them in the way that he had done in the original.

Let me be clear that by "originality" here I mean "uniqueness" or "singularity" rather than "innovation"; on the expression view, every artistic act—and hence every artistic product—is singular: it cannot be replaced by another, mistaken for another, or duplicated without loss because of the personal nature of its creation. Even were we confronted with two pieces that happened to be identical in all apparent respects, they would, as Arthur Danto has well taught us, comprise uniquely individual works of art in part because of the particularity of this originating activity. But this means that the basis for the originality of art lies not in its formal or apparent properties at all, but in the specificity of its meaning or content as determined by the expressive act that produced it. Art in this sense is an act that produces a uniquely executed "one-off" work in every case. And any work that has not been created by this act cannot be art, whatever other aesthetic qualities it might possess. Let me also stress that, while I take originality in this sense to be a defining feature of art for expression theory, it plays no part in what makes art any good. "Original," as innovative, is a normative term and we generally use it as such. "Originality" as uniqueness is meant to be shorn of these normative connotations. If design should lack this feature, it will not be *less* than art, but merely different.

Superficially, we can see an immediate difference between design and art on the basis of originality. For, whatever is involved in the activity of design, its products are not unique particulars. Danto's famous array of red squares in *The Transfiguration of the Commonplace* suggested that there is an important difference between a work of art and an object, and even a number of perceptually indiscernible things can comprise unique works of art because of their originating expressive activity.[64] Danto in a later paper claimed that each of the red squares "was an importantly distinct work of art . . . constituted in part by what could not have met the eye." Instead, one "needed to know something about the provenance of the work, when and by whom it was painted, and what it *was meant to say*" in order to define it as such.[65] Two (or six or eight) different artists engaged in this expressive activity may well produce objects that are indiscernible from each other but each comprises a unique work of art because of its particular *content*. With design, this is not the case. Designed objects are not singular but multiple; we do not approach an array of indiscernible iPhones or teapots with the expectation that each *says* something unique. Designs for the most part are not "one-offs" in the way that artworks on Danto's view must be. If the activity of design is singular and original, it cannot be through the multiple products of an expressive activity that we come to realize this.

This superficial distinction between art and design, however, fades if we switch our model from the visual arts, which Danto depends on, to the literary arts such as poetry, which Collingwood uses as his paradigm example. A poem, such as Emily Dickinson's "Because I could not stop for death," is the product of an expressive activity just as much as Picasso's *Guernica* is. The difference lies in the physical manifestation of the poem, or what Collingwood calls its "fabrication." We can see how poetry for him is much more of a mental act than painting, for the publication of a poem, in a

64 I refer here to Danto's thought experiment in chapter 1, which cleverly describes various different works of art in a gallery that are nonetheless indistinguishable in terms of their visual properties, all being identical square, red, painted canvasses.

65 Arthur Danto, "Indiscernibility and Perception: A Reply to Joseph Margolis," *British Journal of Aesthetics* 39, no. 4 (1999): 325 (my italics).

chapbook or an anthology (or as is more common lately, on a bus shelter or in a metro), is something that typically the poet takes no part in, an action that happens after the poem is complete, and that is external to its composition. Poems—and novels—can also be produced in runs of thousands, and we likewise would not consider each pressing to be a unique particular work of art. Indeed, literary awards are not granted to a particular copy of a book (and its physical features such as colour of paper, typeface, or jacket design) but to the story or poem contained within, however it may have been printed or by whom.[66] With art on the model of literature, we are also asked to see past the physical features of an object to grasp its emotive content, and it is this content that makes it original, just as it does for Danto. But in this case it is irrelevant if there are countless indiscernible instantiations of a final product: they will not be separate works of art, as Danto suggests in his thought experiment, but multiple copies of one.[67] We can ask whether design cannot be original in the same way as literature; after all, when Yves Behar won the NDA in 2004 for his Birkenstock shoes, it was not for a particular pair, but for all of them together, or at least for the designing activity that led to their production. Each pair, we could say, is a token of the type that is Behar's design, just as each copy of "Because I could not stop for death" is a token of the singular artwork that is the poem itself. And this seems to suggest with design, too, we can look past its apparent features to judge its content, or the activity that went into its creation.

66 Of course jacket covers and typefaces can and do win awards for their design. My point here is simply that an award of *literary* merit for a poem or novel does not take these features into consideration.

67 However, a series of prints, too, will be visually indiscernible while having the same content, something not mentioned by Danto in his work. Yet a series of prints, if numbered, will be limited in a way that the print runs of a novel will not be, and will generally be under the control of the artist herself.

The parallel between design and literary art breaks down in one important regard, however. As Collingwood suggested, a poem may be complete before it is ever written down or published. We may need to read it in order to appraise it, but when we do, it is not the physical features of the poem that are being assessed (such as its typeface) but again its putative expressive content or meaning. Danto would agree: we "read" the apparent features of a painting to get at the "work" that it contains, and we evaluate this work in terms of its meaning. But with design, it is the physical artifact with all of its apparent qualities that is the candidate for our aesthetic evaluation: we have to look at and *use* the object itself in order to make a judgement about it because, if our investigation is cumulative, the object's intended function, (and whether it fulfills it) are equally important to our evaluations of it. An attempt at a purely activity-based approach to design may return us with more sympathy to the third term in Heskett's nonsensical definition that "design is to design a design to produce a design." If the locus of design stands between an activity and a manufactured product, in the way that a completed poem seems to lie for Collingwood between the activity of composing and the printed page, or a painting for Danto lies between the artist's expression and the work's instantiation as an object, we could claim that the originality of design lies in its originating activity. But as Heskett saw, this activity results in a middle term that is only a proposal, not a finished work, and it will remain incomplete until it has actually been produced. The particular activity that is design may be as sincere and authentic as that of art, but unlike art on the expression view, it does not on its own produce an object for our appraisal. It is not a proposal that comprises design any more than notes for an early draft of a poem or a study for a painting are the finished products of the activity that is art. For expression theory, not only is the emotive activity necessary for something to be art, it is also—for Collingwood especially—sufficient, and that which results in the originality of art. For design, this is clearly not the case. It seems that, however we describe the activity of design, we still need it to result in a product for us to appraise, and for this product to be complete, it must be an object whose apparent features we cannot ignore in the way that we can ignore typeface or paper quality when we read for literary merit. This is not to suggest that design is without originality but that we cannot define it based on its originating activity alone. Let me turn for a moment to the distinction between art and craft to help tease out this point here.

Works of craft we also tend to think of as unique originals but on the basis of, perhaps, a different kind of originating activity. Collingwood in particular took pains to distinguish craft from art proper and, while he defined craft negatively as lacking what art has, nevertheless he provided the first and most complete analysis of craft in philosophical aesthetics and it is worth considering his distinction here. Collingwood listed a number of features particular to craft-making, the most important of which are the following:

1. Craft involves a distinction between means and end, where the means are actions ("manipulating the tools, tending the machines") that are "passed through or traversed" in order to reach a given end and "left behind" when that end is reached.
2. There is a distinction between planning and execution, where the result is "preconceived or thought out" before being made.

3. There is a distinction between raw material and finished product where the raw material is found ready-to-hand and then transformed by craft into something different.
4. And, in relation to this, form is distinguished from matter, where the matter remains the same in both raw material and finished product and the form is the only thing that changes.[68]

Craft is a skilled activity: Collingwood refers back to the terms *ars* and *technē* and describes this activity as the ability to "produce a preconceived result by means of consciously controlled and directed action."[69] This activity has two discrete aspects, both of which are essential to craft. First, (in reference to the second feature above) is the planning or foreknowledge required: "The craftsman knows what he wants to make before he makes it." This foreknowledge is "absolutely indispensable" to craft and is "not vague but precise": as Collingwood notes, "If a person sets out to make a table, but conceives the table only vaguely, as somewhere between two by four feet and three by six...he is no craftsman." If an object is made without this precise foreknowledge, "it is not a case of craft but an accident."[70] The planning of a work of craft is a mental activity, as art is a mental activity. But in this case the activity is rational rather than emotional, planned rather than spontaneous and exploratory. Second, this plan is then consciously executed upon raw materials to produce a desired product (as with features 1 and 3); crafts are created by skilled makers, and herein especially lies their uniqueness. Each work of craft is hand-made; by a given means and upon a chosen raw material a

68 Collingwood, *The Principles of Art*, 15–16.
69 Ibid., 15.
70 Ibid., 16.

craftsperson himself fashions this copper pot, that wooden bench, and doing so requires skill and knowledge of materials, as well as a preconceived plan. As Robert Kavanagh has noted in his analysis of Collingwood's theory of craft, "the involvement of the human hand may quite rightly be called *the* creative source of this bowl, at this place and time."[71] In contrast to craft, art for Collingwood "is an activity of which there can be no technique,"[72] partly because the primary act of expression is already over before the fabrication of the material object begins, and partly because it is this primary spontaneous and emotional activity and not the skilled execution of an object that defines art proper. A work of art is original in the sense of singular because it is comprised of, or the product of, the sincere and authentic act of expression; a work that is skilfully executed but that expresses no emotional content cannot be art on this view. A work of craft also has an originating mental activity that is necessary to it but an activity that is rational and conscious rather than expressive. And this activity is not sufficient: a work of craft must then be executed by the actual hands of a skilled artisan, and it is the final product of this execution that is singular and the object of our aesthetic appraisal. While Danto may claim that each work of visual art is also a unique particular, executed by the same person as had the expressive vision, still that execution and the apparent features of the object can only be secondary to his theory of art: if indeed a number of artists can produce objects that are indiscernible from each other, it is not primarily the "human hand" that makes them art but the prior singular vision itself as it is communicated through these objects' visible features. What the finished products *look like,* and what degree of skill or technique is

71 Robert Kavanagh, "Collingwood: Aesthetics and a Theory of Craft," *International Studies in Philosophy* 23, no. 3 (1991): 23.

72 Collingwood., *The Principles of Art,* 111.

evidenced in their fabrication, seems as unnecessary for Danto as it does for Collingwood's more literary model of art.

We may immediately object to Collingwood's depiction of the activity of craft as so pragmatic and so without spontaneity or creativity. He would certainly claim that design is equally rational and precise. And we may equally object to the idea that art requires no skill.[73] We must remember the normative thrust of Collingwood's work: his goal was to define craft negatively, as somehow less than art, and to do that he had to devalue the activity itself. I will return to this in a moment when I consider the supposed profundity of art that underlies the expression view. First, though, let us consider what we learn about design as contrasted with craft in terms of its originality. It shares with craft the double-faceted nature of its production: neither finds its originality in—and thus is not defined by—a mental activity alone, or even primarily a mental activity. In both cases, we attend to the apparent features of the actual finished product in our identification and aesthetic evaluation. Even were craft and design characterized by the same spontaneity and self-reflexivity as art, Collingwood is correct to suggest that what makes something a work of craft is *also* its skilled execution, and this forms, I would suggest, an equal part of our appraisal of it. For

73 The idealism that seems to underlie Collingwood's theory is the source of its most trenchant criticism, which I cannot explore here. "Of course," contemporary expression theorists will claim, "the successful execution of the originating expression and its manifestation in a work are necessary for something to be art. A sincerely felt but amateurish painting (or poem) will be a failure." To this sort of claim I can make two responses. First, we must distinguish between what makes something art and what makes it any good: a poorly executed painting will still be a work of art, just not a very good one. Second, however theorists may have tried to correct Collingwood's earlier articulation of expression to include requirements of skill and the fabrication of an object, expression itself not only remains necessary in their definitions of art but it also remains *primary,* if no longer sufficient. With craft, the balance shifts in the other direction: however unemotional or contentless a pitcher may be, what counts is the finished product and the skill displayed in its execution.

craft, as for design, the mental activity is not sufficient, for all that it is necessary. So I would like to claim that design is *like* craft and *unlike* art in that an ontology of the two must attend to the product as much as the process in its definition.

Second, design is *like* craft in that while both activities produce functional objects, it is not their functions that make them original but their formal features instead. (I alluded to this in the last section.) What differentiates a bowl by one potter from a bowl by another is not its function to hold water or fruit but the way it *looks* and *feels*: its colour, shape, material, texture, and so on. The originality of craftsmanship does not stem from the creation or invention of utterly new objects with unique functions but in the re-creation of a familiar object—a bowl, a bench—that nevertheless can be distinguished from others that are similar to it because of its apparent features. We may define objects by their functions, as I noted in the last section, but this, again, yields a class or kind of object—chairs, bowls, razors, cars—and is not sufficient to single one out for particular identification or appraisal.

The same is true of design. The function and mechanics of the disposable toothbrush, for instance, have remained almost static since its invention. What makes the Oral-B "Cross-Action" toothbrush by Lunar Design in 1999 original or different from the rest on the drugstore shelf will be its formal features: colour, shape, proportion, and so on rather than its function of cleaning one's teeth, which is shared by all of the others. And what differentiates the "Paimio" chair by Alvar Alto from the "Barcelona" chair by Mies van der Rohe, for instance, will not be the function that makes them the same, but the apparent features, or form of each, that makes them different. Of course bowls and toothbrushes (and chairs) may well sport functional innovations too—a rim, a spout; a handle-grip, longer bristles—but it would be false to claim that every bowl potted or toothbrush manufactured can be differentiated on the basis of some functional alteration.[74] In fact, it is often the formal features of an object rather than its function that make it an iconic piece of its kind, such as the Coca-Cola bottle by Alex Samuelson, or the Vespa by Piaggio.

Third, design is *like* craft in that rationality and precision must play a part in the mental activity of each. Just as a craftsman cannot conceive a table vaguely, so too a designer must be able to send precise instructions to the manufacturer of the product. Conran and Bayley note that a designer must understand the capability of the machinery to be used in the manufacturing process, as well as the "cost structure and the humdrum facts of distribution and sales. How the product will be sold, displayed and packaged are all vital parts of the designer's task and must be fully understood at the beginning of any project."[75] In fact, for them, design "comprises 98 per cent commonsense and 2 per cent…art or aesthetics,"[76] a ratio that echoes Collingwood's definition of the craft process. Again, I do not wish to suggest that design cannot be creative or spontaneous but that it cannot be only this because the end product, as with craft, is functional and so intended to *work* in order to be successful.

Where design is most clearly *unlike* craft is in the nature of its production. Craft, as I have stated, is hand-made, the product of the skilled execution by the same artisan who also conceived its plan. The activity of design is bifurcated in an important regard because the designer is not the product's final manufacturer. Design, in fact, can be said to have developed with the means of mass production

74 This is, of course, what marketing firms try to suggest to consumers of manufactured goods in order to move their products. But most often the supposed "innovation" is so slight a change as to amount to almost nothing.

75 Conran and Bayley, *Design*, 11.

76 Ibid., 10.

and the development of industrial technologies. From the moment that William Morris's Arts and Crafts movement turned to factory production, what were once craftsmen became designers. Since that time, as Conran and Bayley note, "mass production has evolved and been perfected, and in the course of this evolution the designer has variously been an artist, an architect, a social reformer, a mystic, an engineer, a management consultant, a public relations man and, perhaps, now a computer engineer."[77] But in all of these roles, there remains that bifurcation between vision or planning, and execution. Today with CAD (computer-assisted design) and CAM (computer-assisted manufacture) technologies, it is even less clear how much of the design process can be said to reside in some mental activity on the part of an individual. And with so many designers working in-house for corporations or on contract for them, what proportion of their output is uniquely their own and what proportion is the result of marketing strategies or the demands of their executive officers or clientele is harder and harder to determine. This perhaps contributes to the neglect of design by philosophical aesthetics: the activity-based model for defining and understanding art is so prevalent that if we cannot adequately locate the authors of the work or pinpoint their role in its production, we seem unable or unwilling to assess it.

Yet however much the actual activity and participation of the designer may be murky in the production of a given product, we do end up with an object that has both formal and functional features, that can be identified on their basis, and that can be judged aesthetically. Is design then merely craft "gone industrial"? Not quite. Where design differs from craft is that it is very much a *collaborative* endeavour, involving clients, marketers, manufacturers,

77 Ibid., 55.

suppliers, distributors, engineers, and so on. Some art, too, is collaborative: film requires directors, actors, stage-hands, prop makers, location specialists, sound engineers, special effects experts, distributors, and marketers as well. Perhaps I was too quick in the first section to suggest that the "author" of a film cannot be clearly identified. Perhaps, instead, we should consider design as art along the lines of film, theatre, and opera, where the vision for the whole is generally granted to be that of the work's director, and the film is identified and evaluated on this basis. Perhaps design, rather than being the activity of craft removed from the hands of its maker, is more a collaborative form of art, where the designer is the "author" and visionary of the final product, and responsible in the end for its merit or demerit. The collaboration would certainly be greatly broadened in design, across a larger number of people, corporations, and perhaps countries, but if in the end each member of the production team is working to realize one individual's vision, we may find the locus of design in the designer's activity after all, in the same way we can locate the genesis of a film with its director, and can distinguish a Kieślowski film from a Bergman or Polanski on the grounds of some singular vision. This suggestion will not succeed, however, because art can be distinguished from craft and design in one last important regard: that of its supposed profundity, which no other activity or object seems to share.

I have said all along that on the expression view, works of art stand out by—and are appraised on the basis of—their content or meaning rather than their apparent features. It is this content that makes a work of art profound. Here, profundity differs slightly from the transcendence of art on the formalist view, because it is not an escape from the complexities of human existence but rather an immersion into them in a revealing and intimate way. Art explores and expresses what it means to be human in all its particularity, and it is this depth of expression that we respond to. A child can draw, an elephant can be taught to splash paint on a canvas, a computer can be programmed to create colourful images, but none of these activities can be art because, whatever their apparent or formal features, they lack the depth of intentional meaning that expression theory demands. A work of craft may be creative and may be original in the sense of being a singular object, but at the end of the day it is not art in the same way that an elephant's painting is not. It *says* nothing and *means* nothing; it has no content because the mental and physical acts that produced it were not intentionally expressive of anything; it is an artifact and nothing more.[78] The fourth feature Collingwood outlined reflects this: with craft, there is a distinction between form and matter, where form refers to "the shape of a preconceived plan before being imposed upon the matter" and the matter is the raw material the craftsperson selects for that plan. Collingwood took pains to clarify a frequent confusion of this distinction with one between form and content, which is of a different kind and is relevant only to art proper. Content does not refer to the raw material taken up and transformed by the artist (indeed art proper has no raw material for Collingwood) but is "what is expressed" in the work of art, with the form this time being "that which expresses it" or the way in which the content is expressed.[79] Whether or not such a clear separation between form and content can be made (and Collingwood sees that it needs more analysis), the point is that with art some meaning is expressed in the act and with craft

78 This is certainly Collingwood's view (*The Principles of Art*, 24). But it seems to be echoed by Markowitz and Fethe in their understanding of craft as being distinct on these grounds. While some craftworks (such as the teapot with no spout) can be defended as making a statement of some kind, such stand-out examples show that this is not the norm for the great body of works of craft.

79 Ibid.

generally nothing is expressed at all. However creative the mental activities of craft and design may be, in both cases nothing in fact is being *said*: craft and design have no content. An object is simply being made.

The presumption of the profundity of art's content has developed in tandem with the sophistication of expression theory itself. For Tolstoy, art had merely to express an emotion with sincerity; for Collingwood, the original emotion was explored and finally understood only through its articulation in the expressive act itself. Perhaps the most sophisticated articulation of expression theory, and hence of art's profundity, we find with Arthur Danto. For Danto, art involves an activity of second-order reflection, where the artist is not simply exhibiting her emotions but is reflecting upon them and saying something particular *about* them. This notion of "aboutness" is central to Danto's claims. While "the concept of expression is the most pertinent to the concept of art,"[80] this expression is not merely faithfully representing an emotion like sadness as Tolstoy would suggest, or fully articulating it for the first time as Collingwood would claim. For Danto, the artist is further reflecting upon the sadness itself that she is feeling, and saying something about what this particular emotion might mean. Danto notes that "[t]hings make up the world, but some things . . . are also *outside* the world in the sense that the world is what they are true of."[81] And art, for him, has a profundity that mere real things lack because it is not only of the world but *about* it in that it does not merely represent our feelings but evaluates them and reflects upon what these feelings might mean. And because of the complexity of this expressive content (which Danto

80 Danto, *Transfiguration of the Commonplace*, 165.
81 Ibid., 81.

describes as largely metaphorical), artworks are things in need of interpretation by their audiences. Danto claims that "to understand the artwork is to grasp the metaphor that is, I think, always there."[82] In our encounters with art "the middle term has to be found, the gap has to be filled in, the mind moved to action."[83] We are not merely infected with an emotion, as Tolstoy would have it, nor do we simply recognize the feelings the artist is communicating, as Collingwood seems to claim. We instead have to *work out* the meaning of the piece, and this requires our participation in art at a deeper level than earlier expression theorists saw. This also makes of art a complex, ambiguous, meaning-laden mode of (primarily visual) communication. "What, then, is . . . essential in art is the spontaneous ability the artist has of enabling us to see his way of seeing the world"[84] through our interpretation of the visual content that carries this deeper meaning. This is not to suggest that all art manages to reach Danto's level of profundity—that a work should fail to do so is an evaluative claim, not a descriptive one. For Danto, what makes something a work of art is that it strives to achieve this kind of communicative content, and that nothing else does, in quite the same way.

By contrast, craftworks and designs would be, as I have suggested earlier, "mere real things": saying nothing and carrying no interpretable meaning. Is this claim at all sound? In short, I think it is. Whether or not Danto's theory of art is correct—or Collingwood's, for that matter—it is an abiding intuition we have about art that it carries with it meaning of some kind, says something rather than nothing, and requires interpretation on our part to understand it. Occasionally, it is profound. This is not

82 Ibid., 172.
83 Ibid., 171.
84 Ibid., 207.

to say that craft and design are thereby *superficial*: I think this distinction can be made without such normative implications. Collingwood's depiction of the activity of craft was, as I have noted, a negative one. Certainly the mental activities of craft and design may be spontaneous and creative—it would take a complex psychological study (if even that) to correctly identify them—but what they generally are not is communicative in the same way that art is.

Sally Markowitz calls this distinction "semantic"[85] and generally supports it, noting certain interesting exceptions. Some craftsmen "desire to be more like painters and sculptors...by insisting that one's work be *about* something, often about oneself." The ceramicist Borgeson, for instance, "intends his pots to make a 'personal statement,'" while others continue to make functional objects but title them.[86] These sorts of practices "transform certain mere things into things-in-need-of-interpretation"[87]—or move them from the category of craft to that of art. Some designs, similarly, can be said to be "about" something, or to comment on the nature of design itself, such as the Philippe Stark goblets I have referred to, which are sold in sets of six, one of which is "absolutely perfect" and the other five "imperceptibly flawed,"[88] or Michael Graves's kettle for Alessi with a handle too hot to handle.[89] And William Morris clearly wished to communicate a vision of how we ought to live through his design practice. But that we can pick out a few such examples to me indicates that we see these as stand-out exceptions to the majority of designed objects: we do

85 Markowitz, "Distinction between Art and Craft," 66.
86 Ibid., 64.
87 Ibid., 65.
88 These are the "Un Parfait" goblets, seen advertised in *Bon Appetit* (September 2005): 42.
89 Conran and Bayley, *Design*, 66.

not generally approach our toothbrushes or coffee-pots or hammers as having a content that is the result of the singular vision of their designers. And it is with these more quotidian objects that I am most interested here.

What this discussion suggests is not a conception of craft and design as superficial, but as *mute*, not communicative. Markowtiz's term "semantic" is useful here: the onus is on art, not craft and design, to say something original, to be meaningful or profound, to move us and to engage our interpretive abilities. Such are the demands of an activity-centred view of art like expression theory, and they are instructive. Art's originality rests on its depth of vision: each work is a singular, personal expression that distinguishes it on the basis of what it says rather than merely how it looks, or what it is good for, or whether it works. And this claim is of course also subject to contestation. How can we know, as Collingwood seems so sure, that all art is created by this spontaneous emotive act? And on what grounds can we claim that craft and design are so different? Surely precision and reason—and skill—are as essential to sculpture, dance, and architecture as to carpentry and potting. And surely creativity and spontaneity are as much at play in quilting as they are in painting. There is no doubt that an activity is behind the practice of art, as behind craft and design. And that the definition of each can be reduced to one type of activity—that cannot be witnessed directly—is as tenuous a ground for an ontology as the location of art with a single feature of an object. Nevertheless, as we have seen, the idea of art's profundity or transcendence runs through both object-centred and activity-centred theories and remains important. Whether as significant form and exaltation, or as expressive and aesthetic properties, or as a certain mental act, art has long been considered "semantic" or communicative in a way that craft—like design—does not seem to be.

If we attend to the strong intuitions at play about art, and the phenomenology of our linguistic practices, then we must concede that art is meant to be communicative if not always profound, and that craft and design can be distinguished as practices because they are not. This would mean that design is *unlike* collaborative artworks because, even if a team participates in manufacturing an object that was created by the design of a single individual, that design would not—from first stage to last—be intended to *say* anything or require interpretation, or present a metaphor, or express an emotion, or be about anything at all. That design would be intended to result in a functional—if innovative or even beautiful—object, to be bought, sold, and used.[90]

4. THE DEFINITION OF DESIGN

Let me draw this discussion to a close. I believe we have all the elements we need for a working definition of design, if not for an ontology presented in a priori terms. There will perforce be counter-examples I have not yet imagined to the notion of design I wish to present here; I would be surprised were there not. But because I do not mean to suggest an essentialist definition of

90 Of course, this is not to suggest that designs cannot also be used in communicative practices: many designs become symbols of wealth, power, elegance, and so on. And I think many of our consumer choices involve attempts at self-expression or self-definition through the objects that we purchase and use. My point here is that these objects do not *themselves* speak, or were not created as forms of (profound) communication, however much we may use them in this way, or however much they may have been marketed in this way by the industry. I discuss such mimetic forms of self-expression in "Art and Identity: Expanding Narrative Theory," *Philosophy Today* 47, no. 2 (2003).

design in necessary and sufficient terms, I do not expect any counter-examples to be of lasting harm to my argument. What I have sought to do is to roughly categorize the things we call design, while paying close attention to our intuitions and linguistic practices, to come up with a working definition that is not alien to the way we think and talk about design. And this exercise in (imprecise) metaphysics has been meant to single out a group of objects and practices that merit our aesthetic attention but that must be evaluated in terms different from the appraisal of art and craft.

Design, then, we can conclude, is functional, immanent, mass-produced, and mute. The activity behind a work of design may be creative and spontaneous, is certainly precise, rational, and often collaborative, but is generally uncommunicative. The product of the design process is an intentionally functional object that is thereby distinguished as a kind of thing, and is further original or individual on the basis of its apparent or formal features. We do indeed give praise to individual designers like Stark or Stam or Chanel and show their work in museums, but this kind of approbation I would like to call the "cult of the designer," where the individual is elevated to a position similar to that of the artist and whose products are then assessed in similar ways (i.e., by being merely contemplated rather than used). The cult of the designer moves design from one category to another, just as some craftworks have been mounted in galleries, or created to intentionally make a statement. But in our daily interactions with designed objects, most often we do not know who the designer of our kettles, shoes, or guns has been, and we do not treat these objects as being unique particulars that have something important to say to us. Thus our definition of design must be more object-centred than many theories of art. To be a candidate for aesthetic appreciation, then, a design must have apparent or perceptual features, and must be a manufactured product of some kind rather than a proposal or sketch. This will exclude the DNA structure of living organisms and the (invisible) molecular structure of vaccines and drugs, for with these sorts of items there is nothing available for aesthetic appraisal, even though these too make up part of our everyday lives and activities. But this *will* include weapons, all quotidian objects whose designers we do not know, all virtual objects such as web pages and the like, clothing both couture and not, garden designs even if they are not mass-produced, machinery, structural elements of buildings, vehicles, tools, and the majority of our lived environments.

Once again, we can find a putative tripartite division emerging here between art, craft, and design, one that has more staying power. Art has been defined by both expression and formalist theories as evincing a singularity of vision. They are divided as to whether form or content is supreme in art, but they agree that it has both. Craft has been defined as having its particularity not in expressive vision or even in the mental act of planning but in the physical act of executing that plan by a skilled artisan. Craft, for Collingwood especially, can be understood through a distinction between form and matter, where the matter is the raw material that is transformed by an artisan into an object that has a use.

Form versus content for the one, form versus matter for the other: design differs from both art and craft in that it could better be understood as residing in the distinction between form and function. Known and used by its function, individuated by its form, designs are not always skilfully made, are almost never hand-made, and while they have form, have no content. Designers alter the shape and look of things but they do not manipulate raw materials directly and they do not engage in "content-ful," emotional communicative practices. Design stands alone as a practice and an object: it is distinguished by neither expressive vision nor skilled production by an artisan. This, I would stress, is not intended to make of design a poor cousin to the more exalted practices and products of art and craft. Some designs are exquisite, some extraordinarily innovative, some have changed our lives, while others are simply beautiful. As to why philosophical aesthetics should attend to a group of objects that are functional, immanent, mass-produced, and mute, we can provisionally say that insofar as aesthetics has concerned itself with natural beauty (immanent, mute, but not functional), with craft (functional but not mass-produced), with popular culture, food, wine, and so on, the oversight is inexplicable. And insofar as aesthetics has long been concerned with our responses to beauty or excellence wherever it may occur in the spectrum of our visual or auditory experiences, the neglect in the case of design may be because it has never before been singled out as a particular kind of thing that merits separate treatment. Certainly that is one of the purposes of this work. My present goal has been to find a way to differentiate design from other sorts of things, to "set up" the target so that we can "shoot at it," and in this I hope I have succeeded. By claiming that design can be distinguished from art and craft I am also suggesting that our responses to it will differ from our aesthetic responses to other sorts of things, as the next chapters will establish.

If anecdotal evidence be permitted, I look around myself as I write this and can clearly locate three different sorts of things. The desk upon which I write was hand-made (without great skill) by a craftsman; the pen with which I write has been mass-produced in a factory somewhere in France but bears a designer's label; my plants grow naturally but reside in pots that are likewise mass-produced and come from who-knows-where, with no labels; and on my wall is a small painting, a gift from the artist. There is no other like it, and no copy or reproduction or forgery in known existence. All of these things I've mentioned are perceptible objects, all have some kind of function, and all have distinct formal properties. But only one attempts profundity, only one is (semi-)skilfully handmade, and the rest, whether beautiful or useful or innovative, form the bulk of that with which we surround ourselves, and the majority of our contemporary environments. These, then, are *design*.

Chapter II

Locating the Aesthetic: Beauty and Judgements of Taste

We now have one piece of the puzzle in hand: a working definition of design as a phenomenon with sufficient particular characteristics to suggest that it merits separate aesthetic treatment. Because design can be distinguished in important regards from art and craft, and because it bears little relation to natural phenomena, I will argue that it is experienced or appreciated in a correspondingly unique way. But knowing what design is gets us only so far: there are good and bad designs just as there are excellent and awful works of art, beautiful and ugly things, and even pleasurable and painful experiences. We now need to turn to the question of our interaction with design, and what makes this interaction specifically aesthetic. This question takes us to the heart of philosophical aesthetics at its most complex. For not only are there competing approaches to the location of the aesthetic—in the properties of objects on the one hand, or in the felt pleasures of our experiences on the other—these approaches rest on deeper commitments about the nature of normativity itself.

Locating the aesthetic is the task of the present chapter, and specifying the aesthetic nature of design is my eventual goal in the next. To do this, I will begin by reviewing some of the fundamental problems of normativity in general before considering the nature of aesthetic normativity, and two competing historically prominent schools of thought about where to locate it. I will seek to find a middle path between these, and to defend a position that identifies the aesthetic with our faculty of judgement in particular, because, following Roger Scruton, I believe that the aesthetic is "deeply implicated in our lives as rational beings" and hence constitutes a mental act rather than a property of objects on the one hand or a form of physical pleasure on the other.[1] And I will make this case by turning to Kant's theory of aesthetic judgement as not only the most fully developed account of its kind, but also the most useful for an explication of our appreciation of design. The following two chapters, then, form my response to the second challenge faced by an aesthetics of design as I outlined it in the introduction to this work: it is not enough to identify what design *is*, that which differentiates it from art and craft; we now need to examine in what way our interactions with design are particularly aesthetic ones, and how we can appreciate and evaluate design on strictly aesthetic (rather than moral, economic, or instrumental) grounds. To develop an aesthetic theory of design, my argument will proceed in three discrete stages. First, I must make good the claim that aesthetic excellence resides in a particular form of judgement that we make. I will do this by analyzing the weaknesses of competing theories (sections 1.i and 1.ii) as well as a contemporary account of aesthetic judgement found in the work of Nick Zangwill (section 2). Second, I will explicate and defend the Kantian theory of aesthetic judgement in some detail (section 3). This section is an optional one: I do not expect all readers to be familiar with Kant's *Critique of Judgement*, which is complex enough to require patient attention and thorough exegesis.

1 Roger Scruton, "In Search of the Aesthetic," *British Journal of Aesthetics* 47, no. 3 (2007): 238.

Those who are already acquainted with his work may simply skip to the final argument of the chapter. Finally, in chapter 3 I will build on this foundation to argue for a particular kind of aesthetic judgement that is unique to our experiences of design, one that relies on, and provides an original interpretation of, the Kantian notion of dependent beauty. My position is that a Kantian treatment of design, if properly nuanced, will not only demonstrate that design fully merits aesthetic attention and of what specific kind, but will also provide the benchmark for any further work in this emerging field. It may seem in what follows that we stray from the direct matter that we have established in chapter 1, but we do not: an aesthetics of design, as I understand it, cannot simply ignore the larger problems of the discipline or make specific claims without proper justification. To maintain that design requires separate treatment we must first show how it is very much part of the central concerns of the field.

Let me begin with something of an equivocation: my normative term of choice is "beauty," although I allow that this can be taken to stand for either aesthetic merit or a form of pleasure in some general sense. Beauty came to be seen as an archaic notion in twentieth-century aesthetics, although lately it has had something of a revival.[2] Perhaps the strongest reasons for its decline lie in developments in the arts themselves: while a Cézanne or a Monet (or indeed a Raphael or a Michelangelo) may be considered beautiful, many of the works of Picasso or Francis Bacon or Damien Hirst are clearly not, even though we might give them our enthusiastic approbation. John Passmore once noted that "[t]here

2 See, for example, Mary Mothersill, *Beauty Restored* (Oxford: Clarendon Press, 1984); Eddy Zemach, *Real Beauty* (University Park: Pennsylvania State University Press, 1997); Nick Zangwill, *The Metaphysics of Beauty* (Ithaca: Cornell University Press, 2001); and a recent contribution to the *American Society for Aesthetics Newsletter* by Ruth Lorand, "In Defense of Beauty" (26, no. 3, 2006).

is something suspect ('phoney') about 'beauty.' Artists seem to get along quite well without it."[3] If the arts have moved away from the creation of objects of beauty in favour of the original, the provocative, or the profound, then it can be argued that beauty has to cede pride of place as the predominant normative term in aesthetics, perhaps to be better used in reference to sunsets, flowers, and other objects of nature. This, I think, is to misrepresent the importance of the term. Beauty has come to be associated with the pretty and the delicate, perhaps the graceful or the elegant, certainly with some general sense of the pleasing, but these terms are not synonymous: behind our claims that a narcissus is pretty or a neck graceful is a judgement that the flower or the neck is *thereby* "beautiful," in the sense of providing pleasure or meriting our approbation. That is, something further is going on when we make these claims. Beauty, as I seek to use the notion, is not merely a descriptive term or even one of particular or localized approbation, but one that indicates an evaluation of aesthetic excellence that is presupposed in the descriptors "pretty" and "graceful" or that is the outcome of a certain kind of experience. We would not use these particular terms *unless* the object of our experience also and already was judged deserving of aesthetic merit. Nick Zangwill writes that "[w]hatever we say about the *word* 'beauty,' what is important is that there is a *mental act* of making a pure judgement of aesthetic value. We could just insist that this is all that the word 'beauty' should express, even if there is no one word in the natural language unambiguously marking out the concept."[4] So "beauty" is useful

3 Quoted in Ruth Lorand, "In Defense of Beauty," 1.

4 Nick Zangwill, "The Beautiful, the Dainty and the Dumpy," *British Journal of Aesthetics* 35, no. 4 (1995): 319. I am not in agreement with Zangwill's strong distinction between our linguistic and mental acts, but see no reason to take this up here. It should not detract from the argument I wish to make, or the parts of Zangwill's work on which I shall rely.

as a term that signifies the occurrence of an aesthetic judgement of merit or excellence but one that is ambiguous as to whether this merit is located in the properties of an object or in the pleasures of certain kinds of experience.

There are two further reasons for my preference for the term "beauty." First, as contemporary art moved away from the conscious creation of beauty in the twentieth century, so did philosophical aesthetics narrow its scope to focus almost exclusively on works of fine art, where the term longer applied.[5] To emphasize the notion of the "beautiful" over the "excellent" or the "meritorious" is to also insist on, and applaud the more recent, broadening of the scope of aesthetics beyond the philosophy of art, to include the consideration of nature, popular cultural forms, and indeed the everyday. It is to resist the conflation of the "aesthetic" with the "artistic" and instead to suggest that aesthetic experience—and aesthetic judgements—have as wide a scope as possible.

Second, as I mentioned, the beautiful has come to be associated with the pleasing, and this is an association I am concerned to maintain, not as a quality of beauty narrowly construed but as an integral and indeed constitutive element of our aesthetic experience. Our appreciation of an object, I wish to suggest, is intimately connected with the pleasure we receive in experiencing it, and the more general notions of aesthetic excellence or merit have come to lack this particular connotation. My use of beauty then will

5 Again, there has been a reversal of this trend in recent aesthetic theory, which is laudable. See for example works in such diverse areas as environmental aesthetics (Allen Carlson, *Aesthetics and the Environment: The Appreciation of Nature, Art and Architecture* [New York: Routledge, 2000]; popular culture (Noël Carroll, *The Philosophy of Horror* [New York: Routledge, 1990] and Ted Gracyk, *Rhythm and Noise: An Aesthetics of Rock* [Durham, NC: Duke University Press, 1996]); and feminist aesthetics (S. Gilman, *Making the Body Beautiful: A Cultural History of Aesthetic Surgery* [Princeton: Princeton University Press, 1999]) to name a few.

indicate a particular theoretical and methodological commitment regarding the problems of normativity that I will seek to establish here. While on the one hand I will accept the construal of beauty as aesthetic excellence in some general sense, I will also suggest that it be understood within its historical context as connected with the notion of "taste."

1 THE PROBLEM OF NORMATIVITY

How then do we come to claim that an object or artwork is beautiful or meritorious with any kind of confidence? Let me pose the problem of normativity with the following examples. We make a number of different kinds of normative statements, such as:

Arugula is revolting.
This sunset is beautiful.
This Cartier watch is exquisite.
Abortion is wrong.

In each case, we are making a judgement about the object or action in question, but only in some of these cases do we expect others to agree, or do we think we are making some kind of truth-claim with these assertions. If you love arugula, for instance, and know that I hate it, we will not quarrel over this matter, and you will not (usually) think that you are right and I am wrong; we each have our own gustatory tastes, or experience our own kinds of pleasures, and we tend to let these lie. These sorts of claims are considered fully subjective in the sense of referring to the experiencing subject—me, with arugula—and not providing any information about the object in question (I do not claim that arugula is generally revolting, but rather that it tastes awful to me, or that I simply do not like it).[6] In this sense, *de gustibus non est disputandem*.

Other statements, such as the one about abortion, are asserted with more force and more confidence. If you think abortion is justifiable and I do not, we will not part company with as much equanimity as we did over the issue of arugula (except for the purposes of politeness); instead, we will be expected to give reasons for our views and each will think they are right, or that there is a truth of the matter that is worth arguing about. We tend to think that moral assertions are objective: they are truth-claims about objects (or practices) in the world that can be verified with the same confidence that we can verify other factual matters, and do not merely refer to the preferences of a given subject. In these cases, not only is it a matter of *est disputandem* but it is not *gustibus* that is at issue but *veritas* itself.[7]

Where do aesthetic statements about artworks, sunsets, designer watches, and so on fit into this picture? This is the subject of much debate. My examples have been designed to set up a clear dichotomy between (purely) subjective and objective normative claims, and I have intended that assertions of beauty should appear to fall in the middle (as we will see shortly). On the one hand, when we exclaim at the flavour of, say, a particular kind of

6 Of course you can try to convince me that I am wrong about arugula; you can tempt me with salads and so on. But at the end of the day if I *still* say I don't like it, there is nothing you can do or say to change my mind, other than admit that we have different tastes (even if you secretly think me a philistine in culinary matters).

7 Of course I am taking as the norm here moral realism. This is not because of an unargued belief in moral facts but more for the purposes of juxtaposition. Were I a moral non-cognitivist, I would still have to acknowledge and account for the strength of the intuition towards realism itself. David McNaughton, in his *Moral Vision* (Oxford: Blackwell, 1988) offers a very good general overview of the debate between realists and non-cognitivists.

coffee, we appear to be making a statement about our *feelings* or our *responses* to the world, rather than offering up facts about the way the world really is. Aesthetic claims also seem to be subjective in this sense, and it is a fairly common intuition that in matters of beauty, as with arugula or coffee, each has his or her own taste. On the other hand, we have an equally strong sense that there *is* a truth of the matter to be had in discussions of art and beauty and we are often at pains to defend our positions (imagine watching the sunset with someone who thought the sight was revolting!). The entire notion that there are "classic" works of art, like *Moby Dick* or the *Mona Lisa* or the *Goldberg Variations*, is premised upon our belief that these works *really are* great or beautiful, in some objective sense of the term. If it weren't for the sense in which these matters can admit of right or wrong, aesthetic objects and experiences would no more be of philosophical interest than arugula.

The problem of normativity as I understand it is the problem of how to chart a course between these two extremes; how to write an aesthetic theory that accounts for the truth-tending nature of our claims while remaining sensitive to the subjective feel of the responses that make up our aesthetic experiences themselves. *Are* aesthetic claims subjective, or are they objective at the end of the day? This is a question with a long tradition, and one of the most pressing in philosophical aesthetics. I will begin by considering the more uncompromising responses on either side of the issue, coupled with the problems that are attendant upon each theoretical stance. While I will describe these somewhat starkly for rhetorical purposes, I will try to remain charitable to each approach, and not treat either too lightly. Each general position has been greatly sophisticated in contemporary aesthetics, in ways that it would exceed my brief to describe.

i. Aesthetic Realism

The first broad approach is to adopt a stance of aesthetic realism, and to claim that beauty is a property of objects that—in some way—can be perceived and known. This approach has the merit of objectivity: just as an object has mind-independent properties of squareness or circularity, and we can clearly be right or wrong about its shape, so too is an object beautiful or ugly. The source of normativity here lies in the object itself, external to our feelings and judgements, and is the subject of cognitive belief. Nick Zangwill writes that the motivation for adopting a realist stance "is that it is the theory best placed to make sense of ordinary aesthetic *thought*," particularly our intuitions that "there is a truth of the matter or that there is a correct judgement" to be made about beauty. Realism suggests that this truth lies "*in virtue* of the aesthetic facts"[8] that our judgements represent and that these facts are independent of the judgements themselves. What, the realist asks, "other source of normativity could there be?"[9] On the realist account, an aesthetic experience is simply one in which we perceive the quality of beauty in an object, whatever it is, whether fine art, nature, or even a coffee-pot.

But the problems with aesthetic realism outweigh its benefits, and run parallel to problems with moral realism, so well articulated by J. L. Mackie in his *Ethics: Inventing Right and Wrong.*[10] First there is an epistemological problem of perception: if beauty is a property

8 Nick Zangwill, "Skin Deep or in the Eye of the Beholder? The Metaphysics of Aesthetic and Sensory Properties," *Philosophy and Phenomenological Research* 61, no. 3 (2000): 597–598.

9 Ibid., 599.

10 Harmondsworth: Penguin, 1977. Portions of this work have been excerpted in *Moral Discourse and Practice*, ed. Stephen Darwall, Allan Gibbard, and Peter Railton (New York: Oxford University Press, 1997).

residing independently in objects, what is our mode of access to it? Do we *see* beauty in the way that we perceive squareness with one or more of our five senses? If not, a realist will have to claim that we have a special mode of awareness, a "sixth sense" or "intuition" that allows us to perceive beauty in the way that W. D. Ross and later Martha Nussbaum have claimed that we can somehow sense moral values.[11] Frank Sibley held this view, claiming that our aesthetic responses require "the exercise of taste, perceptiveness, or sensitivity, of aesthetic discrimination or appreciation."[12] But realism is on shaky ground if it depends on a non-sensory, unanalyzable intuition to pick out a non-perceptual, non-physical property such as beauty in an object! We could never know how we could be correct in our estimations of an object's aesthetic value, nor could we prove that one person's sensitivity or taste was more accurate than another's. Beauty would amount to nothing other than a sense *we* have of a *je ne sais quoi* that the *object* is deemed to possess.

An alternative realist strategy is to suggest that beauty is somehow directly perceivable. Zangwill calls this "physicalist aesthetic realism," the claim that "every aesthetic fact is identical with some physical fact" so that beauty can be directly seen: it is "part of the physical world."[13] Physicalism has a long history, dating back perhaps to Pythagorean doctrines of ratio and harmonious proportion as constituting beauty. Much later, Hogarth claimed that

11 W. D. Ross, in *The Right and the Good* (Oxford: Clarendon Press, 1930) offered the first strong articulation of intuitionism; Martha Nussbaum, in *Love's Knowledge: Essays on Philosophy and Literature* (New York: Oxford University Press, 1990) argues that literature can make us "finely aware," that is, can hone our perception of moral value through the training of our sensitivity.

12 Frank Sibley, "Aesthetic Concepts," *Philosophical Review* 68, no. 4 (1959): 421. That he cannot name this sense with any more accuracy is immediate cause for suspicion.

13 Zangwill, "Skin Deep," 596.

beauty was not to be found in angularity or strict proportions but was constituted by the serpentine "line of beauty," a property that underlies all variety and ornamentation.[14]

Physicalism has a different set of epistemological problems attached to it: if, barring defects of our sensory organs, we can directly perceive beauty in ratios or lines, how does the realist explain the extent of *dis*agreement in aesthetics? This approach may explain how we can be correct in our cognitive determinations of beauty but fails to account for how we can be wrong or think others are wrong, and has no purchase on the great variety of aesthetic valuations seen between different cultures or historical eras. If all that is required to convince a skeptic is to point to a serpentine line in a composition, or to measure the proportions of a set of windows, then there should be universal or near-universal accord in aesthetic matters, which is clearly not the case.

These epistemological problems have parallel metaphysical difficulties. The first form of realism is susceptible to Mackie's "argument from queerness" that suggests that if beauty (or a moral property) is unique and mind-independent, it must be very odd indeed: such values "would be entities or quantities or qualities or relations of a very strange sort, utterly different from anything else in the universe."[15] What kind of ontological status do we give to something that is non-physical and imperceptible by our normal sensory organs? Our experience of beauty is an experience of *value*, and realism suggests that value is part of the fabric of the world. But the idea of a value that has a phenomenal character—that can be experienced—but which exists quite apart from

14 William Hogarth, *An Analysis of Beauty, Written with a View of Fixing the Fluctuating Ideas of Taste*, in *Eighteenth Century Aesthetics*, ed. Dabney Townsend (Amityville, NY: Baywood, 1999).

15 J. L. Mackie, *Ethics: Inventing Right and Wrong* (Harmondsworth: Penguin, 1977), 38.

human responses to it would be as odd, John McDowell notes, "as if we tried to construct a conception of amusingness which was fully intelligible otherwise than in terms of the characteristic human responses to what is amusing."[16] It is difficult to make sense of the existence of values apart from human valuations and responses. And this makes the notion of mind-independent values suspect.

But physicalism fares no better. While it does not entail a "queer" metaphysics, in that it does not claim that beauty transcends the physical world, it has a difficult time accounting for beauty's physical instantiation. For example, Zangwill argues that the realist might say that the beauty of music "*is* sound" or "where sounds are—and then give some explanation of how beauty is 'identical with, realized in, or constituted by, a temporal arrangement of sounds,'"[17] however that explanation might go. This strategy does not provide the mind-independence that realism desires, however, for such sensory properties are not generally thought to be independently part of the world: from Locke forward, sensory properties or secondary qualities have long been considered mind-dependent or "response dependent" in Zangwill's terms, and thus not "real" enough to provide the kind of objective locus of normativity that strict realism would require. Taste, sound, colour, texture, and so on do not reside *in* objects but are the products of our interactions with them, and so have an irreducibly subjective aspect.[18]

16 John McDowell, "Aesthetic Value, Objectivity, and the Fabric of the World," in *Pleasure Preference and Value: Studies in Philosophical Aesthetics*, ed. Eva Schaper (New York: Cambridge University Press, 1987), 4.

17 Zangwill, "Skin Deep," 604.

18 While the classicists and Hogarth avoided this problem by identifying beauty directly with mind-independent physical properties that can be measured and calculated, their conjectures were restricted to physical beauty and so could not include the non-visual beauties of music or poetry, for instance, nor could their identification of beauty with only one *kind* of physical property account for the breadth of even physical beauty that might diverge from their notions of proportion or a serpentine line.

Physicalism is a more sophisticated doctrine than I have suggested here, and a number of philosophers have contrived to explain beauty in terms of sensory properties.[19] But even if this can be managed with any degree of credibility, aesthetic physicalism does not escape the epistemological problems noted earlier: even if it can be explained how we experience beauty, these theories do not account for how we can be incorrect in our judgements or the degree to which we quarrel about aesthetic matters, or even the great variety of aesthetic claims across cultural and temporal boundaries. The fact is that beauty is an irreducibly *normative* concept and realism's main challenge is to account for this normativity in non-normative (factual, sensory, physical, or transcendent) terms.

ii. Aesthetic Subjectivism

A second broad approach to the problem of normativity responded to the challenge facing the realists in the negative: as normative, beauty is thereby *not* a matter of some property of objects that we perceive and about which we can form beliefs. Beauty is instead found in the subjective response we have to our experiences and the pleasure we gain from them, and thus our judgements of beauty are subjective rather than objective, closer to judgements about arugula than abortion. The non-realist approach emerged in the eighteenth century with the development of British empiricist

19 See for example, Sibley, "Aesthetic Concepts" and "Aesthetic and Nonaesthetic," *Philosophical Review* 74 (1965); Zangwill, "The Beautiful, the Dainty" and "Skin Deep"; McDowell, "Aesthetic Value" and "Values and Secondary Qualities," in Darwall, Gibbard, and Railton, *Moral Discourse and Practice*. Two current strategies have attempted to either identify aesthetic properties with secondary qualities such as colour (McDowell), or to claim that aesthetic properties supervene upon—are determined by—non-aesthetic properties (Sibley and Zangwill). See below for a further discussion of this strategy.

philosophy, and coincided with a decline in acceptance of classical principles of beauty and art. A brief overview of this philosophical development will make the position clear.

Empiricism focused on experience or sensation as the foundation of knowledge: what could be known was dependent on and limited to mental representations—ideas—that were the product of individual sensory experiences. Locke most famously argued that the mind at birth is without any ideas or knowledge. "How comes it to be furnished?... To this I answer, in one word, from Experience: In that all our knowledge is founded; and from that it ultimately derives it self."[20] What could not be sensed directly, or derived from sensation, was beyond the bounds of knowledge: "Knowledge then seems to me to be nothing but the perception of the connexion and agreement or disagreement and repugnancy of any of our Ideas. In this alone it consists."[21] The empiricist epistemology perhaps inevitably led to skepticism about core transcendent philosophical concepts such as those of God, a substantial self, and the moral good: any and all properties or objects that could not be apprehended directly by the senses.

When the empiricist thinkers in the early part of the eighteenth century turned their attention to aesthetics, they employed the same methodological principles as they used in the sciences, and an early form of physicalism emerged; beauty must be directly experienced in order to be real and the basis of cognitive belief. "Taste" at first gained currency as the term for the "sense" responsible for the aesthetic experience of beauty. We see this with Hogarth, for instance, who, while using new empiricist principles remained committed to the classical belief in the real existence of beauty as a

20 John Locke, *An Essay Concerning Human Understanding* (Oxford: Clarendon Press, 1975), 104.

21 Ibid., 525.

property. He claimed, "now, whoever can conceive lines thus constantly flowing, and delicately varying over every part of the body even to the finger ends…will, in my mind, want very little more than what his own observation on the works of art and nature will lead him to, to acquire a true idea of the word Taste, when applied to form; however inexplicable this word may hitherto have been imagined."[22] While beauty was no longer a transcendent ideal, it was every bit as real and could be perceived empirically by the faculty of taste.

However, the empiricist methodology eventually led to aesthetic subjectivism in the second half of the eighteenth century. Taste, as not one of the five senses, could not be adequately demonstrated; beauty was not directly perceivable as a property of objects, so beauty was therefore not real. Taste instead came to be understood as a *feeling*—primarily of pleasure—that was associated with a subject's response to sensory experience rather than with that experience itself. David Hume's "Of the Standard of Taste" is perhaps the clearest articulation of this position: "All sentiment is right; because sentiment has a reference to nothing beyond itself.… Beauty is no quality of things in themselves: it exists merely in the mind which contemplates them; and each mind perceives a different beauty."[23] Our felt response to objects became the locus of the notion of beauty, and British aesthetics came to be largely concerned with developing a theory of taste as the grounds for judgements of beauty in nature and art.

Here we can see that Zangwill's earlier claim is only partially correct: realism is not the only theory to make sense of our aesthetic thought. Subjectivist theories equally capture the second

22 Hogarth, *Analysis of Beauty*, 226.

23 David Hume, "Of the Standard of Taste," in Townsend, *Eighteenth Century Aesthetics*, 231–232.

common intuition I described: beauty is a matter of personal preference, an individual reaction to our experiences, and in some sense there is no *arguing* about taste. This intuition is the basis for the epistemological problems with realism that I have already noted; it demands an account of variety and difference in taste to equally be part of a fully developed aesthetic. But the subjectivist approach as it developed carried with it its own set of problems that require resolution. First, if taste is not a form of sense perception but rather of feeling, it must be distinguished from other kinds of feelings to explain its relation to beauty and art. For instance, a theory of taste will have to explain why we generally react with pleasure to the *Mona Lisa* but with displeasure to, perhaps, a black velvet painting of Elvis, and further, to explain why the pleasures of a hot bath, a single malt whiskey, a hug, or a good laugh are not the same as, or included in, the sorts of pleasures that the subjectivist view would call *aesthetic*. Second, judgements of taste, as based on feelings and so subjective, seem to have no claim to objective validity or correctness: it is unclear how we can claim to be right about aesthetic matters or resolve aesthetic disputes.

Responses in the eighteenth century to the first problem led to an account of taste being sought in the principles of a common human nature. The dominant psychology of the empiricists was associationist: ideas evoke one another according to various principles of association, such as their similarity, repeated simultaneity, or contiguity of time and place. By these associations, the mind is led through time and habit and by the nature of its particular constitution to classify its responses to external stimuli with a certain regularity and form the ideas that represent knowledge. "Beauty" could be understood as a feeling of pleasure caused by certain associations the mind makes in response to nature or works of art, and theories of taste, in Archibald Alison, Lord Kames, and Edmund

Burke, for instance, were concerned with locating the cause of this pleasure, whether it be in the perception of uniformity, order, variety, proportion, or a combination of like elements. As Burke noted, "the standard both of reason and taste is the same in all human creatures. For if there were not some principles of judgement as well as of sentiment common to all mankind, no hold could possibly be taken either on their reason or their passions, sufficient to maintain the ordinary correspondences of life."[24] Taste may be a feeling, but its subjectivity is tempered by a set of principles that locate the source of normativity internal to a nature we all share, and all share in the same way.

An account of taste as pleasure of a certain kind founded on a fledgling theory of mind may seem to respond well to the first problem I noted, yet it falls short of full resolution. The more extreme tendencies of the eighteenth century that regarded the mind as passive and completely derived from basic principles of association, as we find in Locke, yielded an overly deterministic picture of not just taste but idea formation in general. Much like the realist views canvassed earlier, a deterministic account based on causal principles does not allow for variety in judgements of beauty or explain disagreements in aesthetic matters unless these be the product of a malfunction of associative principles. Less extreme views suggested that the association of ideas with pleasures was in part generated by the imagination, allowing for a greater degree of freedom and subjectivity in matters of taste. But if the free use of the imagination is involved in my associating pleasure with bucolic landscapes, for instance, and yours with urban scenes, we are no further forward aesthetically: we may have

24 Edmund Burke, *A Philosophical Enquiry into the Origin of Our Ideas of the Sublime and Beautiful*, in Townsend, *Eighteenth Century Aesthetics*, 249.

explained how that pleasure arises but not how taste can achieve any kind of objective rationale. Walter Jackson Bate, in his study of taste in the eighteenth century, remarked that "by encouraging aesthetics to take the subjective activity of the mind as the starting point of any investigation, British associationism opened the door even more widely for an inevitable individualistic relativism."[25] The eighteenth-century theorists were caught on the horns of a dilemma: the sentiment of taste was either causally determined and hence too rigidly specified, or it was freely associated, leading to an extreme subjectivism in aesthetic matters. While this makes room for the subjectivist intuition that there is no disputing about taste, it also engenders the second problem: if judgements of beauty are not like judgements about arugula, how do we provide them with any objective normative criteria?

David Hume was one theorist who sought to temper the relativism of aesthetic pleasures by seeking a standard of taste external to the operations of the minds of ordinary individuals. While equally basing his theory of taste on sentiment or feeling, Hume acknowledged it absurd to suggest that anyone who preferred the poetry of Ogilby to Milton was right: it would be as if "he had maintained a mole-hill to be as high as Tenerife, or a pond as extensive as the ocean."[26] Pleasures may be individual, but Hume sought criteria by which they could be assessed as more or less right or wrong, and he found these criteria in the experience and skills of judges and connoisseurs rather than in the psychology of taste itself. Thus, while beauty was determined by the pleasures of taste, these pleasures could be assessed by a class of critics and experts who would set the standards for beauty and aesthetic excellence.

25 Walter Jackson Bate, *From Classic to Romantic: Premises of Taste in Eighteenth-Century England* (New York: Harper and Brothers, 1946), 128.

26 Hume, "Of the Standard of Taste," 232.

Hume's strategy fares no better than any other: how are these connoisseurs to come by their expertise? Have they an innate delicacy of taste and judgement, or is their sensitivity developed through experience? If the former, an account is needed of how some have better taste than others (and how we can be confident that this is the case). If the latter, Hume's argument suffers from circularity: we cannot determine that the experts have had a proper education in the arts when they are the only ones who can determine what aesthetic excellence is. Hume cannot rely on acknowledged "classics" in the arts to ground the training of experts either, without first explaining how these originally become "classic," and so models of excellence upon which young connoisseurs can rely in their training. Hume's famous essay does not resolve this problem, and points to the difficulties of trying to provide external normative criteria for aesthetic excellence within a subjectivist framework. Aesthetic subjectivism faces, perhaps, greater challenges than realism: once the door to relativism has been opened with the coincidence of taste with individual pleasures, it becomes exceedingly difficult to then claim that these pleasures are right or wrong. If a psychology of taste is not to be deterministic, it becomes a red herring: explaining how we experience aesthetic pleasure brings us no closer to providing normative standards of beauty.

2. AESTHETIC JUDGEMENT

This introduction to the problem of normativity should allow us to become clear about a number of important issues. First, that neither a wholly objective nor a wholly subjective account of beauty can succeed: realism must untangle too many metaphysical puzzles before it begins to address important epistemological challenges, and subjectivist theories require both a developed account of the particular pleasures of taste, in psychology or the philosophy of mind, and some further account of a standard that will allow for objectivity in aesthetic claims if it is not to devolve into relativism. It seems as though we are no further ahead in locating the aesthetic than with our two principle intuitions: there both is, and is not, any disputing about beauty. The middle ground of these two extremes still requires formulation if we are to make any sense of aesthetic normativity. A possible way forward begins to emerge from the failures of these two positions. What is implicated in—and often overlooked by—both realism and subjectivism is the notion of aesthetic judgement itself. Indeed, transcendent and physicalist realism or deterministic and free subjectivism all appear to seek explanatory grounds for the activity of making an aesthetic judgement of beauty or excellence.

Judgement is implicated by each side of the debate in different forms: as objective and cognitive in the course of the perception of a property of beauty, or as subjective and sentimental as a response to our experiences of the world. When we speak of beauty or aesthetic merit, we speak in terms of judgement, whichever position we prefer; we judge that an object is beautiful or not, we provide reasons for having judged in the way that we did, we justify our judgements as being correct through internal or external means, and so on. Further, our use of other aesthetic terms seems to follow from an account of evaluative judgement rather than precede it: aesthetic properties are ascribed in aesthetic judgements, aesthetic experiences or feelings of pleasure ground them, and aesthetic concepts are deployed in their use.[27] Yet in each case we can make the claim that what is central to beauty is the aesthetic

27 Nick Zangwill makes precisely this point in his essay "Aesthetic Judgement" for the *Stanford Encyclopedia of Philosophy*, ed. Edward N. Zalta (Fall, 2010 edition), http://plato.stanford.edu/archives/fall2010/entries/aesthetic-judgment/.

judgement itself rather than the properties, experiences, or concepts to which it refers. Frank Sibley calls purely evaluative judgements "verdicts,"[28] and Zangwill adopts this use by calling them "verdictive," which he contrasts with "substantive" judgements.[29] The idea in both cases is that the act of making an aesthetic judgement is a rendering of a verdict upon an object, or the experience of an object, and the investigation of this act is, arguably, a conceptually more fruitful avenue than the consideration of the properties it ascribes or the feelings that ground it. If beauty is to be understood as irreducibly normative rather than transcendent, physical, or psychological, an investigation of our evaluative judgements in particular should serve to illuminate the notion and explain how we can justify its use.

We at last approach the main argument of this chapter: an aesthetics of design, I wish to claim, will not be focused on a metaphysics of designed artifacts, or the (aesthetic) properties that may be peculiar to them, nor will it focus only on the pleasures we derive from our experiences. It will be grounded in a theory of aesthetic judgements and will seek an account of the justification required for these judgements to have claim to validity or correctness. What explains the aesthetic nature of design, and makes it deserving of separate attention, does not lie in its unique characteristics alone, but in the specific kinds of evaluations we make of designed objects, and how these evaluations differ from aesthetic judgements of either the beauty of nature or of fine art and craft. Before we can embark on this project as it applies to design, however, we need to consider the logical form of judgements of taste themselves, for now we must distinguish the aesthetic from other

28 Sibley, "Aesthetic and Nonaesthetic," 136.
29 Zangwill, "The Beautiful, the Dainty," 317.

forms of judgement, such as the cognitive, moral, or practical. Only by first asserting the autonomy of aesthetic judgements in general can we make the further claim for judgements of design.

Eva Schaper, in her excellent paper "The Pleasures of Taste," takes us some way towards understanding aesthetic judgement. She begins by claiming that what is "axiomatic" to any theory of taste is that its central concern should be with "a subject's experience of something or other and the consequent pleasure or lack of it" that this experience engenders.[30] Here Schaper accepts the centrality of feeling and subjective response in aesthetic judgements, but she seeks to temper this subjectivism by claiming that "the important question" for this theory is to show how our felt responses "are related to causes and reasons" that can ground or justify them.[31]

Schaper points out that the problems I enumerated with reference to realism and subjectivism apply equally clearly to a theory of judgement: "On the one hand we believe that taste is bound up with the immediacy of feeling... [and on] the other hand we believe that... taste judgements are reasoned appraisals."[32] Here again, what I have called purely subjective and objective accounts are each insufficient on their own, although their insufficiencies show up a little differently with judgement. For example, our felt responses to objects are not authoritative simply because we have them; they may have to be disregarded if we can discover the response to have been inappropriate for the object, or unjustifiable, as, for instance, were I to feel amusement at Chopin's Piano Sonata no. 2 ("Funeral March") or for that matter rage at a sunset.

30 Eva Schaper, "The Pleasures of Taste," *Pleasure, Preference and Value* (New York: Cambridge University Press, 1987), 40.

31 Ibid.

32 Ibid.

Reasons play a part even in our own pleasures, and this is a further point to the one I made above about distinguishing between kinds of felt pleasurable responses. Similarly, while reasons and justification are as important for taste judgements as they are for cognitive belief, here it is crucial that they be *our* reasons and justify *our* responses, and not be an impersonal set of principles that tell us how we ought to feel in any given instance. Schaper notes that "whether a person has taste . . . cannot be divorced from considerations of his feelings." Any reasons given "must justify *his* feelings and not what, perhaps, he *thinks* he ought to feel," else his judgements will seem insincere.[33] The subjective and the objective commingle in aesthetic judgements in a way that is particular to them.

Schaper seeks a middle ground between these extremes by construing taste judgements in the context of other judgements "whose logical behaviour is both similar to and distinct from them,"[34] and she devises the following schema that plays on our opposing intuitions about beauty, yet this time views these intuitions as kinds of judgements whose structures are logically distinct. She writes, "Taste judgements can be seen as a species of a genus of which culinary and moral judgements, for example, are species also."[35] The difference between these runs in part like this:

> Culinary preferences are never actually in conflict, and we do not feel obliged to defend them. Moral preferences can be inconsistent and in conflict with one another and are always supported by reasons—they can be refuted and may be

33 Ibid., 42.
34 Ibid.
35 Ibid.

> abandoned. Aesthetic preferences, by contrast, whilst never strictly inconsistent with one another, are yet justifiable by appeal to reasons.[36]

There is no contradiction, for example, in my taste for rapini and distaste for arugula, and no reasons for my judgements about them can be demanded of me: I simply like one and not the other and so judge one delicious and the other distasteful. Here again, there is no arguing about taste. With moral judgements, by contrast, the case is reversed: if I lie to my students but declare honesty to be a virtue, I can be called to account for my inconsistency by providing some kind of rational explanation for it, and if I fail to do so, my position is open to refutation.

True taste judgements, Schaper claims, occupy some middle ground between the subjectivity of gustatory pleasures and the objectivity we assign to moral judgements. They "are not merely capricious or idiosyncratic"[37] because we can demand that justifying reasons be given for them. That I should prefer a Braque over a Picasso of the same period is something that I can be obliged to explain. This is the objective character of taste judgements: here argument is possible and reasons can be demanded. Conversely, "the felt delight is primary"[38] in aesthetic judgements and is their subjective character, so long as it is *my* felt pleasure and not some general notion of what I think I ought to feel. Schaper claims that in the aesthetic realm there is a "twin desire to show taste judgements to be based on reasons and yet to preserve the basis of such judgements in the immediacy of feeling."[39]

36 Ibid., 43.
37 Ibid., 44.
38 Ibid.
39 Ibid.

Schaper's logical schematization is helpful as far as it goes: we can say that judgements of taste have, in roughly equal measure, a subjective and an objective component that makes them unique. But Schaper's schema, as she is well aware, does not answer important questions so much as raise them. What becomes clear is that we now need an account of the reasons that legitimate the felt delight that is primary in judgements of taste such that they can make a claim to correctness. The progress we have made is to venture that the problem of normativity is one that centres on evaluative or verdictive judgements themselves, and the dichotomy I presented earlier is one that is to be resolved *within* the notion of judgement itself, rather than in an account of properties on the one hand, or with a psychology of feeling (perhaps coupled with an external set of standards) on the other.

Let me now consider one contemporary effort to theorize beauty as a kind of judgement that may be instructive. Nick Zangwill, in his provocative paper "The Beautiful, the Dainty and the Dumpy," which I have mentioned in passing already, seems a strong ally to the kind of methodology I have suggested we need. He intends to "stick up for beauty" and argues that "judgements of beauty should indeed be the central concern of aesthetics."[40] Further, and more importantly, he seeks to find a way of legitimizing taste judgements that is *internal* to the mental act of judgement itself, rather than relying on either a differentiation of subjective pleasures or a metaphysics of the objective properties of aesthetic objects. To make good this thesis, Zangwill divides aesthetic judgements themselves into two kinds: "verdictive," as we have seen already, and "substantive judgements," where we "judge that things are dainty, dumpy, graceful, garish, delicate, balanced, warm, passionate,

40 Zangwill, "The Beautiful, the Dainty," 317.

brooding, awkward and sad."[41] These judgements are by and large descriptive, even though they employ aesthetic concepts, and need to be accounted for as a central factor in aesthetic discourse. The question Zangwill tries to resolve in his paper is that of the relation between these two types of judgement.

His method, in brief, is this: substantive judgements, he wishes to claim, "have *no evaluative content*," but when we use them, "we *conversationally imply* an evaluation."[42] Evaluation, he claims, "is not part of the *content* or *sense* of the [substantive] judgement. Instead we infer that the person making the judgement also makes the evaluative judgement" that the object is beautiful.[43] Substantive judgements then become supports for verdictive aesthetic evaluations; they legitimize them, they give reasons for our claims, and become the grounds by which we are correct or incorrect in our judgements of beauty.

The source of normativity lies in judgement, Zangwill claims, but this judgement has now been bifurcated into the evaluative and the descriptive, with the latter's role being "to describe that which determines merit or demerit."[44] "Something which is beautiful," he argues, "cannot be *barely* beautiful" [45] or beautiful *tout court* because then no reasons would be available to defend our evaluations. Instead an object "must be beautiful *because* it has various substantive properties [*sic*]"[46] that support and determine our judgements of its beauty, as in a flower being beautiful *because* it is delicate and graceful.

41 Ibid.
42 Ibid., 322.
43 Ibid.
44 Ibid., 328.
45 Ibid., 325.
46 Ibid., 322.

Zangwill's method ultimately fails, and the last claim indicates why. We are now making two judgements instead of one, and only one of these is actually evaluative. But on Zangwill's view, it has no normative force of its own. The second, as descriptive, is what determines the evaluation, but it does this by pointing beyond itself, to properties that objects possess or appear to possess, and Zangwill's elision of the terms "judgement" and "property" comes as no surprise. By the final quarter of the paper, all talk of judgement has been replaced by a discussion of (real) aesthetic properties with by now familiar results.

What is a descriptive judgement except a cognitive one, and how do Zangwill's descriptive judgements of aesthetic properties differ, in the end, from garden-variety cognitive judgements of other sensory properties such as redness or circularity? He does reject the suggestion that his determinative view entails a realist metaphysics, claiming that we could explain substantive determinations by "some kind of Humean analysis of aesthetic properties in terms of projections of sentiment,"[47] but it is unclear how this would operate. If our description of an object as dainty or graceful is based on our felt response to it, are we not making a normative rather than a descriptive judgement? And if we are, then there is no use in categorizing this as a different kind of judgement than one of beauty, for it will neither determine nor legitimize the evaluative judgement, and will require some other kind of support itself when we are tasked to defend our position.

If a theory of aesthetic judgement must bifurcate judgements in the way that Zangwill has done, an explanation is needed of the relation between the two forms of judgement (which he offers as determinative) *and* a further argument to show how these judgements

47 Ibid., 322.

together amount to a claim of beauty that can be objective. At which level do we agree or disagree about an object's aesthetic merit? If the substantive judgement is based on pleasure, the verdictive may as well have been, for we have failed to ground normativity in anything other than subjective feeling. If, however, the substantive judgement is descriptive of some aesthetic properties objects at least seem to possess, we are no longer talking about normative judgements per se but about metaphysics or the philosophy of mind.

Zangwill admits that "we need a rationale for subsuming substantive judgements and judgements of aesthetic value under one category"—of taste judgements—and he acknowledges that he has not provided one. But he dismisses this requirement by claiming that "[w]hether or not verdictive and substantive properties [!] can be usefully subsumed under one category, the latter determines the former."[48] This optimistic claim is simply insufficient: in the end, Zangwill has not provided an account of normativity that is internal to the faculty of judgement at all, but in his focus on the cognitive basis for judgements of taste he has found refuge in *external* reasons and has at least broached—if not arrived at—a realist metaphysics.

Zangwill's account is instructive for a number of reasons. He rightly points to certain kinds of claims we make in support of our aesthetic judgements; when we are asked to give reasons for our approbation or disapprobation of an object, we are likely to do so in substantive terms, such as "it is beautiful because it is dainty and elegant," or "this piece fails because it is dumpy and garish." These aesthetic terms are part of our discourse about beauty, even if the exact role they play in our evaluations is unclear. Zangwill argues that if these substantive terms are meant to be reasons to

48 Ibid., 326.

ground our judgements, then "we need something approaching laws" linking the two. Otherwise, he asks, "how can the presence of one be evidence for the other?"[49] But to ascribe an evidentiary role to substantive descriptions is difficult. Daintiness or dumpiness, Zangwill agrees, "can be aesthetic virtue or vice": some porcelain figures are "horribly dainty" while "neolithic sculptures of women," for instance, are "wonderfully dumpy."[50] Substantive appraisals seem to support evaluations of both merit and demerit, which weakens their evidentiary role. Zangwill's determinative argument circumvents this problem. He claims that evaluating an object is a matter of "understanding which substantive aesthetic properties determine its aesthetic value":[51] that is the *point* of substantive judgements. So the laws that link substantive and verdictive judgements are causal and the task of the critic is to investigate these causal relations. But since for Zangwill aesthetic properties "depend on non-aesthetic properties,"[52] these causal laws will lead us towards a determination of merit by the sensory properties of objects, which we have so far sought to avoid.

Further, we can see that Zangwill's account goes too far: if we claim that this chair is beautiful *because* it is brown and soft rather than yellow and hard as evidence of our approbation, on Zangwill's model we are making a causal claim about what determines its beauty, even if our reasons are not couched in obviously aesthetic terms. The determinative model leads to this: our reasons, for Zangwill, are perforce determining grounds, what he calls the "'because' of determination."[53] And this is precisely where he errs:

49 Ibid., 327.
50 Ibid., 323.
51 Ibid., 328.
52 Ibid., 325.
53 Ibid., 327.

a less rigid interpretation of our discourse would read our substantive claims as post facto or retrospective legitimizing reasons for our prior verdictive judgements. As Schaper saw, we can be asked to account for our aesthetic approbation or disapprobation of objects in ways that we needn't do with purely subjective pleasures. But this accounting is not a causal claim: it is an explanation in terms of reasons by which we try to articulate a judgement we have already made. This is the point of a vocabulary of aesthetic terminology: it helps us to explain ourselves. It is a mistake to reify this vocabulary or to provide it with a causal determining power.

Zangwill's attempt to theorize beauty as a kind of judgement should demonstrate its dangers and pitfalls. It should also make clear that we need a fuller account of verdictive judgements themselves than what Zangwill has offered; we need to demonstrate that the verdict arises from reasons *internal* to the judgement itself, rather than from a series of external causal determinations. In doing this, we need to be clear that we are speaking of judgements of the correct logical form. Schaper's schema is useful here: while aesthetic judgements share some of the qualities of objective moral judgements (as well as the subjective form of culinary judgements), they are autonomous, and this means that their legitimizing reasons should be specific to the judgements themselves. If they find their grounds in external properties, they become overly cognitive, pointing to the way the world is; if they rely too much on felt pleasure, they likewise become overly subjective and psychological. Zangwill shows us just how difficult the middle ground is to find.

What we also learn from Zangwill's account is that a theory of beauty as autonomous judgement must posit a *singular* judgement of taste as its basis. Zangwill's bifurcation of judgement rendered pure evaluations superfluous to his aesthetic theory: once we detect the determining substantive properties of grace, delicacy, and the like, what need is there for a second evaluative claim that the object is *therefore* beautiful? The latter would have been presumed in the former descriptions if these were to have such determining force, leaving it at best merely a stamp of approval on conclusive determinations that have already been made. What we need to seek is an account of evaluative judgements themselves rather than the grounds for their legitimacy. And we now see how easily we can be led away from this central task.

Before we move on, let me pause for a moment to reestablish our goal and consider how far we have come towards meeting it. My argument is that the normative quality of the aesthetic in general can best be understood in terms of judgement rather than the properties of objects on the one hand or felt pleasures on the other. What I seek to do, then, is to "isolate a mental act or state of mind"[54] and locate the aesthetic in this. Our interactions with design, when they are aesthetic rather than cognitive, practical, moral, or merely subjectively pleasurable—when they involve appreciation in the appropriate sense—will require that we make judgements of their beauty or aesthetic excellence, and these judgements will have the following characteristics: (*a*) they will be autonomous of other forms of judgement; (b) they will account for both the subjective and objective aspects of beauty in terms of aesthetic pleasure on the one hand and a standard of correctness on the other; (*c*) they will nevertheless be singular rather than dispersing the aesthetic over two or more claims; (*d*) they will in the end yield an account of the beauty or aesthetic aspect of design that is different from the beauty of art, craft, and nature.

The requirements of this goal can largely be met, I believe, in the aesthetic theory of Immanuel Kant. Kant was well aware

54 Scruton, "In Search of the Aesthetic," 238.

of the problems of realism and subjectivism as they emerged in the eighteenth century and likewise sought their resolution in a theory of the aesthetic as a form of judgement. It is not only judgement that is autonomous for Kant, however: he sought to distinguish aesthetic pleasures from those of the sensory or moral as a particular kind, thereby resolving a lingering problem of their possible confusion. Further, by positing the aesthetic as a singular kind of judgement, his account corrects weaknesses in Zangwill's attempt to theorize beauty. Finally, what is most important for the goals of this project, Kant's account is flexible enough to allow for our active engagement with an object in our appreciation of it—our needing to use it—and specifically contains reference to a particular kind of beauty that can be directly applied to judgements of design.

3. *The Kantian Account*

Kant's aesthetic theory, traced out in the *Critique of Judgement*, is immensely complex and notoriously difficult, containing seemingly as many confusions and inconsistencies as it does insights. It is not my purpose here to rehearse or attempt to resolve the many different problems it presents. My goal is to provide an overview of Kant's account of taste to frame one particular section in the *Critique* that is most significant for judgements of design, and to provide a full treatment of the interpretive difficulties we find there.[55] In doing so, I will demonstrate the ways in which Kant's

55 Of the many other problems that arise throughout Kant's account of beauty in nature and art, I refer the reader to the excellent scholarly work already available, by especially Paul Guyer, *Kant and the Claims of Taste*, 2nd ed. (Cambridge: Cambridge University Press, 1997), Donald Crawford, *Kant's Aesthetic Theory* (Madison: University of Wisconsin Press, 1974), and Henry Allison, *Kant's Theory of Taste* (Cambridge: Cambridge University Press, 2001).

account meets the theoretical requirements I have outlined for a theory of beauty.

Kant's examination of the "faculty of taste" (synonymous with what he termed "aesthetic" or "reflective" judgement)[56] is an attempt to reconcile the subjectivism of aesthetic pleasure with the universality of an objective standard, which he clearly saw the eighteenth-century empiricists had failed to do. Of the earlier empiricist attempts in this regard, Kant wrote, "As psychological observations, these analyses of the phenomena of our mind . . . afford rich material for the favourite investigations of empirical anthropology" (§29, 119) but do not amount to a comprehensive aesthetic theory. "For these only enable us to know how we judge, but do not prescribe to us how we ought to judge. . . . Thus the empirical exposition of aesthetical judgements may be a beginning of a collection of materials for a higher investigation; but a transcendental discussion of this faculty is also possible, and is an essential part of the 'Critique of Taste'" (§29, 120). This "transcendental" discussion is in fact a critique of critique; it is concerned with the status of the critical attitude in matters of taste—not the empirical principles that lead us to judge in one manner or another but with a genuine a priori theory that will itself be "a total justification of the possibility of criticism" itself.[57] In taste, it is not personal preference that is decisive but the operation of a supra-empirical or "transcendental" norm. Yet this norm is not found in external reasons or the properties of objects: it is located within aesthetic judgements

56 Preface, 6. References to Kant's *Critique of Judgement* will follow J. H. Bernard's translation (New York: Hafner, 1972) with section and page number inserted in parentheses in the body of the text. For the German, I have used the Suhrkamp edition (1974), references to which will be by section and page number within the text.

57 Hans-Georg Gadamer, *Truth and Method,* 2nd ed., translation revised by Joel Weinsheimer and Donald G. Marshall (New York: Crossroad, 1986), 40. The first part of this work is concerned with a critical analysis of Kantian aesthetics.

themselves. To see how Kant effects this critique, we need to begin with his conception of judgement in general and the way that he distinguishes its aesthetic function from all other forms.

i. *The Faculty of Judgement*

Judgement (*Urteil*) or the faculty of judgement (*Urteilskraft*) is not only relevant to taste: it is the central point around which Kant's entire critical philosophy revolves. Each of his major works focuses on a particular kind of judgement, or a particular operation of this faculty: cognitive judgements in the *Critique of Pure Reason*, moral (practical) judgements in the *Critique of Practical Reason*, and aesthetic and teleological judgements in the *Critique of Judgement*. As Norman Kemp Smith has noted, Kant's doctrine of judgement maintains "that awareness is identical with the act of judging, and that judgement is always complex, involving both factual and interpretive elements.... Not contents alone, but contents interpreted in terms of some specific setting, are the sole possible objects of human thought."[58] Aesthetic judgement, then, is but one type of human awareness, and for Kant it is not inferior to others, but an essential part of them. The establishment of the conditions and limits of possible judgements forms Kant's main philosophical goal; his considerable legacies in ethics and aesthetics are in fact central to this task, posing a challenge for readers wishing to isolate his theory of taste, for instance, from the greater architectonic, for each of his claims about beauty is designed to contribute to a final exposition of human awareness itself. It is worth remarking, before we continue, that Kant's theory of taste makes beauty a central part of human experience; aesthetic judgements are not

58 Norman Kemp Smith, *Commentary to Kant's "Critique of Pure Reason"* (Amherst, NY: Humanity Books, 1923), xxxviii.

reserved for a small group of objects of fine art, an occasional trip to a gallery or a Sunday walk in the mountains. They are essential to what makes us human beings in the world, and this is what, in part, draws me to his theory.

In the introduction to the *Critique of Judgement,* Kant offers an overview of his entire architectonic. All "faculties or capacities of the soul," he writes, "can be reduced to three: the *faculty of knowledge,* the *feeling of pleasure and pain,* and the *faculty of desire*" (13). The understanding legislates our capacity for knowledge, through making determinant conceptual judgements about the evidence of our senses. The faculty of desire is legislated by our practical reason, and provides the basis for our moral judgements about what we ought to do. Between the two (knowledge and desire) Kant writes that "there is the feeling of pleasure, just as the judgement mediates between the understanding and reason" (15). The third installment of his monumental work seeks to develop the relationship of judgement to pleasure and pain in particular, to investigate its possible a priori principles, and to make the case that aesthetic judgements of taste are different from cognitive and moral judgements.

In terms of Kant's overall system, the faculty of judgement in general is meant to make possible the transition from "the pure faculty of knowledge, the realm of natural concepts, to the realm of the concept of freedom" (15)—from the immanent and determined understanding of natural law to the transcendence and freedom of morality—and the completion of this transition will be found in the reflective aesthetic and teleological judgements of the third *Critique*. Much more is riding on Kant's argument here than the solution to eighteenth-century problems in aesthetics, a prime reason for the complexity of his analysis.

The normal operation of judgement in general is to facilitate our understanding of the world. Kant describes its function in this way: "Judgement in general is the faculty of thinking the particular as contained under the universal. If the universal (the rule, the principle, the [natural or moral] law) be given, the judgement which subsumes the particular under it...is *determinant*" (15). Knowledge requires a mental representation that we have (based on our sensory experiences of, for instance, redness and sweetness) and a concept (apple, strawberry) that determines what that representation is of. The faculty of judgement brings these two together. All mental representations (Kant reserves the term "idea" for a different use) are candidates to become objects of the understanding—to become knowledge. But what determines our knowledge is a set of transcendental principles or laws, and concepts that the understanding has a priori. Because these are already given, the task of judgement is simply to subsume, or fit, individual representations under these concepts. Kant writes that in its determinant use, "the law is marked out for [the judgement] a priori, and it has therefore no need to seek a law for itself in order to be able to subordinate the particular in nature to the universal" (15–16). And it is these a priori laws, not a determining regularity in the way the world is, that make our mental representations objective and provide us with universalizable knowledge.

But judgement does not always function in this determining manner, as an assistant to understanding. Sometimes, "if only the particular be given for which the universal has to be found, the judgement is merely *reflective*" (15), and it is judgement in its reflective or aesthetic capacity that accounts for beauty and the nature of taste. Briefly, for I will return to this in detail below, there are certain times when we have mental representations for which there are not predetermined principles or laws, when we do not know or do not seek to identify what is before us. In these cases, our judgement must look for these principles, and in so doing it is reflective and operates in a manner that is free rather than determined; the act of searching for the universal is what is foremost here, not the actual conceptual determination of the object. Our mental representations have what Kant calls a "subjective element" (26) that is referenced to the subject (they are *our* representations), as well as an objective element that refers outward to objects in the world and is the basis of cognition. The subjective element of a representation is the "*pleasure* or *pain* which is bound up with it" (26) and it is this element that is engaged by the judgement when it is free. This pleasure is also a result of a judgement of beauty, and forms the subjective aspect of Kant's aesthetic theory.

But taste has another aspect as well. Just as the understanding and reason are rule-governed and have a priori principles or laws that guide them, so too must the faculty of judgement, even in its reflective capacity when these principles do not have a determining function; this apriority provides judgement with its necessity and universality, turning thought into knowledge, a sense of duty into moral law, and pleasure into an objective account of beauty. All of the faculties are rule-governed, but in the case of reflective judgement, this rule or principle can only be subjective and internal, as it is concerned with the feelings that attend our mental representations. Still, as ultimately rule-governed a priori, judgements of taste can claim a necessity and universality (of a sort), and it is this that allows Kant to counter the subjectivism of empiricist theories of taste and argue that we can indeed be right or wrong in our aesthetic judgements, and expect these judgements to have universal validity.

We can already see that Kant's analysis of taste will proceed along the lines enumerated by my argument thus far: his account of beauty finds its source within evaluative judgements themselves, judgements that, we will see, are autonomous and singular but which nevertheless incorporate within them both the subjectivity of felt pleasure and the objectivity of standards of correctness. "Beauty" is not a property of objects of experience, for Kant, but neither is it simply a pleasurable feeling: beauty is a verdictive judgement we make in response to our experiences, and as such it is irreducibly normative. The complexity of Kant's theory in this area alone stems from just how much work he needs this notion of judgement to do: he must show its ties to pleasure as well as to universalizable standards, its autonomy, and its singularity, and he must differentiate this reflective judgement from judgements of all other kinds at the same time. Much of the difficulty in grasping Kant's account of taste lies in not separating out these various strands of argument and seeing the importance of each for a full account of normativity. But each, as we have seen, plays a vital role in resolving many of the problems encountered in trying to frame a theory of taste or beauty. Kant begins the *Critique of Judgement* with an "Analytic of the Beautiful," or analysis of aesthetic judgements of taste in general, where he lays out the subjective and objective aspects of reflective judgements, their relation to pleasure, and their autonomy from cognition. I will take these aspects in turn, although there is considerable overlap in his argument.

ii. The Subjective Aspect of Beauty

Kant begins his analysis of taste by distinguishing three different kinds of pleasure: that of the pleasant or the agreeable; the good; and the beautiful. In each case the pleasure refers to a feeling we have, but only in the third instance is this feeling properly or purely aesthetic. Right away we encounter a complication, for while Kant wishes to relate aesthetic judgements to pleasure, there is not one but three different *kinds* of pleasure, only one of which is properly or purely aesthetic, although all three are the result of judgements that are reflective rather than determinant. We need to first distinguish these. Because Kant's argument depends upon terminology that is highly technical, I will begin by unpacking some of the terms he uses. Remember that we are dealing now with subjective mental representations and the feelings of pleasure or pain they engender, and not with properties of objects in the world. A mental representation (*Vorstellung*) is, as Donald Crawford has noted, "simply any object of awareness, anything of which we are immediately aware." This can include sensations, feelings, empirical objects, or even, Crawford suggests, "universals" or concepts.[59] Representations are thus candidates for cognition, but they need not become knowledge, and judgements of all kinds "are functions of unity among our representations,"[60] synthesizing them under a singular law or concept. Different representations, however, can engender different kinds of pleasures, or no pleasure at all.

The most potentially confusing terminological distinction we need to make is between sensation and feeling, particularly because these terms are often used interchangeably in English. By "sensation" (*Empfindung*) Kant means "an objective representation of sense" (§3, 40) in the way that the "green colour of the meadows belongs to *objective* sensation, as a perception of an objective sense" (that is, directed outwards, to objects in the world) (§3, 40). Nick Zangwill notes that sensation "is thus a matter of perceptual representation; sensations have representational or intentional content."[61] Pleasure, for Kant, is *not* a sensation: it is a "feeling" (*Gefühl*). So the pleasantness of the green meadows "belongs to

59 Crawford, *Kant's Aesthetic Theory*, 39.

60 Kant, *Critique of Pure Reason*, trans. Norman Kemp Smith (New York: St. Martin's Press, 1965), A69/B93. All references to this work will be provided in text, prefixed by *CPR* and using the standard Akademie numbering.

61 Nick Zangwill, "Kant on Pleasure in the Agreeable," *Journal of Aesthetics and Art Criticism* 53, no. 2 (1995): 168.

subjective sensation by which no object is represented, i.e. to feeling" (§3, 40), or what Zangwill calls the "'subjective' hedonic tone (*what it feels like* to have it) of pleasure."[62] Thus we sense green or yellow, but we feel pleasure or displeasure from that sensation.

When Kant distinguishes three kinds of pleasure, he means three kinds of feelings, and this is important because the first kind of pleasure, the agreeable, is based on sensation, as Kant uses the term, and this means that it depends on the existence of external objects, as those that furnish sensations. With the assistance of two further notions—interest (*Interesse*) and desire (*Begehr*)—Kant's analysis proceeds in the following way (he writes):

> The satisfaction [pleasure] which we combine with the representation of the existence of an object is called "interest" [and is based on sensation].
>
> Whereas,
>
> When the question is if a thing is beautiful, we do not want to know whether anything depends or can depend on the existence of the thing, either for myself or for anyone else, but how we judge it by mere observation.
>
> And
>
> We wish only to know if this mere representation of the object is accompanied in me with satisfaction, however indifferent I may be as regards the existence of the object of this representation. (§2, 38–9)

62 Ibid.

The pleasures of both the agreeable and the good depend on the real existence of objects—they are "interested" in the Kantian sense—and thus they also bear an intimate relation to desire. A judgement of the pleasant, for example, stems from pleasurable sensations we experience and "excites a desire for objects of that kind" (§3, 41). For example, with gustatory pleasure, as Paul Crowther suggests, "to enjoy the taste of a certain kind of food, the food must really be as good as it looks. The appearance of agreeableness is not enough."[63] Chocolate cannot simply look delicious, it must really be so, and the pleasure of agreeable food provokes desire, as we represent other similar food as the potential source of more pleasure.[64] In this way, the agreeable does not just please us immediately, it "*gratifies*" us (§3, 41).

The pleasure of the good is also interested and likewise requires an object's real existence, but this time our desire is mediated by reason. That food we find pleasant may also be *good,* as in good for us, but in this case it must not only exist, we must know something about it. Kant writes that "in order to find anything good I must always know what sort of thing the object ought to be, i.e. I must have a concept of it" (§4, 41). For example, Kant notes that in judging the health that good food brings us, we find that it (health) is "immediately pleasant to everyone possessing it," but to be good it "must be considered by reason with reference to purposes, viz. that it is a state which makes us fit for all our business" (§4, 42) and that we desire it for this reason. The good does not gratify, but instead is "esteemed" or "approved" by us (§5, 44), in the way that rapini, for

63 Paul Crowther, "The Significance of Kant's Pure Aesthetic Judgement," *British Journal of Aesthetics* 36, no. 2 (1996): 111.

64 I am glossing quickly over the nature of the relationship between pleasure and desire. Nick Zangwill gives it a full and interesting treatment in "Kant on Pleasure in the Agreeable."

instance, whether or not as agreeable to our palates as chocolate, will give us a feeling of pleasure in the eating that is reasoned, and based on knowledge of its health-giving properties.

Disinterested pleasure—that is, the beautiful—can be contrasted with the agreeable and the good in the following manner: first, "the judgement of taste is merely *contemplative*" (§5, 43), by which Kant means that it is not interested in whether or not the object of a mental representation really exists, but compares only its appearance as a mental representation with a feeling of pleasure. Second, this pleasure does not depend on sensation, as physiological, but is directed inward, to our feelings. Third, this indifference to the actual existence of an object underlying the representation means that taste is free of desire: "All interest presupposes or generates a want" (§5, 44), which is absent here, so that the beautiful does not gratify us, is not esteemed by us, but merely "pleases" us (§5, 44). And finally, the contemplative judgement of taste "is not directed to concepts" and so "is not a cognitive judgement" (§5, 44): we can make judgements of beauty without any knowledge of the object of our experience.

What Kant offers here is a picture of taste as a judgement thoroughly grounded in subjective pleasure, but he is concerned to delineate this pleasure in a way the empiricists did not do: pleasantness or agreeableness, he notes, "concerns irrational animals also" (§5, 44)—it is a pleasure based upon sensation alone, one that presumably a cat can feel when stroked or offered tuna. The good is mediated by the faculty of reason and so its pleasures require rational beings with knowledge of the objects under consideration. By contrast, beauty provides a pleasure that is utterly free of desire for the object on the one hand and cognitive estimations of its worth on the other. What is beautiful is what pleases us directly, absent any desire, any knowledge, or any interest. It is a pleasure that arises as a response to the mere appearance of things in front of us that is grounded not in our physiology or sensory faculties, nor in our reason and understanding, but is a feeling free of the determinations of each. This is not to suggest that aesthetic pleasure is somehow less real, or refers only to simulacra of real things but that it is an intellectual pleasure that results from engagement with a mental representation instead of a response to an actual object, a pleasure that importantly involves freedom from the constraint of both our animal natures and our law-giving reason. It is the intellectual character of the aesthetic that will keep its pleasure from being wholly subjective.

Judgements of the agreeable, such as "chocolate is delicious," ought more properly, Kant claims, take the form of "It is pleasant *to me*" (§7, 46). The immediate pleasure of the food is caused by a private sensation that we have, and is individual in that it is grounded in our private desires, experiences, and physiological make-up: some of us take pleasure in hot baths, some of us do not, and as with chocolate, the preference is purely subjective. The agreeable, then, is "nothing different from the mere pleasantness of the sensation" and so can have "only private validity, because it is immediate and dependent on the representation through which the object is *given*" (§9, 51). So there is no arguing about pleasures of this kind: with the agreeable, Kant claims, "the fundamental proposition is valid: *everyone has his own taste* (the taste of sense)" (§7, 47). Not only is the agreeable purely subjective but it is determined—by our sensations, by our desires, by our personal tastes.

By contrast, when we make judgements of beauty, we "speak of the beautiful as if beauty were a characteristic of the object"; we "demand" agreement of others and "*blame* them if they judge otherwise," and so we "cannot say that each man has his own particular taste" (§7, 46–47) but that taste must somehow be shared or at least shareable. The feeling of pleasure that is beauty is not so immediate: it is not based on external or bodily sensations at all. So what, then, is its basis? And how does it stand out from other forms of judgement?

What is unique about the pleasure of taste is that it is a mediated pleasure, not by concepts or properties of objects that are already determined, in the way that cognitive and moral judgements are, and not by desires or reason in the way of the agreeable and the good. This pleasure is instead the result of a reflective judgement that stems from the free and harmonious play of our cognitive faculties when they are released from their normal operations. Kant's argument here is complex, and requires reference to the roles of our faculties in the course of normal cognition.

For cognition to occur, the imagination must gather together our mental representations, and subject them to an a priori rule or concept provided by the understanding that determines what these are representations of. With aesthetic judgements, there "can be no rule" if we are to maintain their reflective character (§8, 50), yet they still involve the same mental faculties of imagination and understanding. In this case, though, the faculties operate somewhat differently. The imagination gathers together our representations (redness, sweetness), but it is "not regarded [here] as reproductive, as it is subject to the laws of association, but as productive and spontaneous" (§22, 77) because it is free in this instance from the determining rules of the understanding, and this actively contributes to what gives us aesthetic pleasure. Kant writes,

> The cognitive powers which are involved by this representation, are here in free play, because no definite concept limits them to a definite rule of cognition. Hence the state of mind in this representation must be a feeling of the free play of the

> representative powers in a given representation *with reference to a cognition in general*." (§9, 52, italics mine)

The imagination is released and feels a pleasure in that release from its normal functions. But the imagination is not completely released to an infinite freedom of fancy in reflective judgements; the determinations of the understanding are not completely disregarded here. It is not a matter of "anything goes" as though we could put representations together in any manner at all; the imagination cannot be completely without limit because it continues to attempt to fulfill its normal role by seeking the rule for the particular representation that in this case is not pre-given or a priori. Thus the freedom of the imagination is tempered by its need to operate in concert or harmony with the general rules of cognition, if not in this case with any particular one.

Harry Blocker describes the simultaneous independence and dependence of the cognitive faculties like this: "The imagination in aesthetic experience is free from the servile relations to the understanding which it has in its cognitive employment" in that it can range across a broad number of possible combinations of intuitions. But the imagination is simultaneously "influenced by the understanding in that the form of the representation . . . is . . . bound, *like* those representations of the imagination which become objects of cognition."[65] Even as it ranges freely over possible determinations, the representations of the imagination continue to take the form of possible cognitions, and so remain in harmony with the law-giving nature of the understanding. And this free play of the imagination gives us a feeling of pleasure in our temporary release

65 Harry Blocker, "Kant's Theory of the Relation between Imagination and Understanding in Aesthetic Judgements of Taste," *British Journal of Aesthetics* 5 (1965): 45.

from rule-bound and concept-driven determinant judgements, even while the essential operations of the mind remain intact. Judgements of beauty are, then, not wholly private, like those of the agreeable, because they are distanced from the particulars of individual sensations and desires. But they are not wholly objective, either, because they are not determined by concepts, as we find with normal cognition, or by moral laws. They are autonomous. Yet because the pleasure of beauty *is* dependent upon faculties that Kant claims are universal (imagination and understanding), it is a pleasure that we can have in common, as we shall see.

How does this complex process actually work in our everyday experience? Imagine that in walking down a tree-lined street in summer, you see a dappled pattern on the road (made by the sun shining through the canopy overhead). You think, "How beautiful," but this response is to the mere representation itself, not requiring you to find its source in the elms or the angle of the sun, but in the immediacy of its appearance to you and the pleasure that this brings. What Kant wishes to claim is that in this instance the imagination has gathered together your sensory impressions but the mind has not made a determinant judgement of what they are; it has experienced a freedom from its normal role and has given itself over to the mere pleasure of the appearance itself. This—fleeting— experience is beauty and is the result of a singular, autonomous, verdictive judgement made in that moment of freedom. Because this experience required you to be in that place at that time, see that pattern, make that judgement, and feel that pleasure as your own, beauty is inherently subjective. You might have missed it were you preoccupied with your shopping list, and you would not have experienced it if you were focused on the species of the trees overhead, or the time of day as indicated by the direction of the sun. The mind must be in repose—reflective, as it were—and desire must be held in abeyance. There is nothing in the trees or the sun themselves—no properties—that will provide an external cause for the feeling. It arises from the functions of the mind alone. Beauty in this sense "happens" upon us, rather than the other way around, and cannot be intentionally sought out in the world. Further, were we together, if we did not have identical experiences—I was a minute behind you and a cloud obscured the sun, I was preoccupied—we would not agree on what is beautiful in this instance, not because you find trees graceful and I do not, but because we had different experiences and thus had different responses to our mental representations. Yours was aesthetically pleasurable, mine was perhaps cognitive (look, an elm!), or agreeable (god, but the shade feels refreshing), or it went unnoticed altogether. Beauty is not determined by the properties of a particular object, and can emerge from the relation of a number of factors in a given experience. But beauty need not be so indeterminate; as we will see in the following chapter, we can also make aesthetic judgements about discrete things. What is at the forefront in both cases is a certain mental activity rather than a set of properties or qualities that we call aesthetic.

What we have thus far is an account of beauty that is internal to the faculty of judgement, that is subjective insofar as it references our personal pleasures, and that is autonomous of other forms of judgement, whether determinant like cognitive and moral judgements, or reflective, as resulting in other kinds of pleasures. Not only is this singular judgement a unique kind, but so too is the pleasure itself, on Kant's view. What remains in Kant's analysis is an explication of what makes these reflective judgements objectively valid, and what makes these personal pleasures universalizable. For, as it stands, his theory is simply a more complex version of the subjectivist or anti-realist approach to beauty we considered much earlier. The challenge is to now draw this out and give these judgements some applicability to the world.

iii. The Objective Aspect of Beauty

In the first part of the Analytic, Kant was concerned with how aesthetic judgements function, and what operations of the mind produce them. But all judgements—cognitive, moral, reflective—presuppose a relation between the subject and the object being judged, and Kant must turn to the other half of this relation: to its objective character. What are we judging when we say "X is beautiful"? For aesthetic realists such as Hogarth and Zangwill, the answer is some property or properties of a given object, be it a certain waving line that can be empirically demonstrated, or more intangible qualities such as grace, delicacy, and the like. Because Kant's theory of taste is committed to an internalist explanation of beauty, he must forgo this route (and all of its attendant problems) and instead locate the objectivity (as object-referring) nature of beauty within the judgement itself. He does this by producing some of the most difficult and abstruse discussion of the third *Critique*, centred around the notion of *Zweck*—purpose or end. The objective principle upon which aesthetic judgement operates Kant describes like this: "Schöneit ist Form der Zweckmäßigkeit eines Gegenstandes, sofern sie, ohne Vorstellung eines Zwecks, an ihm wahrgenommen wird" (§17, 155): it is the form of purposiveness without purpose, or mere formal purposiveness. To understand this formulation we need first to consider real purposiveness and the notion of purpose in general as it relates to other forms of judgement. This section is crucial for our later discussion of different kinds of beauty, one of which will be central to judgements of design. In this regard, while I will be returning to these notions in the next chapter, we need to linger long enough here to get a clear grasp of Kant's argument.

"Purpose" (*Zweck*: also translated as "end") and "purposiveness" (*Zweckmäßigkeit* or "finality") are defined "according to [their] transcendental determinations" like this: "purpose is the object of a concept in so far as the concept is regarded as the cause of the object," and "the causality of the *concept* in respect of its *object* is its purposiveness (*forma finalis*)" (§10, 54–55). Purpose or purposiveness seems to be a property of a concept, not of an object. It does not refer to the utilitarian purpose to which an object may be put, such as a tire becoming a swing, or to its general usefulness. Purpose, in this way, is a very misleading term. Kant instead wants to suggest that a purposive object is something we judge could only exist through an action that involves some *prior* conception of what it ought to be, that it has been created by a will (human or divine) according to a plan that precedes its existence.

Paul Guyer describes purpose like this:

> An end [purpose] is the product of an action, but by calling something an end we do not refer it to the desire which presumably motivates the action. Instead, we assert that it is an object whose nature is such that it could come into being only by a process which involves a representation of its nature prior to, and as a condition of, its existence.[66]

A pencil, for example, in our cognitive judgements of it, we consider to be a purpose, or the product of a purpose—not because it has a use, but because we judge that it was created or designed according to a plan (to make *this* thing and not another) that is a

66 Guyer, *Claims of Taste*, 188.

prior conception of what it ought to be. A chalky stone found on the beach may serve the same purpose (in our sense of the word) as a pencil in that both make marks on a surface, but the stone is not a purposive object qua marker—it was not designed, we imagine, with this use in mind. Purpose is not equivalent to *use*. And purpose, in the Kantian sense, is an a priori principle: the concept of the object is prior to and a condition of the object's eventual existence, which aids in our intellectual grasp of it.

Now, an object, Kant claims, can be purposive without having a purpose, when "we do not place the causes of this form in a will, but yet can only make the explanation of its possibility intelligible to ourselves by deriving it from a will" (§10, 55). In his discussion of teleological judgement, he provides the following example of this:

> If in a seemingly uninhabited country a man perceived a geometrical figure, say a regular hexagon, inscribed in the sand... [he] would not regard as a ground of the possibility of such a shape the sand, or the neighbouring sea, or the winds, or beasts with familiar footprints, or any other irrational cause. (§64, 216)

No—this hexagon is understood as purposive because it appears as though it could only have been brought about by a will; it is an intentional object, or we judge it as such, even if we cannot name its creator. Its intentionality is how it is intelligible to us; purposiveness here also underlies determinant judgements of cognition. As Donald Crawford notes, we can also go further, and "place the cause of this form (this purposiveness) in a will"—another human, an extra-terrestrial being, a god—and if we do, "we then attribute a [real] purpose to the object."[67] So there are

67 Crawford, *Kant's Aesthetic Theory*, 95.

objects that are clearly purposive (like pencils), and others which are merely purposive in respect to cognition (hexagons found in the sand). This takes us some way towards the notion of purpose, but we need to link this basic understanding to aesthetic judgements, which is more difficult. The heading of section 11 is that "the judgement of taste has nothing at its basis but the form of purposiveness of an object," and so we need to distinguish the form of purposiveness from actual or real purposiveness to make the connection to beauty.

Kant's argument in this section, as Henry Allison has noted, proceeds by elimination:[68] the goal is to elucidate judgements of beauty as distinct from judgements of the agreeable and the good, but also from the cognitive—purpose and purposiveness have a role to play in all of these. Thus we must rule out, for example, chocolate *and* rapini, pencils *and* hexagons, in order to uncover the specific kind of purposiveness to which judgements of beauty refer.[69] We judge pencils to be the products of real purposes: they have been created with an end in mind as the effect of a conceptual cause that we locate in an agent. With hexagons we are also making cognitive, determinant judgements about them, even if in this case we do not attribute real purposes but only purposiveness to our cognitions. We judge that they had been created with a concept in mind but we do not determine any specific agency and thus no real purpose to them; our cognition of them is limited in this case. Rapini displays what Kant calls objective purposiveness in a different sense: it is bound up with a concept of the good in that we

68 Allison, *Kant's Theory of Taste*, 125.

69 As we will see in the following chapter, we can make judgements of beauty about pencils, for instance, as designed objects. But these judgements are a particular sub-category of the beautiful that requires further elucidation. For now, I wish simply to explicate the Kantian notions of purpose, and of beauty, in their most general terms.

judge that it is *as though* rapini were designed, created to fulfill the rational objective of making us healthy, and the pleasure (of the good) that we find in rapini is due to this. In our judgement "the concept of *what sort of thing it is to be* must come first" (§15, 63), before the object itself. The difference between hexagons and rapini is presumably that the former involve a cognitive determinant judgement and the latter, as reflective, refer to a judgement that, while including an element of cognition (and relying on a concept), produces specifically a kind of pleasure in the subject: we judge rapini to be good, on the grounds of its benefits for health, which seem to be purposive (but we do not judge that they really are), and we merely identify the pencil and the hexagon without any attendant pleasure.

We are left with judgements of the pleasant and the beautiful. Judgements of the pleasant, as of chocolate, are not objectively purposive as they are not cognitive or based on concepts such as the good. They are instead pleasurable sensations (yumminess, for instance) that involve a notion of subjective purposiveness. Henry Allison is the first to admit that "Kant does not explain what he means by this," and indeed the brevity of this section belies its maddening complexity. But Allison conjectures that Kant "presumably has in mind some object in which one is interested on subjective or desire-based grounds, that is, something agreeable."[70] It appears that a judgement of subjective purposiveness is one that is reflective rather than cognitive, but the pleasure we receive from it involves our judging this object as though it were created to gratify us, or satisfy our desires. While objective purposiveness makes reference to cognition, subjective purposiveness makes reference to desire gratification. And neither form of judgement is directed

70 Allison, *Kant's Theory of Taste*, 125.

towards real, or actual purposes and their agents, as in the case of the pencil and (to a lesser degree) the hexagon.

Reflective judgements of beauty must be distinguishable from all of these other forms of judgement while still retaining their a priori (and hence objective) character *as* judgements and while still exhibiting some relation to the object being judged. Kant describes them in this way (and I will quote him at length):

> Every purpose, if it be regarded as a ground of satisfaction [pleasure], always carries with it an interest—as the determining ground of the judgement—about the object of pleasure. Therefore no subjective purpose can lie at the basis of the judgement of taste. But also the judgement of taste can be determined by no representation of an objective purpose, i.e. of the possibility of the object itself in accordance with principles of purposive combination, and consequently by no concept of the good, because it is an aesthetical and not a cognitive judgement. It therefore has to do with no *concept* of the character and internal or external possibility of the object by means of this or that cause, but merely with the relation of the representative powers to one another, so far as they are determined by a representation. (§11, 56)

The purposive character of judgements of taste cannot be real or actual—neither subjective nor objective—yet it must be present in some way, for our judgements to relate to the representations being assessed because purpose is the a priori determining ground of *all* judgement. Kant locates the relational nature of aesthetic judgements as internal to our cognitive faculties themselves: we judge the appearance of an object to be beautiful when our judgements have the *form* of purposiveness without really being purposive. And the formal character of our judgements is the determining ground of beauty. He goes on in this way:

> it [the determining ground of beauty] could be nothing else than the subjective purposiveness in the representation of an object without any purpose (objective or subjective), and thus it is the mere form of purposiveness in the representation by which an object is *given* to us, so far as we are conscious of it, which constitutes the satisfaction that we without a concept judge to be universally communicable; and consequently, this is the determining ground of a judgement of taste. (§11, 56)

Let me unpack this statement. When we have an aesthetic experience of an object, we have no concept available—the cognitive faculties are in free play—and the pleasure we feel is based only on the appearance, or form, of our mental representation rather than its cognitive content *as* being such and such a thing. That is fine as far as it goes, but you were pointing to something on the street that you called beautiful (and that I failed to recognize). If beauty is not external to us, it can also not be purely personal, else we would claim dreams, fantasies, and the like to be beautiful too. Something about our judgements must be objective. What Kant adds to this free play of the faculties is the claim that our mental representations must also *seem to be* purposive, as all regular cognitions are, without our being able to discern any real purpose in them. As Donald Crawford suggests, "if judgements of taste are to be legitimate, they must be based on the formal purposiveness (designedness, rule-governedness) of the object, without that object actually being judged to have a definite purpose, to be designed, or to be the exemplification of a concept."[71]

71 Crawford, *Kant's Aesthetic Theory*, 95.

The merely formal purposiveness of aesthetic judgements responds to the representation of an object that we do not cognize—it responds to the way a thing looks, (or sounds), and the pleasure we receive from its appearance alone. It is formally purposive because it is so lovely, so seemingly perfect, that it appears as though it has been planned or designed, but we do not conclude that it has been. The pleasure we experience in the perception of this object is one of "fit": the faculties in free play find it "fit" for cognition, according to the a priori principle of purpose, even though this too is held in abeyance and is not determinant, and this fitness is what produces the pleasure we find in beauty. We at minimum recognize that this mental image is not a chimera, a dream, or a hallucination. Aesthetic experiences, or judgements of beauty, are, as I have noted, one of the forms of human awareness. And this awareness requires a relation to objects in the world, one that for Kant must be consistent with all other kinds of awareness.

What Kant has added to his elucidation of taste here is but a further factor in the freedom of our reflective judgement, but this time as it refers to the object of that judgement: purposiveness is an integral element of determinant judgements of cognition, just as it underlies practical judgements of reason in moral matters, and so it must also operate in aesthetic judgements of the agreeable, the good, and the beautiful. In all cases, purposiveness is a priori. With cognition, we have seen, purpose is the a priori ground of the intelligibility of our concepts: the hexagon is intelligible *as* an intentional object and not a random series of lines in the sand. With the agreeable, there is real (subjective) purposiveness in our judgements of objects based on sensation and desire; with the good there is real (objective) purposiveness in our judgements of the utility or perfection of a thing for our needs or desires (as dictated by reason). But with taste, this a priori element is not determining: we judge a representation *as if it were purposive* but we do not conclude that it actually is. The free play of our faculties is circumscribed, first, because of the laws of the understanding, and now further when we see that, not only do they play in a rule-governed manner, but they do so according to the principle of purpose. When the feeling of "fitness" for cognition is experienced, it is not empirical, based on sensation, nor driven by reason and desire, but is still a priori in that it has a purposiveness that, while law-like, the judgement provides for itself.

To what, then, do our judgements of beauty refer? To any and all objects the appearance of which we judge to be formally purposive. This objective quality of our judgements does not specify kinds of objects or properties of objects that display beauty, and this is why providing examples of beauty here is so difficult. It is not that some things are beautiful and others not, but that any experience of the representation of a thing could yield a judgement of beauty if the right conditions are in place. The objective nature of our judgements is once again internal to the judgements themselves: so long as we judge *in this manner*, so long as we relate to objects in terms of merely formal purposiveness, we will find these representations of objects beautiful. Paul Guyer has claimed that this argument "represents Kant's attempt to accomplish the traditional objective of aesthetics: that of directly specifying certain properties or even kinds of objects which will license judgements of taste,"[72] but this, I believe, is to misunderstand Kant's intention in this section of the Analytic. Yes, he is certainly responding to the "traditional objective of aesthetics" in providing a theory of beauty or aesthetic experience, but he is doing so in a way that precisely does *not* circumscribe the objects or properties we call

72 Guyer, *Claims of Taste*, 185.

beautiful. To do so would be to defeat the purpose of the Analytic as it has unfolded, which has been to forge a middle path between purely objective and purely subjective accounts, by focusing on the faculty of judgement itself.

In the Analytic, Kant is arguing in a way analogous to the Copernican revolution for cognitive judgements he undertook in the *Critique of Pure Reason*: there he saw that it is not that our knowledge must conform to objects, but that we will understand cognition only if the objects of experience must conform to our ways of knowing them (*CPR* B xvi–xviii). Similarly here, our aesthetic judgements do not conform to the beauty objects possess (formal or otherwise), but rather they are beautiful because we judge them to be so, in an admittedly very complex way.[73] We can still agree with the realist that a sunset pleases us *because* we find it beautiful, as against the subjectivist claim that it is beautiful only because it pleases us, but our finding it beautiful is a product of the form our aesthetic judgements take and not because of some independent properties the sunset possesses.

What Kant provides with the notion of purposiveness is a way to understand beauty as having an objectively rational component by relating these judgements to all other forms of (cognitive, moral) judgements about the world. Without this account, beauty would remain wholly internal to the judging mind (and its attendant pleasures) and have no external application whatsoever. But even in a theory that claims beauty is internal to judgement, this cannot be construed as being merely imaginative, or private, if we seek an aesthetic theory that lays claim to any kind of objective validity.

73 Allison has noted that Kant's earlier argument about the harmony of the faculties displays this Copernican analogy, although I find it most striking here (*Kant's Theory of Taste*, 110–111).

Let me conclude this discussion by briefly considering how Kant construes the universal validity of aesthetic judgements.

The question that remains is how aesthetic judgements as subjective can carry "objective necessity" such that we can say that "everyone *will feel* this satisfaction in the object called beautiful" (§18, 73). Kant calls the necessity of pleasure "exemplary": "a necessity of the assent of *all* to a judgement which is regarded as the example of a universal rule we cannot state" (§18, 74). With judgements of beauty, we "*ask* for the agreement of everyone else" because our judgements are founded on "a ground that is common to all" (§18, 74 italics mine) in the feelings that result from the play of our faculties and in the a priori principle of purposiveness that guides the faculty of judgement in all of its applications or uses. But we cannot demand this agreement of others because taste has a subjective nature grounded in feeling rather than thought. Because Kant has maintained throughout that reflective judgements of beauty are subjective and based on feeling, he is vulnerable to claims of aesthetic relativism, where taste is localized, if not individual. Without objective properties determining the beauty of objects, it seems as though our judgements can carry no necessity with them that would allow us to be right or wrong in our aesthetic appraisals. Kant counters this threat by again locating the necessary character of beauty within the judging subject.

Because of the complex workings that make up a judgement of taste, Kant claims we are licensed to presuppose a "common sense" or feeling to humanity, and ground the "ought" of our judgements in this sense. And he argues that he has foundation for presupposing such a sense in us, for if our cognitive judgements carry with them necessity and universal communicability, why not our "state of mind" (§21, 75) that plays with the same elements as cognition? These elements in reflective judgement are harmony or "accordance" with cognition in general, and this accordance "can only be determined by feeling and not by concepts themselves" (§21, 76). If we are to agree that aesthetic judgements work in the way Kant suggests, the feeling that is derived from this mechanism must be as universal as the individual faculties and their interactions are. This "common sense" can then be assumed "without relying on psychological observations, but simply as the necessary condition of the universal communicability of our knowledge" (§21, 76), which all but the most committed skeptic would presume.

While feelings are subjective, Kant claims that with judgements of beauty they are not wholly private or individual as they are in judgements of the agreeable, but instead, their particular make-up renders the feelings themselves "common" (§22, 76), as common as experiences and concepts are. And with the presumption of this common feeling, we can with confidence prescribe our judgements of beauty to everyone else having the same experience as us, without requiring either some objective property of beauty or a psychology of sensation, or the notion of an external standard to ground the idea of taste.

With this conclusion, Kant claims to have resolved the seemingly contradictory nature of taste that vexed the empiricists: on the one hand, there appears to be no disputing about taste because we *each have our own*; on the other, we claim for beauty a certain objectivity—we quarrel about aesthetic matters in the belief that there is a *truth* to them. The solution to this "antinomy," Kant claims, "depends on the possibility of showing that two apparently contradictory propositions do not contradict each other in fact, but that they may be consistent" (§57, 185). And he renders the two sides of the antinomy consistent based on the foregoing argument. The subjectivity of taste means it cannot be based on concepts, else it would be "determinable by proofs" (§56, 184), which it is not. Conversely, taste must seemingly be based on concepts if we want to claim "the necessary assent of others" (§56, 184) because concepts as the basis of knowledge are the foundation for truth and objectivity. Taste is not conceptual because it is not cognitive, which allows it to maintain its basis in feeling, and allows for dispute in aesthetic matters. But taste is similarly based on an a priori principle by which the judgement is law-like (in the way that concepts are), and which allows us to resolve our disputes, albeit through prescription rather than determination. There is a necessity to our judgements, if it is a necessity based on feeling rather than fact. "Thus the two apparently contradictory principles are reconciled—*both can be* true, which is sufficient" for a theory of taste (§57, 186). The methodology Kant uses here is the same as elsewhere in his system: he seeks to reconcile empiricism with rationalism, subjectivism with (aesthetic) realism, and in following this (admittedly complex and often convoluted path) he locates beauty *within* the faculty of judgement itself, providing a fully normative account of taste.

4. NORMATIVE BEAUTY

Two immediate questions present themselves at this juncture: does the Kantian account deliver a normative theory of beauty that meets the requirements as I articulated them at the end of section 2? And did it have to be so hard? The answer to both is a qualified yes. Let me return to those requirements. I have maintained that an adequate theory of the aesthetic experience of beauty must be grounded in judgements rather than in felt pleasure on the one hand or in the properties of objects on the other. Only this route, I argued, would satisfy the conflicting intuitions we have about aesthetic matters. But "judgement" is neither a simple nor a straightforward notion. I concur with Kant about its centrality to human thought, in all its great variety. We make a number of kinds of judgements, often about the very same object. For instance, of a canvas we may judge that it is a Rothko of 1951, or that it is oil rather than charcoal; that it is 189 × 101 cm in size, rectangular rather than oval. These are cognitive judgements. We may further judge that this work is morally reprehensible or uplifting, that we desire to own it or that it is too expensive, that it amuses us or that it clashes with the wallpaper. All of these judgements must be differentiated and distinguished from purely aesthetic judgements of a work's excellence or beauty, but on what grounds? We are attempting to theorize an internal mental phenomenon: do the judgements *feel* different? Do they have different consequences? Do they refer to different objects? How can a singular faculty give rise to such diversity? Kant has delved further into these questions than any other thinker, and the complexity of his account reflects the difficulty of the task itself.

His discussion of *Zweck* and *Zweckmäßigkeit,* for instance, is a sophistication of Hume's earlier claim that all of our knowledge concerning matters of fact in the world is founded on the relation of cause and effect. Hume argued that it is only by this relation that our knowledge can extend beyond the immediate evidence of our senses. "A man, finding a watch or any other machine in a desert island, would conclude, that there had once been men in that island. All our reasonings concerning fact are of the same nature."[74] In Kant's terms, these reasonings must be purposive. But

74 David Hume, *An Enquiry Concerning Human Understanding* (Indianapolis: Hackett, 1993), 16.

if judgement is a singular faculty, then this purposiveness must be present—and must be accounted for—in each of its various applications. Part of Kant's task has been to maintain the singularity of this specific mental faculty, even while somehow distinguishing the great variety of actual judgements it generates, and this leads us decisively to the theoretical complexity of the Analytic.

Similarly, while I claimed that beauty requires an account that is internal to judgement itself, this account must simultaneously explain both the subjective and objective aspects of judgement such that it satisfies our conflicting intuitions without becoming overly psychological or overly metaphysical. Here Kant's argument is at is most original and perhaps its most contentious. He locates beauty within the mental act of reflective judgement, but in order to do so, he must separate the resultant pleasures of this judgement into three kinds, which seems as though he is merely carrying forward a problem without resolving it. Instead of bifurcating judgements into the verdictive and the substantive as Zangwill did, Kant maintains that reflective judgement is a unique form but that it yields three different sorts of pleasure, one of which he calls beauty. While there is intuitive appeal in this move, it will be difficult, on independent grounds, to assess his claim that the pleasures we feel differ according to factors present in the reflective judgements we make. Kant is consistent with the British empiricists in claiming that the pleasure in aesthetic judgement must be *ours* in order for us to have taste. But we will need a complex psychology of that pleasure in order to distinguish the beautiful from the pleasant and the good. It satisfies many of our intuitions about aesthetic experience to claim that our appreciative response to a Rothko is different in kind from our appreciation of a piece of chocolate or a hot bath, and that we can tell the difference between them. Kant attempts to formalize these intuitions by situating the pleasure of the agreeable in physical sensation, the pleasure of the good in the faculty of reason, and the pleasure of beauty in an intellectual feeling that somehow stands partway between the two. But he, no less than any theorist of aesthetic pleasure, will have trouble demonstrating his case to a modern skeptic. Nevertheless, he captures a commonsense feeling implicit in many contemporary theorists that aesthetic experience, or the pleasures of art and beauty, is importantly different from more quotidian physical pleasures on the one hand and wholly intellectual pleasures on the other. However contentious this may be, Kant at least has attempted to explicitly articulate these differences and is one of the first to do so.

There is a lot riding on Kant's presupposition that our mental faculties are universally the same, and that, barring accident, they will proceed in the same way all the time. In this, he is indebted to Enlightenment notions of the universality of reason. In his defense, however, even Zangwill's more contemporary account shares these presuppositions in its suggestion that certain properties of objects will cause similar hedonic responses in all spectators, and this is a problem that any internal account will share, Kant's no less than others'. His advance on Hume and the eighteenth-century theorists of taste lies in his intellectualization of our aesthetic pleasures as a way of attempting to make them universalizable, and hence remove their overly subjective and contingent character. But the cost of this approach is the presupposition that there is but one way in which the human mind works, cognitively, morally, and aesthetically.

Kant's account is also unique in its attempt to make aesthetic judgements objective and necessary without reverting to an ontology of beautiful objects; to locate that objectivity within the faculty of judgement is a philosophical coup that has not been repeated or superseded. But he achieves this through a set of theory-laden claims about the rule-governed yet free operation of the cognitive faculties that is seemingly overly complex and indeed abstruse. And none of it, in the end, seems to tell us precisely *what* is beautiful, or *how* to be sure that it is, or even how to resolve disagreements about taste; the applicability of Kant's account is questionable at the ground-level of assessing how any works of art or design or even natural phenomena can gain our approbation.

Part of the frustration aesthetic theorists feel in the face of the Kantian account is similar to moral theorists seeking a normative ethics from his metaphysics of morals: this simply was not his goal, as I cautioned at the outset. However, in spite of these problems, the Kantian account is the most consistent and complete theory of beauty available to date. This is not to damn him with faint praise: even given the concerns I have noted, Kant's theory for the most part meets the requirements I have listed, and where it does not, it points to the challenges any normative aesthetic theory must face, rather than particular weaknesses in his argument. Kant locates the aesthetic in our experience of beauty as the product of an autonomous and singular judgement that contains within it both subjective hedonic feeling and the objective necessity that accounts for aesthetic appraisal as a unique response to our experience of the world. Can we still quarrel about taste? Of course, as our judgements impute but do not postulate the agreement of others. Can we make aesthetic judgements without actively taking pleasure in the objects themselves? Assuredly not. We can approach but cannot cross the threshold from subjectivity to full objectivity. If this brings with it corollary problems in an analysis of the faculties of the mind, it is the price any account must pay that focuses on elucidating the particular richness of aesthetic judgements.

But I had said at the outset that this discursus into aesthetic normativity and Kantian theory was meant to establish the basis for judgements of design as particular kinds of judgements of taste, meriting separate treatment. Indeed, were the foregoing complexity not enough, Kant follows it by differentiating *types* of beauty with a further detailed discrimination within the aesthetic judgements he has worked so hard to explain. And it is within this further discrimination that we will find a place for design as a beauty of a particular kind. We can, at last, turn to this analysis.

Chapter III

Design and Dependent Beauty

Kant's aesthetic offers a theory of beauty that meets the conditions I laid out in the last chapter: it is an account that escapes the problems of realism and subjectivism both, and that posits beauty as the result of a particular kind of judgement we make. But, as anything at all can be beautiful on (my reading of) the Kantian account, we have not yet distinguished the beauty of design as a particular kind of aesthetic appraisal that can be marked out from judgements of the beauty of nature, fine art, or even craft. Indeed, from the foregoing, it seems that beauty is the same, or operates in the same way, in all things as referenced to our disinterested responses to objects as they appear to us. However, as we saw in chapter 1, while art, craft and design all have *form* (as does nature), this form is coupled with, respectively, content, matter and function, and if I am to satisfy my contention that the beauty of design is different from that of art and craft (and natural beauty), our judgements of design will have to then differ from our judgements of these other kinds of beauty in a significant and parallel way. The Kantian account, with careful interpretation, can achieve this without reference to the particular properties of designed objects in terms of some necessary and sufficient conditions that would mark them out from other kinds of things. Kant's further work in the third *Critique*, on the aesthetic ideas of fine art and particularly on dependent versus free beauty, is a refinement of his analysis that delineates the various species of the genus that is beauty or aesthetic judgement writ large. And it is within the species of dependent beauty in particular that we will find the locus for judgements of design.

What do I mean by genus and species of beauty? And how can Kant make such qualifications to his theory without reversing or contradicting the structure of aesthetic judgements as he has laid it out? Kant sought, as we saw in chapter 2, a "transcendental discussion" (§29, 120) of the faculty of taste, or the preconditions for the possibility of aesthetic judgements. That is, he was concerned to provide an a priori analysis of the logical structure of taste in general, one that I think we can interpret as a *regulative ideal,* just as Eva Schaper delineated the logical structure of aesthetic judgements as opposed to moral and gustatory judgements, without having anything further to say about how we *do* actually judge at the phenomenological level of our everyday experiences. She, like Kant, was interested in the solution to a theoretical problem, not in its application. The demands of these transcendental requirements satisfied, Kant is able then to turn his attention to the much messier business of how our actual aesthetic judgements rarely achieve the purity of this ideal, how the faculties of the mind rarely work in such complete isolation from each other, and how our responses to the world more often contain an admixture of knowledge, pleasure, and desire.

As Marcia Muelder Eaton notes, "'pure,' conceptless, valueless uses of 'beauty' are rare," and it "has been a mistake for aestheticians to take this [pure] sense of beauty as the paradigm aesthetic concept."[1] That is, while Kant's analysis in the Analytic was

1 Marcia Muelder Eaton, "Kantian and Contextual Beauty," *Journal of Aesthetics and Art Criticism* 57, no. 1 (1999): 13.

theoretically consistent, it was not, perhaps, wholly realistic, or intended to actually describe our aesthetic appraisals of this or that thing. Robert Wicks would agree: "it is undeniable that in concrete circumstances, our judgements of beauty are typically mixed"—with pleasures of sensation, for example, or pleasures of the good. And he suggests that Kant's further discussion is meant simply "to clarify the structure of a large portion of our everyday experiences."[2] The refinements I wish to consider, then, are not a reversal or denial of the analysis Kant has provided but simply a grounding of that analysis in everyday life. I believe that without inconsistency we can concede that what is ideally the case—that we make pure judgements of taste in the manner Kant has described—is not actually the case, for the greater part, and thus the previous analysis needs to be tempered by this more sober realization. In particular, we can read §16, on dependent beauty, and Kant's discussion of the aesthetic ideas of fine art (in §43–50) as his attempt to do just this.

There is a precedent for such an interpretation, in Kant's equally transcendental analysis of moral judgement in the *Foundations of the Metaphysics of Morals*. There, while he also laid out the logical structure of moral judgements (as being purely rational), he was well aware that, by and large, we do not operate as purely rational creatures with fully autonomous wills, and that many of our choices and deliberations result from empirical and contingent factors such as our desires, sympathies, and the like. His concern in that work was nevertheless "with actions of which perhaps the world has never had an example, with actions whose feasibility might seriously be doubted" because a "completely isolated metaphysics of

2 Robert Wicks, "Dependent Beauty as the Appreciation of Teleological Style," *Journal of Aesthetics and Art Criticism* 55, no. 4 (1997): 388, 389.

morals [is] ... an indispensable substrate of all theoretically sound and definite knowledge of [moral] duties."[3] Similarly, an analysis of pure aesthetic judgements, such as we saw in chapter 2, can be read as a theoretical substrate that resolves the logical problems inherent in an internal account of taste but that nevertheless grounds our actual understanding of beauty. It is no more meant as a field guide to actual criticism and appraisal than the *Foundations* was meant to provide a normative ethic. But while in the *Foundations* Kant merely conceded this point, in the *Critique of Judgement* he goes further and offers some explication of how our impure, mixed aesthetic judgements actually operate. And one of these impure judgements will be applicable for the beauty of design.

Before I turn to this discussion proper, however, let me note that while Kant contrasts pure and impure beauty in §16 we should not take him to be suggesting a hierarchy of forms, from the falsely, to the partially, to the fully beautiful in a way that would suggest design and craft, for instance, are objects of lesser aesthetic value than fine art or the beauty of nature. This is why I suggested the metaphor of genus and species: just as design is different from art but in no way inferior as a potential object of aesthetic appraisal, so our so-called "impure" aesthetic judgements differ from their pure form even while retaining the overall structure that makes them judgements of taste. Indeed, our impure judgements of beauty are in fact the more complex of the two, because of the additional factors that are present but that must be held in delicate balance in

3 Immanuel Kant, *Foundations of the Metaphysics of Morals*, trans. Lewis White Beck (New York: Bobbs-Merrill, 1959), 24, 27. Beck, in his introduction to the volume writes, "Kant insists that man is neither completely rational nor completely moral; but he also insists, in a way reminiscent of Aristotle and in many ways anticipating Dewey, that morality is conduct guided by reason. But reason is never claimed to be all-powerful, and Kant is, in fact, rather more pessimistic about man's rational competence than either Aristotle or Dewey" (xviii).

our appraisals. With this in mind, we can turn to the refinements of these judgements themselves.

1. FREE BEAUTY

Kant begins §16 by claiming that there are "two kinds of beauty; free beauty (*pulchritude vaga*), or merely dependent beauty (*pulchritude adhaerens*)," and he differentiates the two as follows:

> The first presupposes no concept of what the object ought to be; the second does presuppose such a concept and the perfection of the object in accordance therewith. The first is called the (self-subsistent) beauty of this or that thing; the second, as dependent upon a concept (conditioned beauty), is ascribed to objects which come under the concept of a particular purpose. (§16, 65)

The characteristics of free beauty, in fact, render it identical to the overall genus of beauty we've already seen: these judgements are disinterested, non-cognitive, provoke pleasure from the free play of the faculties, and take the form of purposiveness without any purpose. In this section, Kant at last offers examples of free beauty, and what is interesting is that these examples are couched in negative terms. For instance, flowers, some birds, and seashells are free beauties found in nature. He notes that "[h]ardly anyone but a botanist knows what sort of thing a flower ought to be; and even he .... pays no regard to this natural purpose if he is passing judgement on the flower by taste" (§16, 65). Similarly, of manufactured or intentional objects, Kant mentions "delineations à *la grecque*, foliage for borders or wallpapers" as free beauties that "mean nothing in themselves" and "represent nothing," along with "all music without words" (§16, 66).

With free beauty our judgements of taste "can only be pure if either the person judging has no concept of this purpose or else abstracts from it in his judgement" (§16, 67). In some instances of free beauty this requires us to disregard—or have no knowledge of—the function or real purpose of the object, while in other cases we treat it as having no content when we respond to its form alone. Free beauty is at the outset defined negatively as that which lacks cognitive content, or ignores it. And while we can make judgements of free beauty—achieve the regulative ideal—such judgements are rare. The botanist, for example, who recognizes "in the flower the reproductive organ of the plant" (§16, 65), must ignore what she knows in order to judge it freely beautiful; she must respond to the flower as if she is unaware of its purposive nature. Similarly, I presume, the interior decorator will have to disregard his knowledge of the functions of wallpaper and the pianist must abstract from all he knows about a given composition when he listens to it in order to make a free judgement of beauty about the way it appears to the listening ear. By contrast, the example I offered in chapter 2 was much simpler: there was no actual *object* that was judged in that moment of beauty but simply a pattern, an image, and thus perhaps not so great a demand on us (dendrologist, meteorologist, or otherwise) to disregard our knowledge of trees and sun in order to respond to it. The dappled pattern on the street really had almost nothing but formal qualities.[4] But this example was also perhaps too easy: the majority

4 When I use the, perhaps infelicitous, term "formal qualities" I mean this as a shorthand for "the way things appear to us as mental representations without cognitive content" and in no way suggest that, following Bell, beauty resides only in the formal properties that objects actually possess. All objects have form, as I contended in chapter 1; beauty resides in the judgements we make *in response to* our experiences and not in the objects themselves.

of our aesthetic experiences will be encounters with actual objects that we know, that we use, or that we value, and thus in the majority of cases judgements of free beauty will be harder to effect. Hence, I think, the reason for Kant's negative description of free beauty.

Eaton, for instance, notes of the invasive flower purple loosestrife that while she finds it beautiful, her friend the ecologist cannot: "she tells me she finds it ugly—even repulsive" and "has a poster on her office door urging us to wipe it out."[5] The abstraction (or ignorance) required for a judgement of free beauty is considerable—for the ecologist or botanist with knowledge of the purposes of flowers, no less than for the pianist with knowledge of the content of a musical composition, or any of us when faced with objects that we know, use, and value.

Free beauty, while coincident with the structure of aesthetic judgements in general, is at the same time a limit case: an experience that may come upon us in certain circumstances, but not representative of the norm. What I suggest *is* more common is dependent beauty, an aesthetic judgement that does not prescind from—that somehow includes—conceptual knowledge of the objects we encounter. The problem, of course, is that the notion of dependent beauty appears to do violence to Kant's theory as we have so far understood it. Beauty, as a reflective judgement, must be free of concepts yet dependent beauty, as having conceptual content, contradicts the theory on this central point. Our task, then, is to unravel this seeming contradiction and render the discussion in §16 consistent with Kant's broader account.

If we can make good Kant's claims here, we will be able to locate the particular beauty of design, and distinguish it from other kinds of aesthetic appraisals. In order to do this, we must return to the notion

5 Eaton, "Kantian and Contextual Beauty," 11.

of *Zweck* or purpose because, I will argue, it is only in this regard that dependent beauty differs from free beauty. Judgements of dependent beauty will also be autonomous, singular, require the free play of the faculties, result in a particular kind of disinterested pleasure, and remain subjectively universal: in all other respects, dependent beauty will be coincident with free beauty. If we consider the discussion of purpose in chapter 2, we can see why this one element is so important: the reader will already have noticed that my example of a real purposive object, the pencil, was precisely a designed object, yet the discussion of purpose in that chapter appeared to exclude it from true aesthetic judgements. It is only through the notion of dependent beauty that we can make real purposes apt objects of aesthetic appraisal. Yet what Kant means by dependent beauty—and whether it is a coherent notion—has been the subject of a great deal of debate, which we will have to consider. In the following section I will focus on our knowledge of purposes and leave aside for the moment dependent beauties that have content or that represent something. Kant mentioned the latter in §16, I think, because it foreshadows his fuller treatment of fine art in §43–50. Our judgements of art are judgements of dependent beauty because of the particular content that art expresses through aesthetic ideas. I will return to this below, when I juxtapose judgements of design with art and craft.

2. DEPENDENT BEAUTY

i. *Beautiful Things*

Let us begin with Kant's examples of dependent beauty: he mentions human beauty, the beauty of a horse, or of a building (church, palace, arsenal, summerhouse), each of which "presupposes a concept of the purpose which determines what the thing is to be, and consequently a concept of its perfection" (§16, 66). As with free beauty, these examples include both natural and manufactured objects. How, then, does a horse differ from a seashell, or a palace from the wallpaper in its rooms? Or perhaps I should ask how our *judgements* of these objects differ because here we meet our first interpretive hurdle.

Paul Guyer would seek to claim that Kant distinguishes between kinds of *things* that are either freely or dependently beautiful rather than kinds of judgements we make. "[C]hurches and horses *must* be regarded from the point of view of their purposes," and he notes that Kant speaks as if "these things could be beautiful only in connection with such a concept or as if the nature of these objects themselves required that they be judged as dependent beauties." Further, "If a thing has a purpose, it seems, it can *only* be judged according to that purpose, or as a dependent beauty."[6] This association of dependent beauty with objects rather than judgements is important for Guyer's "negative" or "external" account whereby the purpose of an object imposes a "constraint on the freedom of the imagination" in our response to it: we on principle cannot find such things freely beautiful.[7] I will consider the substance of Guyer's negative account in a moment; first, though, we need to properly locate dependent beauty and, *pace* Guyer, it is inconsistent (and not at all useful) to read Kant as though these examples were meant to provide instances of things that *really are* beautiful.

6 Paul Guyer, *Kant and the Claims of Taste* (Cambridge: Cambridge University Press, 1997), 221, 222.

7 Ibid., 220. It is Robert Wicks who called Guyer's account both negative and external (see Wicks, "Dependent Beauty," 389) but Guyer in a later exchange did not disagree with this appellation (see Paul Guyer, "Dependent Beauty Revisited: A Reply to Wicks," *Journal of Aesthetics and Art Criticism* 57, no. 3 [1999] as well as Paul Guyer, "Free and Adherent Beauty: A Modest Proposal," *British Journal of Aesthetics* 42, no. 4 [2002]).

While Kant did state in the opening of §16 that "there are two kinds of beauty," the remainder of the section juxtaposes pure and impure judgements of taste, so the textual evidence for Guyer's interpretation is scant. Further, if we claim that horses and churches can only be dependently beautiful, we would have to, for the sake of consistency, also claim that flowers, seashells, and wallpaper are only freely beautiful (or that some things are one, some the other, and some can be both). But surely a botanist, if she does *not* abstract from her knowledge of flowers, could find one dependently beautiful (if not, perhaps, purple loosestrife), just as a pianist surely can make an impure judgement of taste about a piece of music. What seems to be at issue is the determinative role these examples play for Kant, and in keeping with my interpretation of this section as concerned with our actual (as opposed to ideal) aesthetic judgements, I can only read them as empirical observations rather than logical distinctions between beauties of different kinds. That is, in Königsberg of 1790, we just may not have been disposed to judge a horse freely beautiful—in the way that, perhaps, we do not today find trucks or tractors freely beautiful with any ease. And it may have been as difficult to make a pure judgement of taste about a church or palace at the time as it is for me to abstract from my knowledge of my own home in order to find it beautiful *tout court*.

Guyer does stress that, on his reading, the purpose of an object does not "fully determine"[8] our approbation of it, but his interpretation does suggest that these purposes *do* determine the latitude the imagination has for free play in its response to them. Thus, while I cannot charge Guyer with taking a strongly realist stance whereby beauty is a property that resides in this or that thing, it does seem that an object's other substantive properties—or our

8 Guyer, *Claims of Taste*, 219.

substantive judgements of those properties—do determine our aesthetic responses in a way that is similar to the determinative role substantive properties played in Zangwill's conception of beauty from chapter 2. In Zangwill's case, substantive properties had a positive evidentiary role in determining what is beautiful; in Guyer's case the purposes of objects play a negative role in that they "function to exclude certain forms as imperfections in objects to which they apply."[9] Robert Wicks reads this negative claim strongly as one of incompatibility: a church without a cruciform floor plan, for instance, "would be an instance of a form that is incompatible with what is necessary for the church's beauty, and would be one whose presence precluded the church's beauty."[10] And this reading of Guyer does suggest that purposes play a determinative (if negative) role in our judgements, *and* that some things cannot be freely beautiful in principle, both of which claims we must reject.

As we have seen, I am committed to the position that, because beauty is a singular judgement—and is internal to that judgement—anything at all can be freely *or* dependently beautiful, as beauty resides not in an object but in our felt responses to it. This commitment will be important to my overall conception of design as being functional—a real purpose[11]—but the knowledge

9 Ibid., 247.

10 Robert Wicks, "Can Tattooed Faces be Beautiful? Limits on the Restriction of Forms in Dependent Beauty," *Journal of Aesthetics and Art Criticism* 57, no. 3 (1999): 361.

11 In what follows I will use the terms "function" and "purpose" interchangeably, but I assert that this does not result in a problematic confusion of the two notions. If an object that is a real purpose must have a prior concept as its determination, it will also have a function: we do not intentionally conceive of objects that we will make as having no function whatsoever. These, following Collingwood, would be mere accidents. In the case of real purposes and functional objects alike, what underlies these notions is knowledge of what the object is meant to be, one of my defining characteristics of function from chapter 1. Nevertheless, it is important once again to note that by purpose/function here I do not mean *use*, nor do I refer to the relative success or failure of that object in meeting the purpose we had in mind when we conceived it, or if it is fulfilling the function we intended it for.

of that function as being historically and culturally localized. If I belong to a culture that does not understand the function of a (Christian) church, or that does not recognize that such places of worship need to have a cruciform floor plan as Guyer suggests, then I may indeed not find these buildings dependently beautiful, but this does not mean that I cannot find them beautiful at all. This should be apparent simply from the way that we can appraise the decorations on Tibetan monasteries or the roofs of Shinto temples to be beautiful without having any idea of the intended contributions these elements make to the religious functions of these buildings. Guyer's claim that some objects cannot be freely beautiful moves towards—if it does not arrive at—an ahistorical and essentialist conception of what things must be, or be *good for*, which I believe is unrealistic particularly where artifacts are concerned.

Finally, note that in claiming that some objects really are (or cannot be) beautiful, Guyer is shifting the role that the notion of *Zweck* plays in Kant's theory, from the necessary form our judgements take, to an actual substantive property an object seems to have. But that a thing is objectively or merely formally purposive is *not* a (substantive) property of an object; it is part of our judgements of that object that can change depending on how much knowledge we bring to our experiences, or how much of it we disregard. It is therefore more fruitful for understanding Kant's discussion of §16 to locate the difference between free and dependent beauty within our judgements themselves, especially as these judgements are now going to include some amount of conceptual knowledge of the purposes we attribute to the objects we encounter. It will then be an empirical matter whether we judge in one way or the other, whether we include or disregard our knowledge of purposes in our judgements, and a historically contingent matter whether we have that conceptual knowledge available in our experiences in the first place.

ii. Pure and Impure Judgements of Taste

Locating dependent beauty within aesthetic judgement itself, however, brings us to the crux of the problem: if judgements of beauty in general are conceptually free, how can *some* of them have conceptual content and still be reflective judgements of taste? Here the debate about §16 is at its most acute. Kant claims that judgements of dependent beauty "presuppose" a concept of the purpose that determines what a given thing is and "consequently of its perfection" (§16, 67). It is these two elements—the presupposition of a purpose and the idea of perfection—that must somehow be reconciled with what we already know of aesthetic judgement to render that judgement one of dependent beauty. Let me consider briefly a few attempts to do this.

Donald Crawford, for instance, claims that the distinction between free and dependent beauty is just the logical distinction between "judging that something (which happens to be a rose) is beautiful and judging that something is a beautiful rose." To claim that a rose is dependently beautiful is an "assessment of close approximation to the perfection or ideal of the kind"—that the rose has a purpose and is nearly perfectly suited to that purpose. A judgement of dependent beauty will thus have the same kind of validity as a cognitive judgement: it is a "conceptual judgement in disguise."[12] This move can be quickly rejected, as it excludes dependent beauty from the realm of aesthetic judgements altogether, although Crawford is correct to suggest that knowledge of

12 Donald Crawford, *Kant's Aesthetic Theory* (Madison: University of Wisconsin Press, 1974), 113–114.

purposes is more than *some* information we have about an object, but must include the idea of perfection, as of its being a good thing of its kind. But rather than reconciling the cognitive and the reflective elements in dependent beauty, he has merely ignored the latter and opted for the former, which does not get us very far.

Malcolm Budd, on the other hand, conceives of dependent beauty as a compound judgement, a combination of the judgement that something is beautiful and that it is a good specimen of its kind. "In other words, 'O is a beautiful K' = 'O is a qualitatively perfect K and O is (freely) beautiful.'"[13] This compound judgement also includes a "twofold pleasure [that] is a combination of pleasures of different kinds," those of the beautiful and of the good.[14] While Budd seeks to claim that dependent beauty is a different kind of judgement from that of free beauty, he does not sufficiently explain how this compound judgement operates. One pleasure is interested, the other is disinterested; one judgement is determinant, the other requires the free play of the faculties. There is a similarity here with Henry Allison's "essentially additive"[15] approach (although Budd would disagree), where dependent beauty "is not *purely* a judgement of taste, though the taste component within the complex evaluation remains *pure*."[16] Allison conceives of dependent beauty not as a singular complex judgement but as the combination of two judgements—the aesthetic judgement of free beauty and the cognitive judgement of purpose. Taste in this case "plays a subordinate role without compromising its inherent purity"; the beauty of an object can be seen "either solely in its own terms, or

13 Malcolm Budd, "Delight in the Natural World: Kant on the Aesthetic Appreciation of Nature. Part I: Natural Beauty," *British Journal of Aesthetics* 38, no. 1(1998): 10.

14 Ibid., 12.

15 This is Guyer's appellation, from "Free and Adherent Beauty," 361.

16 Henry Allison, *Kant's Theory of Taste: A Reading of the Critique of Aesthetic Judgement* (Cambridge: Cambridge University Press, 2001), 290.

as an ingredient in a larger whole."[17] In both cases, whatever role our cognitive determinations play—as merely additive for Allison or as combining to form a new complex judgement for Budd—the *aesthetic* element in judgements of dependent beauty is the same as that in judgements of free beauty. And this means that all dependently beautiful objects will also be freely beautiful, at least in part. The (pure) aesthetic judgement in each case will be the same and proceed from the same conditions we have seen, although with dependent beauty there will be (some kind of) a presupposition of the object's purpose and its perfection and with free beauty there will not.

Both Budd's and Allison's suggestions allow for a flexibility in our aesthetic responses: we either abstract from our conceptual knowledge and judge an object to be freely beautiful, or we have that knowledge but judge it (freely) beautiful anyway, and call this complex or compound judgement dependent beauty. The advantages to this view are that (*a*) dependent beauty is located within our judgements rather than in the properties of objects; (*b*) one thing—a flower, a horse—can be both freely and dependently beautiful; and (*c*) the reflective element in this compound or complex judgement is consistent with Kant's Analytic of taste. However, this reading of dependent beauty renders the notion *superfluous* to aesthetic theory simply because all dependently beautiful judgements would *also* be judgements of free beauty, at least in part. In some cases these judgements would include knowledge of the object; in other cases they would not. What makes something beautiful will be our response to its form alone; the element of beauty in fine art, nature, and design will thus always be the same.

17 Ibid., 140, 142.

Such a reading is insufficient for our purposes. For our judgements of design would be pure judgements of beauty that do not include the function of the object in any substantive way. We might know what the object is meant to be, but our appraisal of it will rest on the same grounds as our appraisals of flowers or dappled patterns on the street. And this is patently *not* how we evaluate design: in design competitions, design museums, and our daily lives, we do not make note of the purposive aspects of objects only to then make pure aesthetic judgements about the harmony of their line, the balance of their elements, the pure *look* of them in a way that likens them to works of art. Our approbation of a given design not only occurs on the presupposition of our understanding of what the thing is (and whether it is successful in its purpose), but these cognitive elements inform our judgements in a significant way. It would be easier, for Budd and Allison, to simply claim of an object that it has aesthetic value—it is beautiful—and that it is *also* a good thing of its kind. Why confuse the issue and call this appraisal dependent beauty? If we do not take up the object's purpose in the aesthetic part of our compound evaluation, then we really are by default judging it to be freely beautiful, and the notion of dependent beauty as a different kind of judgement becomes redundant for Kant's theory of taste.

While Crawford erred in one direction, by placing the emphasis in dependent beauty on the conceptual component of our judgements (and rendering them indistinguishable from cognitive judgements), Budd and Allison err in the other direction by placing too much emphasis on the free and reflective aspect of these judgements, rendering them in effect judgements of free beauty. In none of these cases is there a clear sense of why Kant made the distinction between free and dependent beauty in the first place, or how dependent beauty might stand out as an aesthetic response of a unique kind. For it to do this, the conceptual component of dependent beauty (whether of purpose or content) must be taken up and directly inform our evaluations so that, while we still make a judgement of taste, it is *not* the same as the pure response to free beauty. What we need, then, for this notion to become useful to a theory of design is an account that will allow an object to be dependently beautiful without also being freely beautiful (at least at the same time); one that, while acknowledging the separate elements that must be admixed in impure judgements of taste, still combines them in such a way as to produce a judgement that is more than—and different from—the sum of its parts.

One such account has recently been offered by Philip Mallaband, who uses the following illustration to focus his interpretation of §16:

> The mayfly is a small insect. It cannot fly far, and is a weak flier; many live only for less than a day, so that often they die before producing any offspring. Without these considerations, one would not be inclined to judge these insects as beautiful; they have dull colourations, are small, and are barely distinguishable from countless other insects. However, when in possession of [this knowledge] about the mayfly, one might perceive the insect to possess a rare fragility, and thus judge it to be aesthetically valuable in virtue of this.[18]

That is, the mayfly is dependently beautiful. Let us see how Mallaband applies this example to Kant's discussion.

18 Philip Mallaband, "Understanding Kant's Distinction between Free and Dependent Beauty," *Philosophical Quarterly* 52, no. 206 (2002): 75.

Mallaband is concerned to keep the subjective nature of aesthetic judgements in the foreground, and he notes that our experience of an object must please us in the appropriately disinterested way in order for us to call it beautiful.[19] Yet, while the pleasure we feel is singular (*pace* Budd), there are different kinds of experiences that are appropriate to judgements of free or dependent beauty. Any experience, Mallaband tells us, will have both a conceptual and a non-conceptual or perceptual component, even if that conceptual component is very minimal. Our experience of a dappled pattern on the street does not take place in a conceptual void, even if we make no conscious determinations about the representation in front of us. So he claims that "it will then be the case that if a conceptually thin experience of [an object] causes [pleasure], then we can claim that [it] may be judged freely beautiful."[20] If this experience does not lead to the appropriate pleasure, then it was *not* an experience of free beauty. But if we then add more substantial conceptual content and we are pleased, we can say the object is dependently beautiful. So for Mallaband, a judgement of free beauty—as of a flower—is a judgement that is "thin": we do not know or care what the thing is or how it came about, responding only to its formal appearance with pleasure. But a judgement of dependent beauty is "thick" because it is based on an experience that includes knowledge of the thing in question. The mayfly, for example, will not cause the appropriate pleasurable response *unless* our experience of it is accompanied by such concepts as "is a weak flier," "is unlikely to produce offspring," and so on. Without these concepts the insect is ugly or displeasing, but once they are added, it has the "rare fragility" Mallaband has noted, and our experience of it can then be one of dependent beauty.

19 Ibid., 79.
20 Ibid., 80.

So far so good. Mallaband makes the point that Kant's examples are not intended to illustrate that horses, buildings, and the like are of such a *nature* as to require our experiences of them to be conceptually thick in order to see them as beautiful. Mallaband agrees with my interpretation that Kant "is making an empirical claim about us": we are just "not disposed to respond with pleasure to our conceptually thin experiences of these kinds of objects."[21] And his interpretation of Kant has, at first sight, greater applicability to judgements of design because we can say that a conceptually thin experience of, for instance, a truck or a pencil will not generally produce the pleasure that grounds a judgement of taste—that, in fact, only once we have a degree of knowledge about the object will our experience of it be appropriately aesthetic. The difference between our appraisal of a mayfly and a pencil will turn on the type of purpose that is invoked: mayflies, like hexagons, have objective purposiveness whereby they are made intelligible to us by their seeming intentionality, whereas pencils are the result of real purposes, the design of which we locate in an actual agent. Both real purposes and objective purposiveness are forms of cognitive or thick conceptual content, the former "thicker," as it were, than the latter, but both functioning in similar ways in our judgements because purposiveness in general is the ground of all cognition.

Mallaband's account, however, runs into trouble on a number of fronts, the consideration of which will lead us closer to the heart of the problems with dependent beauty. First, notice from his description that the mayfly becomes dependently beautiful only once we attend to its perceived *weaknesses*: it cannot fly far and is unlikely to produce offspring. These are, for Mallaband, *imperfections* or

21 Ibid., 81.

design flaws in the mayfly.[22] He notes that "the mayfly could be considered to possess a property that is a bad-making property for insects (extremely short lifespan) but which is the ground for the good-making aesthetic property (rare fragility)"[23] that underwrites a judgement of dependent beauty. So we perceive the mayfly to be purposive but somehow flawed in the execution of its concept, and we find it beautiful not despite these imperfections but rather *because* of them.

Compare this account with the sorts of appraisals we make of designed objects: the winner in the product design category of the NDA in 2004 was Yves Behar, for such things as Birkenstock shoes, a lighting fixture, and a Toshiba laptop computer. Each of his products *work*: the shoes fit, the chandelier provides light, the laptop runs. We do not give our approbation to designs that are *flawed,* such as teapots that do not pour, or lamps that shed no light; we in fact would exclude these sorts of objects from our judgements of them as dependently beautiful. Mallaband's understanding of thick conceptual content seems to be that this content is negative but that it nevertheless somehow provides a *positive* contribution to our aesthetic appraisals.

This should not be confused with Guyer's negative account that I mentioned earlier, although comparing the two may be useful here. For Guyer, as I've noted, the conceptual component of our judgements does not "fully determine our approval"[24] of an object: the imagination and understanding must still engage in free play.

22 Of course, these may not be imperfections at all, but rather exactly what the mayfly needs to perpetuate its species; that is, the mayfly could be fulfilling its purpose just through these traits. My point here is simply that for Mallaband, these are *perceived as* weaknesses against some nominal physical ideal of being able to fly, live a long life, and produce offspring.

23 Mallaband, "Understanding Kant's Distinction," 75.

24 Guyer, *Claims of Taste*, 219.

But with dependent beauty this free play operates within certain constraints or limits set by the purpose of the object. So, for example, the requirements that make a church a good thing of its kind (a cruciform floor plan) will limit "what can please us in a church" in terms of its form, without actually determining that pleasure.[25] But note that these constraints are *positive* contributions to the success of a given object's purpose rather than flaws that detract from it, and that the negative role they play is to merely limit the kinds of churches we find beautiful. The conceptual content—in the form of constraints—remains in the background, or is merely presupposed, in our experiences, thus allowing our response to the object to involve the free play that brings about disinterested pleasure.

For Mallaband, our pleasure may indeed remain disinterested, but it involves an unusual sense of our presupposition of the purpose of the object, as he dwells on precisely those properties that apparently detract from the mayfly fulfilling its function. And these negative substantive properties are somehow transmuted into positive *aesthetic* properties that play an evidentiary (or even determining) role in our appraisals. In this sense, his interpretation of §16 also puts him closer to Zangwill than to Kant: we have conceptually thick experiences of substantive properties that become aesthetic properties that in turn determine what we will find beautiful. The mayfly is beautiful *because* it has a rare fragility, an aesthetic quality determined by the substantive properties of its various weaknesses.

Further, and because of this similarity to Zangwill's account, Mallaband does not explain how the imagination and understanding engage in free play about the mayfly. Our thick experience seems to be determinant in that it requires us to have specific knowledge

25 Ibid.

of the object in question, knowledge that becomes an awareness of a determining aesthetic property. The most charitable reading of Mallaband's claims I can offer is that, perhaps, we engage in a kind of free interpretation of the meaning arising from our conceptual knowledge of the mayfly such that it comes to represent or express a metaphor for fragility. But this reading, as we will see below, aligns our experience of the mayfly with that of an expressive work of art, rather than a quotidian object of either nature or design. And if our aesthetic evaluation is based on (metaphoric) association, then we are not judging the appearance of the mayfly *itself* to be dependently beautiful but rather the ideas that we generate on the basis of our experience. So Mallaband's account needs, first, to attend to the actual purpose of an object and, second, to explain how knowledge of that purpose can still lead to the free play of the faculties: our judgement of an object must remain reflective in spite of its thick conceptual content.

Finally, Mallaband's account dismisses entirely the notion of perfection that is integral to Kant's definition of dependent beauty. In fact, he concludes his discussion by stating that "Kant's talk of meaning and purpose, then, was a red herring"[26] but this cannot be the case. It is not enough that we have *some* conceptual content about the object we experience; we also need to judge that it is a good thing of its kind. Budd's and Allison's earlier readings of Kant at least maintained this insight: that Kant does not intend us to judge faulty or deficient things to be dependently beautiful. What we also need to add to this idea of "thick" conceptual content is an understanding of how Kant intends the notion of perfection to operate in impure judgements of taste. Were this notion present in Mallaband's account, the thick content that supports our

26 Mallaband, "Understanding Kant's Distinction," 81.

judgements of the mayfly would be that which makes it a *successful* thing of its kind, the qualities that we perceive contribute to its perfection, rather than the other way around. And still, somehow our judgements of an object's perfection must allow the free play of the faculties that is the basis for a reflective judgement of taste.

A number of commentators seem to suggest that a judgement of the perfection of an object as a good thing of its kind is identical to a reflective judgement of the good as opposed to the beautiful. We have seen this with Allison's and Budd's accounts, for instance. And Geoffrey Scarre claims that dependent beauty, along with a concept of purpose, includes a "restriction of a moral sort" on our aesthetic judgements, one that he associates with *decorum*.[27] He notes that for Kant "it is a kind of perversion of the proper objects of aesthetic experience to judge free beauty without looking to the moral limitations on how an object may be presented. We must not be mere seekers after sensory experiences but must think too of what is morally proper."[28] Both the beautiful and the good do indeed involve a concept of the purpose of a thing, but judgements of the good are interested judgements, and so their pleasure rests upon (rational) desire. Were this what Kant meant in §16, then dependent beauty would differ from free beauty not only in terms of the cognitive element of purpose in these judgements but also in terms of the pleasure the judgements produce, and this would sorely tax our ability to reconcile dependent beauty with the conception of taste in general. As I've noted, my intention has been to read §16 as differing from Kant's general analysis on one point alone. There is, however, a different way to understand the notion of the perfection of an object, one that contrasts it with the good.

27 Geoffrey Scarre, "Kant on Free and Dependent Beauty," *British Journal of Aesthetics* 21, no. 4 (1981): 357.
28 Ibid., 359.

In §§4–5 Kant distinguishes between the mediate and the immediate good: what is "useful or good in itself" (§4, 42). The mediate good is "pleasing as a means towards pleasantness somewhere" (§4, 43), and so will involve interest in the existence of the object, and desire insofar as we think it will bring about the end we seek and satisfy us in that regard. The immediate good is "good absolutely and in every respect, viz. moral good, which brings with it the highest interest" (§4, 43), and this interest is a function of pure practical reason that operates a priori without reference to our particular—contingent, subjective—desires and interests. In both cases, when we judge something to be good, we mean it is good *for us*: either qua contingent individuals or qua rational beings, and so we have an interest in it and we desire it either personally, for what it can do for us, or rationally, for the good that it is.

Our judgement of the perfection of an object, by contrast, is that it is a good thing of its kind: it involves empirical reason instead of practical reason, and is disinterested in the way that all cognitive judgements are. That is, we can make a cognitive judgement that an object fulfills its purpose without wanting the thing for ourselves, or having any interest in its actual good for us. The purpose of an object is the realization of a given function or concept that precedes its existence; it needn't be a function that we want it to perform. The problem here has been to confuse function with use, on the one hand, and success in that function with moral goodness on the other. Some things are mediately and contingently good because they will bring about an end we seek, and we desire them on this ground (like money or rapini, for instance). They are useful in this regard. Others are immediately good—good *tout court*—and our rational desire for them will be universal: all of us desire happiness or health, for instance. But an object that displays perfection in the accomplishment of its purpose we may not desire at all, and may not even find good: we don't all want olive pitters (find them mediately good) no matter how perfectly they pit olives, nor do we all find Scud missiles to be good in the immediate moral sense even if we acknowledge them to be extremely successful in delivering their payload. Thus when Kant writes that the purity of a judgement of taste is "injured by the combination with beauty of the good," he should be taken to mean good as "that manifold which is good for the thing itself in accordance with its purpose" (§16, 66) and not good for us, either mediately or immediately. Perfection, then, is an objective concept, wrapped up with our cognition of an object, and its purposiveness is unrelated to our desires or the particular pleasures that we get from the (interested) good of a thing for us. My interpretation of Kant's claim that dependent beauty requires the presupposition of an object's purpose as well as of its perfection is not that we thus make two reflective judgements—of the beautiful and the good—but that the conceptual content presupposed in our knowledge of an object's purpose includes its perfection as being successful, or a good thing of its kind, without any desire and without any moral implications. It is this notion of perfection that Mallaband's account must include, along with the aforementioned acknowledgment of the free play of the faculties in our response to it.

3. THE APPRECIATION OF FUNCTION

From the problems with the foregoing readings of §16, we can now see what a proper interpretation of dependent beauty will require for my argument to gain purchase on design:

1. That it be a distinct kind of judgement
2. That this judgement be conceptually thick

3. That this thickness be directed towards the positive features that contribute to an object's success in fulfilling its purpose (with perfection)
4. That this judgement nevertheless allow the imagination and understanding to engage in free play that produces disinterested pleasure
5. And finally that we distinguish the dependent beauty of design from that of art, nature and craft

If we have in some part addressed the first two requirements already, let me approach the last three by turning once again to Guyer's negative account. Apart from the concerns I've noted (that he locates dependent beauty in the object itself and that he describes the purpose of that object in overly determinative terms) he also does not allow that the functional element of an object can *itself* be a source of its dependent beauty. Function or purpose, for Guyer, plays no positive role but merely constrains the kinds of forms that can please us. As Parsons and Carlson note, in Guyer's account function "[r]ather than contributing positively to aesthetic pleasure as one of its constitutive elements ... now serves only to restrict the occurrence of that pleasure" in terms of the formal elements that we can freely appreciate.[29] And this seems insufficient for a robust account of dependent beauty whereby we appraise the object *because of* the perfection in the way it fulfills its purpose.

However, in spite of these concerns, I do not think we should dismiss Guyer's account altogether, for he does make note of an important element in judgements of dependent beauty that, as I have mentioned, resolves one of the weaknesses in Mallaband's

29 Glenn Parsons and Allen Carlson, *Functional Beauty* (New York: Oxford University Press, 2008), 23.

interpretation. That is, if an object fails to fulfill its purpose, we will not find it beautiful.[30] So, for instance, a bicycle has certain requirements: it must have two wheels, pedals, a seat, and handlebars. If it lacks any of these it will either be a poor specimen of a bicycle, or it will not be a bicycle at all (and perhaps be a unicycle). Guyer is correct to suggest that we do not judge faulty things to be dependently beautiful, which means that we do indeed need to know what they are supposed to be in our evaluation of them. The problem lies in Guyer's reading of these elements as fixed, as though the essence of a bicycle *requires* it to have various features, and this essentialism does not allow for historical or cultural variations, or for innovation in design in general. Many of us, for instance, would consider brakes a standard feature of a working bicycle, but fixed-gear bikes have none, nor do they need them. And recumbent bicycles, while they *do* have two wheels, a seat, and so on, fulfill their functions in a very different way than the more common upright models. Nevertheless, if we can soften his more essentialist stance, Guyer's account provides an important set of minimal criteria for dependent beauty, something like an adequacy condition, whereby if an object does not meet the (necessary) minimal requirements to be a thing of its kind, we will not find it dependently beautiful, and this, I think is quite correct in terms of item 3 above, even if it remains a negative condition rather than a positive source of the beauty we find in a bicycle. What I seek to add to this is, first, that the perfection of an object's purpose be a positive contributing factor in our

30 Yuriko Saito notes in *Everyday Aesthetics* (New York: Oxford University Press, 2007), that our aesthetic rejection of the old, shabby, dilapidated, etc. has to do with the decreased functionality of these things: we do not judge something to be beautiful if it does not work. However, she also observes that our negative reactions to objects can be "directed exclusively toward their *appearance* even when their functionality is unaffected," as in the case of threadbare couches, chipped dishes, and clothes that have gone out of fashion (157). That is, judgements of beauty extend to the formal as much as the functional aspects of things, which I will take up below.

finding it beautiful, and second that if an object can fulfill its function in a variety of ways, these ways themselves should also be part of our overall appraisal of it.

Guyer's account makes a second important point in that it is the only one I have canvassed that provides an explanation of how the faculties can engage in free play in spite of the conceptual background of purpose in our judgements, as with requirement 4. He notes that one church that satisfies the conditions required to *be* a church may "yet be ugly, perhaps because of the coarseness of its stone or the crude proportions of its columns," while another equally adequate church may "also be beautiful, perhaps because of the elegance of its columns or the delicacy of its stained glass." And, he asks, "who can say what may turn out to be a bar to or a necessary condition for beauty in any particular case?"[31] What Guyer wants in our judgements is that once the minimal conditions of a thing are met, we can freely play with the non-essential or formal qualities of the object, and that herein lies its beauty. My concern is that Guyer reads dependent beauty as lying in these formal qualities alone. But if I wish function to play a positive role in our judgements of beauty, I will have to somehow show that the imagination and the understanding can freely play with that conceptual content in a way that is consistent with Kant's general account of taste. Guyer avoids this problem by limiting free play to an object's formal elements. Thus while I seek a more positive role for function and perfection in our judgements of beauty, Guyer's interpretation does provide a cautionary note to my search: if two objects both equally satisfy the requirements of their purposes—if indeed both do so perfectly—on what grounds will we

31 Guyer, "Dependent Beauty Revisited," 357–358.

find one more beautiful than the other except according to their nonessential, formal qualities?

Steven Burns has suggested that the account of dependent beauty I am looking for may be one-sided if it emphasizes function over form, and provided the following illustration to make his case:

> When I was a teenager, my family distinguished itself by owning a series of Studebakers. By 1958 the Studebakers had spectacularly non-functional fins, and were advertised as designed by Raymond Loewy, the famous Parisian industrial designer.... Clearly Loewy had started with an acute angled triangle and its simplicity was so un-boxlike, and was sufficiently well-preserved in the finished product, that it stood in a class of its own, and made the surrounding Fords and Chevys and Cadillacs—though they also had fins—look like Edsels.[32]

Burns, like Guyer, suggests that the non-functional parts of a designed object must contribute to our judgements of its beauty. The Studebaker, after all, would fulfill its function without fins, but its fins are integral to our approbation of its design, just as the delicacy of a church's stained glass is integral to our judgements of its dependent beauty.

There are two routes I can take to respond to Burns's concern. The first is to distinguish ornamentation from the essential elements of an object's purpose and claim either that ornament is extraneous to our judgements of dependent beauty (but relevant to free beauty), or attempt to include it as part of an object's overall

32 Stephen Burns, "Commentary on Forsey's 'From Bauhaus to Birkenstocks,'" Canadian Philosophical Association Annual Congress, Toronto, May 2006.

aesthetic merit.[33] The former is unsatisfactory because the style of its fins is one of the reasons we merit the Studebaker above the Chevy and cannot therefore be omitted in our appraisal of it as dependently beautiful. But if I claim the latter, my account looks either formalistic, along the lines of Guyer's claim that even dependent beauty stems from the inessential formal properties of objects, all other requirements being met, or my account bifurcates judgements of dependent beauty into two separate types—of utility and ornamental beauty—in a way similar to Allison's additive account.

The second route, and the one I must take, is to acknowledge the importance of these non-functional or contingent features in our appraisal of objects but claim that they are nevertheless of a piece with dependent beauty while not being the sole focus of our attention; that while we can aestheticially appreciate the function of an object we can also appreciate the *way* it fulfills that function by considering its *style*. To finally complete an account of dependent beauty, then, we need to make room for a more positive contribution of purpose as a source of beauty even while retaining the insights of Guyer's negative, more formalistic interpretation. In fact, in a later paper,[34] Guyer also revisits his discussion of §16 and concedes that it could be enriched by just these elements: that a fuller understanding of dependent beauty would be one that includes the possibility of a full integration of functionality with (formal) beauty in our appreciation, and he locates such an account in the work of Robert Wicks.

Wicks argues that "what we appreciate in positively judging the object in reference to dependent beauty" is not only that it is

33 This is the route David Pye took in *The Nature and Aesthetics of Design* (Bethel, CT: Cambium Press, 1978), as we saw in chapter 1, where he claimed that design is embellishment or ornamentation, "doing useless work on useful things" (13).

34 Guyer, "Free and Adherent Beauty."

successful in fulfilling its purpose with perfection but also "the *contingency* of the way the object realizes its purpose so very well. In short we appreciate the object's 'teleological' or 'functional' style when we appreciate it as a dependent beauty."[35] For Wicks, an object's purpose (and the perfection of its realization) indeed operates as a "fixed category" in the way that Guyer suggests. But rather than being merely backgrounded or acting as a constraint upon our judgements of beauty, Wicks conceives of this purpose as having "further contingent and systematic structures [that] can be presented and then appreciated as beautiful."[36]

It is not simply that we take the church with the cruciform floor plan, or the bicycle with its two wheels and so on, as being purposive and then go on to appraise its inessential or merely formal qualities—its appearance to us—as that which constitutes its unique beauty. Instead, the object's purposive structure directly contributes to our finding it beautiful when we "reflect upon the contingency of the object's systematicity in view of other imagined configurations."[37] A bicycle may or may not have brakes or gears, for example, and these factors are not directly constitutive of the bicycle's function as something that will transport us. But they *are* directly constitutive of this bike's dependent beauty, Wicks would claim, because they are the (contingent) ways in which it realizes its purpose and so must be part of our appraisal of it. He notes that with judgements of dependent beauty "we compare alternative means to a single purpose, as we reflect upon the contingency of an object's form insofar as this form realizes the object's purpose".[38] The fins of the 1958 Studebaker, then, are not mere extraneous

35 Wicks, "Dependent Beauty," 393.
36 Ibid., 391.
37 Ibid., 392.
38 Ibid., 393.

ornamentation: they are the product of a design decision to create an object *in a particular way*. They may not be directly contributive to its function as a car in general—Chevys and Cadillacs also run—but they are contributive to the way that function is realized in this given product as opposed to any other, and thus part of what makes it the unique thing that it is as an object of aesthetic appreciation. Teleological style can also refer more directly to the realization of an object's function, as when we compare the way that a recumbent bicycle fulfills its purpose as opposed to an upright one. The virtues of this notion are that it applies to our notice of the functional as much as the formal elements in an object, and that it conceives of these as together contributing to an object's perfection as well as to its beauty.

Wicks is also careful to note that our appreciation of teleological style does involve the free play of our faculties, albeit in a slightly different way than in pure judgements of taste. He claims that in a judgement of dependent beauty "we run through many determinate images in view of their suitability for realizing an object's given purpose. Each image is determinate, but there is a free play within the imagination insofar as none of these images (at this stage) is selected as a concrete way to realize the object's purpose."[39] In general, he notes, "there is no 'definitive' way to realize any given purpose" (*pace* Guyer): the purpose of an object like a church or a bicycle "is an abstract concept," and for that reason we can "never fully determine every contingent detail of its concrete instantiation," which keeps our judgements from becoming determinant and cognitive.[40] But further, in dependent beauty it is not only that we play upon the many ways to realize a given purpose,

39 Ibid.
40 Ibid.

but that we directly "appreciate how the actually presented object realizes the given purpose in its specific way"[41] when we judge it to be beautiful. It is not that it could have been made like this or like that (and have fulfilled its function)—have fins or not, have brakes or not—but that we find the object dependently beautiful when we appreciate how it "was actually done, in view of other possible, and far less elegant [pleasing, efficient], ways."[42]

Guyer is critical of Wicks's construal of free play here because he reads it as being an explicitly comparative judgement[43] that requires too much conscious conceptual content. He would prefer that "one simply feels" the simultaneous freedom from determination and harmony of the faculties "without any conscious, semi-conscious, or even unconscious comparison of the actual form … with other possible forms."[44] But I believe Wicks is right in that, following Mallaband, *no* aesthetic experience takes place in a conceptual void. Kant notes that we make "intelligible to ourselves" (§10, 55) (i.e., consciously) the purposiveness of an object, and if purposiveness in general is part of the free play of aesthetic judgements, then intellection must be as well, as we have seen. Further, if we have conceptual knowledge of the purpose of an object, we cannot have it in isolation from other, similar, kinds of things. Wicks notes that this knowledge "can only be determined against a background of rich experience, so a wealth of comparisons must be presupposed in order to recognize an intelligibly organized form as such."[45] If we judge this to be a bicycle, or a good one of its kind, it has to be because we have experienced other (lesser) bicycles in the past, and we pass judgement based on this experience.

41 Ibid., 394.
42 Ibid.
43 Guyer, "Dependent Beauty Revisited," 359.
44 Ibid., 360.
45 Wicks, "Tattooed Faces," 363.

Wicks's account, then, provides us with what we need to fully understand dependent beauty, and understand it in a way that is consistent with Kant's Analytic of beauty in general. Dependent beauty is part of our aesthetic judgement, is in fact a particular form of judgement, and results in a singular form of disinterested pleasure. It differs from free beauty because not only is a certain amount of conceptual knowledge presupposed in our appreciation but that knowledge is directly taken up in the free play of our faculties and informs—without determining—what we find beautiful in a given instance through our attention to the way that a particular object fulfills its function with teleological style. On Wicks's account, we appreciate the specifics of function aesthetically as much as we enjoy an object's form when both are present to us, and our ultimate approbation comes when we find the two as fully integrated or complementary as possible (i.e., when the object approaches perfection). Wicks's account further integrates Guyer's negative conception of dependent beauty because (*a*) the general function of an object is presupposed in our appreciation (we know that it is a bicycle and what bicycles are supposed to be); and (*b*) this function or purpose constrains our appreciation in that whatever qualities detract from its fulfilling this function will also negatively impact our aesthetic appreciation of it.

Finally, there is room in Wicks's formulation for both real purposes and merely objectively purposive objects—for pencils *and* hexagons, churches *and* horses—if we note that the amount of conceptual content with which we play will be more sophisticated or complete in the former than in the latter. So, for example, we can judge that the way in which one natural object fulfills its purpose seems better than, more beautiful than, another, without locating its purposiveness in a particular agent or designer. The difference between the dependent beauty of nature and of design will continue to turn on the notion of *Zweck*, and how it applies to these different sorts of things. Natural objects are not designed objects, and our knowledge of them is therefore more limited. Some, like flowers, we may more frequently judge freely beautiful, but others, like horses, may require that we attribute to them a purposive nature without having any definite, certain, knowledge of a purpose determined by an agent who made them. Designs, instead, have specific purposes devised by their creators, and if we are to judge them dependently beautiful—that is, make aesthetic evaluations as to their excellence—we must know what these purposes are and whether they fulfill them reasonably well, or perfectly. And this knowledge itself will be historically specific and culturally localized: if we are presented with an object whose function we cannot determine, we can only, at best, find it freely beautiful if at all.

In terms of Kant's overall theory of taste, and if we adhere to Wicks's formulation, we can say that judgements of beauty have a synchronic aspect in that the same criteria must always be present for that judgement to occur: disinterested pleasure and the free play of the faculties, for instance. This is the genus of beauty in general. Judgements of dependent beauty also have a synchronic aspect in that they share these characteristics even while they add a further dimension to their structure: the presupposition of a concept of purpose. But judgements of dependent beauty have a further diachronic aspect in that what we find dependently beautiful will change across time and space: we cannot judge a thing to be well designed if we do not know what it is supposed to be and whether it fulfills its purpose. And this knowledge will depend upon what, at a given time, we know, use and value. Here we can see how judgements of dependent beauty will be of things familiar to us, but how we may pay closer attention to them when they work extremely well (approach perfection) than when they fail to fulfill their purposes. Further, as we will see below, dependent beauty becomes useful to explain the location of the aesthetic in design: to ascertain whether an object fulfills its function we will have to actively engage with it, use it, handle it, wear it, and not simply judge it by its appearance alone. And this engagement will make the aesthetic experience of design qualitatively different from our experience of works of art.

What remains, then, is to distinguish judgements of design from those of fine art and craft as other forms of dependent beauty, and I will turn to this briefly before concluding the chapter by looking at design directly. There is a great body of scholarship that explores the Kantian account of fine art in detail.[46] I will offer here nothing more than a brief outline for the purposes of juxtaposition, and I will say even less about craft: it has been my intention to argue that our aesthetic experiences of design require a unique form of appraisal, but to give a full account of our judgements of art and craft (never mind nature) in contrast to design far exceeds the purposes of this project.

4. FINE ART AND CRAFT

While Kant's theory of taste does not offer us a fully developed philosophy of art in particular, Kant nevertheless did single out fine art for some detailed discussion. As much as in the past he has been (mis)read as a formalist about art in the manner of Bell, his

46 Here I am thinking of Guyer, of course, as well as Allison and Crawford. But also please see Salim Kemal, *Kant and Fine Art* (Oxford: Clarendon Press, 1986), and *Kant's Aesthetic Theory* (London: St. Martin's Press, 1992) as well as articles by these authors and others too numerous to name.

account of genius and aesthetic ideas has also been seen as offering a fledgling expression theory that describes art as a particular kind of dependent beauty because of a unique and profound *content* that we judge it to possess. Artworks are intentional objects, the products of an endeavour by an agent who has a concept of some kind as its cause: they are real purposes in the way that pencils are. And our responses to art do not ignore what it is in the way that we prescind from our conceptual knowledge of trees and sun when we delight in the mere appearance of a dappled pattern on the street. This is not to say that it is impossible for us to make a judgement of free beauty about a painting or sculpture, just that it would be, empirically, an impoverished description of our rich experiences of art. But unlike our responses to horses or bicycles (where we attend to the purpose of the object (and its perfection)), with art we respond to its meaning or content that is the product of the talent of "genius" and that is uniquely responsible for the pleasure we get from our experiences. This content itself produces a free play of the cognitive faculties "in which concepts are manifest but never sensed as constraining or determinative."[47] That is, while the free play of the imagination and understanding occurs spontaneously in pure judgements of, for instance, nature, art has instead been specifically engineered to produce the same effect. This is the source of Kant's somewhat misleading remark that "the purposiveness in the product of beautiful art, although it is designed, must not seem to be designed, i.e. beautiful art must *look* like nature, although we are conscious of it as art" (§45, 149). Looking like nature here does not refer to representational verisimilitude but to a content that affects the mind in the same sort of way as free

47 Guyer, *Claims of Taste*, 357.

beauty does, producing a disinterested pleasure in our response to it. And only fine art produces that pleasure in this particular way.

To explain the content of art, Kant makes use of the notion of "idea" and contrasts the aesthetic ideas of art with the rational ideas that are the product of pure reason. In the Kantian system, there are things we can think but cannot know, and the purpose of the *Critique of Pure Reason* was to demarcate the limits of our objective knowledge. Beyond that knowledge, we can speculate—about God, freedom, justice, death, and so on—but we cannot make determinant judgements about these ideas because knowledge requires both a conceptual component *and* a mental representation based on sense experience, and we can have no experience of a rational idea. Kant cautions that if we try to establish the objective reality of these ideas "we are asking for something impossible, because absolutely no intuition can be given which shall be adequate to them" (§59, 197): they extend beyond the bounds of possible human experience. Rational ideas are thus *indemonstrable* in this regard: while they can be defined in the abstract, they cannot directly be shown as mental representations with substantive content.

Aesthetic ideas are the counterparts to rational ideas. Kant defines an aesthetic idea as "that representation of the imagination which occasions much thought, without however any definite thought, i.e. any *concept* being capable of being adequate to it" (§49, 157). Whereas a rational idea can be made intelligible by reason but not represented otherwise, an aesthetic idea is presented as a sensible intuition (or mental representation), which, Kant says, "cannot be completely compassed and made intelligible by language" (as all knowledge must be) (§49, 157). Aesthetic ideas are the products of artistic genius, and form the expressive content of works of art that stimulate the imagination to "spread itself over a number of kindred representations that arouse more thought than can be expressed in a concept determined by words" (§49, 158). Aesthetic ideas are so abundant in intuitive content that no single determinant concept is adequate to capture them. Like rational ideas, they reach beyond cognizable experience, but while rational ideas are indemonstrable because of a paucity of intuitive content, aesthetic ideas are *inexponible* because they are too intuitively rich to be nailed down.

The activity of the artist is to "[venture] to realize to sense, rational ideas of invisible beings" (§49, 157); this Paul Guyer calls the "content or theme of the work of art,"[48] whether it be heaven, hell, destiny, or the like. What the artist produces is a work that has empirical content we can sense (Kant's primary example is "Jupiter's eagle with the lightning in its claws [as] an attribute of the mighty king of heaven" [§49, 158]) but which cannot be a direct representation of that rational idea because none is possible. The content of the work—as a mental representation—moves the imagination to search for a determinant concept, or seek the universal, but to fail because none can be given. And thus in our response to art, the mental faculties engage in free play. But art is dependently beautiful because we judge it to be a real purpose, rather than merely formally purposive: we know it as an intentional object devised to create this effect.

Some theorists have ascribed to aesthetic ideas a theory of art as metaphor,[49] and indeed there are similarities between Kant's account and, for instance, Danto's, which I canvassed in

48 Ibid., 358.

49 See for example A. T. Nuyen, "The Kantian Theory of Metaphor," *Philosophy and Rhetoric* 22 (1989), and Kirk Pillow, "Jupiter's Eagle and the Despot's Handmill: Two Views on Metaphor in Kant," *Journal of Aesthetics and Art Criticism* 59, no. 2 (2001), and my critical response to these views in "Metaphor and Symbol in the Interpretation of Art," *Symposium: Canadian Journal of Continental Philosophy* 8, no. 3 (2004).

chapter 1. But whether metaphorical or not, artworks for Kant have a unique content, even a profundity in their attempted depiction of rational ideas, and require interpretation on the part of the audience to sort out. As with Danto's account, here too the mind must be "moved to action"[50] as it attempts but fails to find a concept adequate to the representation it is given. And in this free but rule-governed search, the judgement is reflective, the faculties are in harmony, and we find works of art (dependently) beautiful. With art, too, we have all of the elements in place that are consistent with the genus of beauty in general. And art's difference from free beauty again revolves around the notion of *Zweck*: artworks are real purposes, and hence some cognitive content informs our responses to them. Where they differ from the dependent beauty of design is that this cognitive content is not directed to our knowledge of purpose (and perfection) but to the—profound, expressive—content this purposive object seeks to convey.

And so we can make some very clear distinctions between art and design, and between both of these and the beauty of nature, and these distinctions should be consistent with the argument as it commenced in chapter 1. Natural beauty, for instance, if it is not free (as referenced merely to the appearance of a thing) is dependently beautiful because we do not prescind from our knowledge of the object before us. But this knowledge in our judgements takes the form of merely objective purposiveness and thus is somewhat limited. Designed objects we take to be real purposes—manufactured, intentional—and we appraise them in terms of the (contingent) way in which they succeed in

50 Arthur Danto, *Transfiguration of the Commonplace* (Cambridge: Harvard University Press, 1981), 171.

fulfilling their purpose as it was conceived. But, contrasted with art, design is mute: it says nothing, and has no expressive content. Fine art, when we judge it to be dependently beautiful, is also the product of a real purpose but in this case one that has been created with an ambiguity of content that itself stimulates the free play of the faculties as they seek to determine its meaning but ultimately fail to do so. We interpret works of art (in the way I suggested Mallaband's response to the mayfly was a matter of interpretation), but we come to no determination because, as Kant has described the relation of rational and aesthetic ideas, no determinate knowledge is ever possible. With design we have a relation between form and function, with art one between form and content, but with our adoption of the Kantian approach neither function nor content is simply a substantive property of objects in an ontological sense. In aesthetic terms, function and content are the forms our judgements take when we are confronted with the appearance of things.

Finally, Kant has almost nothing at all to say about craft, although he acknowledged even in 1790 the difference between it and fine art. As opposed to the "free" activity of art (an "occupation that is pleasant in itself") craft, or "handicraft," is "mercenary" because it "is regarded as if it could only be compulsorily imposed upon one as work, i.e. as occupation which is unpleasant (a trouble) in itself and which is only attractive on account of its effect (e.g. the wage)" (§43, 146). This depiction of craft is, first, as negative as Collingwood's was, in this case directed to such "crafts" as blacksmithing and other (guild) professions of the time; and second, it is, of course, terribly insufficient for our understanding of craft today. Kant does, however, make a further comment that is more interesting: to differentiate between artists and craftsmen (in more marginal cases) we would have to consider "the proportion of talents which must be assumed requisite in these several occupations" (§43, 147). And it is this reference to talent or skill that may be of some use. I noted in chapter 1 that if the distinction between art and design was one between form and content on the one hand and form and function on the other, craft could be distinguished by its relation between form and *matter* as the raw material that has been skilfully transformed into a product with a use. Craft, I asserted, was hand-made, and the skill of its execution would be important to our aesthetic appraisals of its beauty. Kant's mention of "talent" suggests that it would also be important for him in an account of the appreciation of craft (which he then declined to provide).

I can only gesture towards what a normative account of the beauty of craft would entail; it has not yet been written. Certainly craftworks are the products of real purposes, and thus our judgements of them would be more often ones of dependent beauty. And indeed we can even see that our judgements of craft would include presuppositions not only of purpose but also of perfection in the way that a work of craft fulfilled its function. Craftworks, as having no content, would not be analogous to works of art on either Kant's account or mine. But while a depiction of our aesthetic appraisals of craft would also have to be consistent with the genus of beauty in general (as those of art, design, and nature are), something is missing if we suggest that we judge craft in exactly the same way as we judge design. That is, skill or talent in execution—by hand—which plays no part in our appraisals of design, will have to inform our judgements of craft.

It may be possible to construct such an account with an expansion of Wicks's claims. For instance, while the purpose of the crafted object is presupposed in our judgements of it, we can say that its perfection lies not simply in how well it fulfills its purpose (in general or in a given instance) but more specifically in how much talent the craftsperson has displayed in taking up and transforming her raw materials to effect that desired end. We may freely play at the contingency of the way that a given object realizes its purpose, but this contingency will be constrained by what a (single) individual can manage to do with the raw materials she has chosen and the talent she evinces in her work on them. So there is a place here too for Guyer's negative account: it is not only that imperfections in the fulfillment of purpose will constrain our positive appraisals of a crafted object, but also that imperfections in execution, or deficiencies in talent, will likewise constrain what we will judge to be dependently beautiful in this particular thing.

If we consider Guyer's example of two churches, each adequately fulfilling its function but one being beautiful and one not, and if we consider the carving of columns (by hand) and the making of stained glass to be activities of craft, we could then suggest that the church that is ugly because of the crude proportions of its columns displays a lack of finesse in (crafted) execution, while the church that is beautiful because of the delicacy of it stained glass is beautiful in part because of the perfection or degree of talent in that portion of it which has been handwrought. This seems not inconsistent with Guyer's intentions in his example. Clumsy execution will detract from our pleasure in a crafted object, even if it sufficiently fulfills its purpose (as, for instance, a place of worship).

This would allow us to say, as I suggested in chapter 1, that craft is *like* design in that objects are created to fulfill specific functions, and we can judge how well they do this. But craft is also *like* art in that it is hand-made, and the talent or skill in its execution is also the focus of our judgements. The difference between the talent of art and the talent of craft, on the Kantian account, will be that art produced with "genius" will express aesthetic ideas that are the content of the work and that initiate the free play of our cognitive faculties, while the talent of craft will display the skill and creativity with which the craftsperson has used the raw materials at her disposal to create a functional thing. And the free play of the faculties when faced with a work of craft will consider the contingency of the way that object fulfills its function *by means of* the individual skill at creating it from a given raw material. With judgements of design, we do not attend to this aspect of the object: we feel no individual hand at work when we appraise a laptop computer or a car, and we do not judge it according to how a single individual has manipulated some raw material to produce it. With design, we merely judge the relative perfection of the thing in fulfilling its function, absent any knowledge of—or often any interest in—who actually did the work. This of course does not mean that we do not attend to the materials used in a work of design in our appraisal of it: a car made of fibreglass may be inferior to one made of metals, or a wine goblet of crystal superior to one made of plastic. But these are also part of the contingent way in which an object fulfills its function, and we can make these judgements without acknowledging the individual (hand) behind that object's manufacture. With craft, that hand is something we simply cannot ignore. And the talent of the individual I think can be included in a normative account of the beauty of craft that would render it consistent with the general criteria necessary for a theory of taste and at the same time distinguish it from our appraisals of nature, fine art, and, especially, design.

5. THE BEAUTY OF DESIGN

I will conclude this chapter—and our lengthy discussion of beauty—with one final example that will help to consolidate the foregoing and tie up a few loose ends. It is the story of two coffee-pots, mine and his. Both are stove-top espresso makers, both of Italian design, and both function in the same way: water in the bottom half of the pot, coffee grounds in a metal filter fitting into it, and a holding pot that screws into both and into which the coffee is forced as the water boils and passes through the filter. Here the similarities end. Mine: a knock-off of the classic Bialetti Moka Express, originally designed in 1933 by Alfonso Bialetti, that is a familiar sight in every Italian kitchen. It is octagonal, made of aluminum, with a black Bakelite handle that angles out from the body like a crooked arm and Bakelite knob at the top. From years of repeated use the aluminum has begun to corrode from contact with water and the finish is now dull, spotted, and has some rust on the inside. His: a Vev Vigano Itaca Oro, designed by Alessi, of stainless steel with a brass knob and straight brass handle that runs parallel to its body. It is conical in shape, tapering from the slightly bulging rounded bottom towards the lid, and the brass has some detailing on it. It shines and looks as new as the day he bought it because it is stainless. It is also slightly larger than mine, and so makes a larger cup of coffee.

But his coffee-pot, I want to claim, has flaws that are hidden behind that newness and shine, that detract from its beauty. First, brass conducts heat, and each time you reach for the handle, or put your finger on the lid, you burn yourself. Bakelite remains cool. Second, the sleek rounded design makes it very hard to unscrew the two halves, especially if you already have soapy hands. My octagonal pot turns as easily as a nut in a wrench, whether wet or dry. Third, the conical shape of his means the opening of the top pot is too narrow to fit even a small hand in to clean it, whereas mine, as wide at the top as at the bottom, welcomes a quick scrub. These are perhaps minor quibbles: both pots make very good coffee and both perhaps do it equally well (if I hesitate here it is, I am sure, out of prejudice alone that I prefer mine). And his is, admittedly, better looking.

When it comes to judging the aesthetic merit or beauty of these two pots, their similarities and differences tell us a number of important things about the nature of our approbations of design:

1. We have to know what they are, and what they are meant to be. For those who do not drink coffee, or have never made it, these little pots will be mystifying, and a judgement without this conceptual content cannot be a judgement of design excellence (although it could be one of free beauty). But this means that the necessary conceptual knowledge that underpins our judgements will be quite culturally and historically specific: there are also many ways to make coffee, from a drip filter maker to throwing grounds in the bottom of a cup and pouring boiling water over them. Not only must we be coffee drinkers, but coffee drinkers of a certain kind.
2. This conceptual knowledge is not directed at the content of the object: a coffee maker says nothing and expresses no meaning. Knowledge of what these objects are, while a minimal condition, must also be directed at their purposes: we must know whether they perform their functions

well—whether they fulfill their intended purposes—and are good things of their kind, in order for them to gain our approbation. Design is not art, nor judged in the same way as art.

3. This judgement of perfection cannot be made by looking at the coffee-pots alone. Designed objects are meant to work, but to ascertain whether they do, and whether they are good things of their kind, requires us to use them or put them to the test: is the coffee any good? Can we lift the lid to serve it? Does the pot leak or the metal corrode? Some of these virtues and deficiencies will not be apparent to the eye alone, and this means that judgements of design excellence, first, require more than observation and, second, are more integrated into our everyday lives and activities than aesthetic judgements of fine art. To judge a design by its formal qualities alone, even with the minimal conceptual content from (1) above, is to approach it as an object of contemplation or mere visual appreciation, and not as a functional object meant to be used. The true beauty of design requires perfection in fulfilling its function, to more than a minimal standard of managing to squeeze out a cup of coffee, or appearing to manage it.
4. We can know that these are intentional, manufactured objects without knowing who designed them or who actually made them, or we can know the former but not the latter, and neither bit of information is relevant to our judgements of their aesthetic merit. Even were my pot an original Bialetti, it would not be *better* than his because of this: we do not feel the hand of the designer in the pot in front of us because Alfonso Bialetti did not actually make it. With fine art too, knowing that a painting is a Picasso does not

make it any good (although it may make it valuable), but both art and craft require that the object be hand-made and that we know it has been because we evaluate the genius of its expression in the first instance and the skill of its production in the second when we judge it to be beautiful. With design, we evaluate the beauty of the object absent this further knowledge because designs are divorced from their manufacture—lie between conception and completion—in a unique way. Design is thus also not craft, and it is not judged in the same way.

5. The factors that contribute to a judgement of design excellence are the *contingent* ways an object fulfills its function. The decisions to use brass instead of Bakelite for the handle, or a conical instead of a octagonal shape, are not necessary to the pots' *being* espresso coffee makers (although they must have some shape and some way of being picked up), but they are directly contributive to both their beauty and their being any good. Certainly the Vev Vigano needed no detailing on the handle to perform its function, but this is part of the way in which his pot was realized as the particular thing it is. Form and function are symbiotically related in our judgements of design, and both contribute to a given object's beauty.
6. Judgements of design excellence then will be comparative, or work against a background of knowledge about the thing in question. We needn't have a perfect specimen available as an ideal with which to compare the relative success of the object—indeed perfection may not yet have been achieved—but to make a considered judgement of the thing we must know or at least imagine other contingent ways its function could have been realized and

judge it against a backdrop of past attempts or a projection of future modifications to achieve its purpose. We may give credit to design for innovation, but innovation itself works from within the history of previous attempts to create an object that functions in a certain way. A hitherto unknown and radically new thing will not win our approbation as a design if we do not know what it is or is meant to be. This comparative element of our judgements will also be historically and culturally specific as with number 1 above.

7. This means that in order to judge design as beautiful it must also be familiar to us, part of the everyday, and part of the things we interact with in our quotidian lives. Without being a botanist, I cannot judge a flower to be dependently beautiful; without being a rocket scientist, I cannot appraise the excellence of a rocket. But we are, in fact, "specialists" in living out our lives and days, and we do have the expertise to appraise a mop or broom, teapot or bicycle, as dependently beautiful provided that these are objects with which we regularly and actively engage.
8. Differences between objects—and innovations to objects—can be both formal and functional, and both elements contribute to their beauty, not separately but in the fully integrated teleological style that they display in the contingent way that their purposes are realized. There is no perfect coffee-pot: it is unhelpful to suggest that if both mine and his equally perform their functions adequately (or even well: they do both make good coffee) that this is sufficient and their beauty will then be determined by their formal elements alone. Shine, for instance, is a product of decisions about materials used but also has functional

implications: mine makes coffee more quickly than his, but mine corrodes. Because these are objects that are used, their formal elements will contribute to that use as well as to the appearance of the thing.

9. Factors that are irrelevant to the beauty of a designed object include monetary value (his is more expensive but still burns my fingers), and age (his is also newer). While the age of my pot and its signs of use may detract from its appearance or formal beauty, this need not be the case: some objects, particularly those made of wood or leather, become more beautiful with the patina of age. Irrelevant too is the quantity of objects made from a given design (producing one or ten thousand does not make the design any better), and the means of production. That mine was made in China and his in Italy, or that his was, perhaps, made by a workers' collective and mine in a third-world factory under dismal conditions will certainly affect our moral judgements of the objects depending on our views on international trade and labour laws but not our aesthetic judgements of their beauty. And we may even prefer his on these grounds, but doing so is not an aesthetic judgement of the coffee-pot itself.
10. The beauty or excellence of a given object produces a pleasure that is disinterested, and must be distinguished from other kinds of judgements we make about the same thing, including both those of the pleasant and the good. This is a fine distinction: many of us may not make an aesthetic judgement of the beauty of an espresso maker, or ever make an aesthetic judgement of a mop. The former may be useful to bring about the sensuous pleasure of a hot cup of coffee, and the latter may be (mediately) good insofar as it functions to

clean the floor. But *when* or *if* we make aesthetic judgements of those objects, they will be disinterested: absent a current need for a cup of coffee (but dependent upon my being a coffee-drinker and one who makes coffee in this way) I can with disinterest avow that my Bialetti is a beautiful design. A hot bath may be pleasant; it may be good, too, in warding off a chill; but whether this bathtub or that one is beautiful is a judgement we make within the context of our knowledge of these things but *absent* any interest or desire at the time of our appraisal.

11. For all of their cognitive content and situatedness, aesthetic judgements of design remain subjectively universal, and disagreements between individuals about matters of beauty are possible. These can be acknowledged—or even resolved—"by showing that one is speaking of free, the other of dependent, beauty—that the first is making a pure, the second an applied, judgement of taste" (§16, 68). Attendance to the sleek conical shape, the shiny brass handle, the harmony of proportions that cause him to say, "I know it burns your fingers but I still think mine is more beautiful" is a judgement that disregards the functional elements of the object in favour of its appearance. We disagree because we are making different kinds of aesthetic judgements, not because beauty is a matter of personal taste. Even within judgements of dependent beauty there remains room for disagreement because of the fine balance between form and function in our complex appraisals. It could be that for one judge the beauty of the brass mitigates the heat, while for another this is too high a price to pay for a good cup of coffee. Judgements of the dependent beauty of design are "all things considered" judgements,

and it is an empirical matter whether, in fact, each judge is considering all of the elements of the object in her appraisal of it. Here again use is important—you will not know the defects of his until you make coffee—as is the amount of experience and knowledge brought to bear on the judgement (I didn't know that aluminum would corrode when I bought mine). But there is no ideal critic or final arbiter of taste in design because extent of knowledge and experience will always be limited. No one knows *all* of the elements involved in creating the perfect espresso maker.

12. Familiarity, or the relative extent of knowledge brought to bear in a given judgement, does not entail that the beauty of design is *itself* merely relative, or that aesthetic judgements make no attempt at some kind of objectivity. Judgements of beauty have a synchronic aspect that will determine that these *are* reflective aesthetic judgements and not some other kind, and this aspect must be present in each and every case. This requires that we make a singular judgement, one that involves the free play of the imagination and understanding, and one that produces the appropriately disinterested pleasure. This is simply what beauty is. Within this synchronic framework there is also a diachronic aspect to judgements of design (and indeed to all dependent beauty) because of the shifting conceptual knowledge of form and function that is presupposed in our appreciation of the things that are integral to our lives. If this is relativism, it is of a very weak sort, and is directed towards who is *competent to judge* in a given case, and not towards what is *actually beautiful*.
13. As an analysis of the beauty of design, this pertains to one type of judgement we make about designed objects but

is not meant to preclude the great variety of assessments that make up our everyday experiences of things. Of some objects—surgical instruments, toilet plungers, mops—we may make only practical judgements of the good: do they perform their functions well? And we may even judge them excellent in this regard. Of others, we may appreciate the luxuriant feel of silk sheets, or the smell of a new car, but our judgements then would be those of the pleasant and not the beautiful, as they attend not to the purpose and perfection of a thing but to the sensation of pleasure it brings us, and this pleasure requires no knowledge of the object at all. And, when admiring foreign but pretty things in museum display cases, we may make free judgements of the beauty of the mere appearance of them, without any knowledge of their purpose or function. These are other forms of reflective judgements we can make about design. There are more ways to experience and judge designed objects than by aesthetic judgements of beauty, but our judgements of beauty, I contend, are of a particular kind. What I have set out to argue here is that the specific form of our aesthetic response to design is a judgement of dependent beauty. When we approach design as an aesthetic phenomenon and give it our appraisal, *this* is the way that our judgements operate. That we do not always respond to design in this manner is an empirical rather than conceptual matter: it does not disqualify an object as a work of design or as a candidate for aesthetic appreciation in the way that a failure to feel aesthetic emotion disqualifies an object from being art for Bell. We may not be disposed today to regard toilet plungers as beautiful, but after all, once upon a time chamber pots were considered purely functional too, for all that they now appear regularly in antique shops and museum displays.

14. Equally, vice grips, Scud missiles, and frozen pizzas may earn our approbation or disapprobation. but we must be careful to distinguish moral, political, economic, cognitive, or practical judgements about design from, first, reflective judgements and, second, the specific aesthetic appraisals I have focused on. Design, because it is functional and intersects with our lives more immediately and more often than fine art or craft, is perhaps more easily seen as the object of these other forms of assessment. This is an important reason why design has been neglected by my discipline: the mundane and quotidian nature of our interactions with it has masked the aesthetic quality of our experiences and has obscured its candidacy for aesthetic evaluation. We have failed to notice design, in an echo of Wittgenstein, because it is right before our eyes.
15. Finally, if we consider the project thus far, we can see that my primary goal has been to make design visible as an aesthetic phenomenon and argue for its inclusion as a candidate for theoretical attention by my discipline. That we do make aesthetic judgements about design has never been in question—design competitions and design museums attest to that fact. But that we also, and more often, make aesthetic judgements about design in our day-to-day lives has not been properly articulated or theorized because the particularly aesthetic aspect of our interactions with design has never before been singled out for theoretical consideration. Singling it out has, initially, required subjecting design to as rigorous a philosophical treatment as is merited by any other aesthetic object.

> But design is not *like* any other aesthetic object. To focus merely on the famous or the classic designs that have been lauded in award competitions and museums would remain an artificial approach that obscures what makes design unique; my example of the two coffee-pots was calculated to direct our attention away from the exceptional, the branded, or the celebrated, towards the ordinary and immanent as the more proper locus of our experiences of dependent beauty.

While thus far I have perhaps emphasized the synchronic structures of design ontology and design beauty to make my philosophical case, it is the diachronic nature of our experiences of design that renders it truly unique as an aesthetic phenomenon and form of experience, and it is to this that we must now turn our final attention in order to complete this study. A direct focus on our day-to-day interactions with design will not only help to consolidate the theory that I have advanced here, it will also have two important ramifications for philosophical aesthetics that the following discussion will make clear. First, to understand design aesthetically we must direct our focus to everyday objects, experiences, and judgements and away from the more rare or select occurrences of natural beauty or fine art—or celebrated designs. A recent movement in philosophical aesthetics has attempted to highlight the everyday, and I will consider its work in the following chapter. I will show, however, that attention to the everyday without the strong philosophical structure I have provided quickly dissolves into a series of broad gestures that are theoretically inconsistent. We must focus on the everyday, but it is *how* we do so that is important for the viability of our theory. Second, I will argue that, properly articulated, a theory of design as part of our everyday experiences in fact challenges the way in which aesthetics has traditionally approached its subject matter, and can function as an eloquent corrective of the discipline. Through design, we come to have a deeper understanding of beauty and of the significant ways that the aesthetic directly intersects with our defining concerns as human. This second consequence I will take up in my final remarks.

Chapter IV

Everyday Aesthetics and Design

Everyday Aesthetics is a very recent movement in the discipline that is motivated in ways similar to my own: it seeks to make visible the beauty and significance of the apparently mundane and familiar, and to demonstrate that this is a rich and important part of our lives. Contemporary work in Everyday Aesthetics undertakes a twofold task: it argues for broadening the traditional aesthetic categories and concerns to include familiar objects and quotidian experiences; and it also functions as critique: of the narrowness of scope of philosophical aesthetics as primarily art-centred, and as neglecting the myriad ways in which the aesthetic—as object and experience—directly touches our lives.

But the freshness and enthusiasm evident in writing on Everyday Aesthetics masks a certain lack of philosophical rigour: the literature provides more calls *for* an aesthetics of the everyday than it provides actual theories *of* the emerging field. Even Yuriko Saito, who has written the most sustained treatment of the area to date, characterizes her work as "an initiation for further exploration rather than a definite theory of everyday aesthetics."[1] Many of the sweeping claims made by this new movement require critical assessment: not all of them can be sustained and not all of

1 Yuriko Saito, *Everyday Aesthetics* (New York: Oxford University Press, 2007), 243.

them are relevant to an aesthetics of design, as I will seek to demonstrate in this chapter. Nevertheless, there are signs that current attention to the everyday is providing an impetus for broadening the scope of philosophical aesthetics, and this will assist me in articulating the contribution that a theory of design can make to the discipline.

In the sections that follow, I will consider, first, the directly aesthetic claims made about the everyday, and their relevance to design, and second, I will distinguish these from the moral or more broadly ethical claims made on its behalf. My contention is that the movement turns to these other areas of value theory to bolster its account of the significance of the everyday precisely because its aesthetic account of this significance has failed to do the job. With a stronger theoretical foundation in place it would not have needed to legitimize our attention to the quotidian with moral or ethical theory but could have found these legitimizing reasons within aesthetics itself.

1. THE CRITIQUE OF AESTHETICS

Everyday Aesthetics rests upon a critique of the discipline that begins with a number of meta-theoretical observations about its traditional approach to its subject matter. While philosophical aesthetics has a long and varied history, it has come to be dominated by the model of fine art as the quintessential aesthetic object,[2] so much so that "aesthetics" and "the philosophy of art" are almost interchangeable as designates for the discipline. This is not to disregard the body of work that focuses on our aesthetic responses

2 Ibid., 13.

to nature, for instance, or to a lesser degree popular arts and craft, but even these fields largely use the fine arts as their theoretical model. As Thomas Leddy has noted, "although many aestheticians insist that aesthetic qualities are not limited to the arts, even *those* thinkers generally take the arts as the primary focus of their discussion."[3] Sherri Irvin, in a recent paper, offers empirical evidence of this: in the five years from 2001 to 2006, of articles printed in the two major English language aesthetics journals (the *Journal of Aesthetics and Art Criticism* and the *British Journal of Aesthetics*) 95 percent focused on fine art, 3 percent focused on nature, and less than 2 percent dealt with anything else.[4] These facts are not themselves a critique of the discipline: art has long been considered a singular form of human expression and an important source of some of our most profound aesthetic experiences. However art, especially if limited to the fine arts of the museum and concert hall, the poetry chapbook and the art-house cinema, is not a significant part of the lives of a great number of people, a great part of the time. To mark it as the norm for aesthetic experience in general is to suggest, as Irvin remarks, that many of our lives would be "rather lacking in aesthetic texture,"[5] which is what Everyday Aesthetics seeks to challenge. This challenge comes on two fronts: that critical of fine art as the prototypical object of our aesthetic experience and that critical of our response to fine art as the form all aesthetic experience should take. Together, these sketch a

3 Thomas Leddy, "Everyday Surface Aesthetic Qualities: 'Neat,' 'Messy,' 'Clean,' 'Dirty,'" *Journal of Aesthetics and Art Criticism* 53, no. 3 (1995): 259. Also cited in Saito, *Everyday Aesthetics*, 13. Note that, as this book goes to press, Thomas Leddy's new work in Everday Aesthetics is scheduled for publication. Please see *The Extraordinary in the Ordinary: The Aesthetics of Everyday Life* (Toronto: Broadview Press, 2012).

4 Sherri Irvin, "The Pervasiveness of the Aesthetic in Ordinary Experience," *British Journal of Aesthetics* 48, no. 1 (2008): 29n.

5 Ibid., 40.

picture of philosophical aesthetics as alienated from human lives and concerns, and indeed as therefore alienated from the guiding interests of philosophy in general.

The pervasive view that our aesthetic experience is directed to works of art—or to things analogous to art—overly circumscribes the scope of the aesthetic.[6] Artworks are, first, geographically and temporally distanced from our lives: as objects on display in museums and galleries, as concerts and operas performed in symphony halls, these are things we must make a point of traveling to experience, taking "time out" from our everyday lives to attend this opening or that concert, willfully seeking out our encounters with different art-forms. The identification of the aesthetic with fine art excludes from this domain our casual and more frequent encounters with objects that have not been singled out for special attention. Instead, our aesthetic experiences take place in artificial environments that shut out the quotidian and natural worlds and that are controlled and directed by curatorial and directoral professionals who strive to create an atmosphere that is "pure" and without distraction so that we can give our entire attention over to the object in front of us. As M. H. Abrams has noted, "the paradigmatic situation, in defining and analyzing art, is that in which a lone perceiver confronts an isolated work ... and simply attends to the features that it manifests to his exclusive attention."[7] Such an

6 I will not dwell here on the theoretical, historical, or sociological reasons for this preoccupation with the fine arts. For relevant background, see my "The Disenfranchisement of Philosophical Aesthetics," *Journal of the History of Ideas* 4, no. 64 (2003). Some good discussion of this phenomenon can also be found in Roger Scruton, "Modern Philosophy and the Neglect of Aesthetics," *Philosopher on Dover Beach* (South Bend, IN: St. Augustine's Press, 1998), and "The Aesthetic Endeavour Today," *Philosophy* 71 (1996); and M. H. Abrams, "Art-as-Such: The Sociology of Modern Aesthetics," *Doing Things with Texts: Essays in Criticism and Critical Theory* (New York: Norton, 1989) and "Kant and the Theology of Art," *Notre Dame English Journal* 13 (1981).

7 Abrams, "Art-as Such," 138.

experience, if identified with the aesthetic in general, will indeed make the objects of our aesthetic experiences rarified and removed from our daily lives.

Artworks are further distanced from the everyday by their metaphysical isolation as presented in a determinate frame. A painting, as Saito notes, is confined to the "visual elements of one side of the canvas," requiring us to bracket out such non-essential features as the surrounding wallpaper and the smell of the paint. A symphony "consists of sounds conforming to a score" and normally excludes outside traffic noise, rustles in the audience, or the texture of the seats.[8] Even when a frame is not literally apparent, there still remains a "conceptual understanding" of the boundaries of the object "such as the conventional agreement concerning the medium, the artist's intention, the cultural and historical content and the like."[9] As enframed objects demanding focused attention, artworks have been considered a sui generis form, autonomous of ordinary human purposes and values, singled out for a profundity and significance that is deeper than other objects or forms of communication. In this way, Arthur Danto has called art "a kind of ontological vacation place from our defining concerns as human."[10] It is distinctive precisely because it is *not* part of our everyday lives, and this distance is responsible for its unique status. But this view of art as metaphysically singular serves to render philosophical aesthetics an esoteric discipline because it concerns itself with

8 These examples, and the discussion of enframing are from Yuriko Saito's paper "Everyday Aesthetics," *Philosophy and Literature* 25 (2001): 89, and are repeated in expanded form in her monograph *Everyday Aesthetics*, 18–22. In the latter work, Saito acknowledges the obvious musical exception of John Cage's *4′33″*.

9 Saito, *Everyday Aesthetics*, 18–19.

10 Arthur C. Danto, "The Philosophical Disenfranchisement of Art," *The Philosophical Disenfranchisement of Art* (New York: Columbia University Press, 1986), 9.

a phenomenon that it has itself defined as esoteric: singular, autonomous, a non-natural kind wholly removed from human interests, concerns, and values.[11]

What could be called the methodological disenfranchisement of aesthetics is compounded by taking our response to fine art as the norm for all aesthetic experience. This "spectator model,"[12] which attends to the apparent features of the art object and brackets what is outside its frame, is paradigmatically one of distance and disengagement, experienced alone, and in a manner that is merely contemplative. We must prescind from our "defining concerns as human" so that we let the works speak; we bring with us nothing from our lives, or as little as we can. Arto Haapala has called this model of aesthetic response one of "strangeness": "Art is the paradigmatic example of a phenomenon that is supposed to be something special," that is "supposed to stand out from the stream of the everyday"[13] in the way that unfamiliar objects or places arrest our attention and call for dispassionate examination. Our proper aesthetic response to a Bach concerto or a Vermeer, for example, is to attend to the singular (significant, profound) aesthetic qualities of the object as they are presented to us and take from them an appreciation or satisfaction that is itself different in kind from our normal responses to objects we encounter in the course of our lives, a satisfaction and experience that more often than not has been couched in terms of aesthetic ecstasy and transcendence.

11 I explore this in some depth in "The Disenfranchisement of Philosophical Aesthetics."

12 I owe this notion to Lambert Zuidervaart, in "The Artefactuality of Autonomous Art: Kant and Adorno," *The Reasons of Art*, ed. Peter J. McCormick (Ottawa: University of Ottawa Press, 1985), who writes, "'The aesthetic' which anchors fine art's autonomy, is a category of commerce between recipients and objects. Where 'the aesthetic' is made central, the philosophy of art becomes a spectator aesthetics" (258).

13 Arto Haapala, "On the Aesthetics of the Everyday: Familiarity, Strangeness and the Meaning of Place," *The Aesthetics of Everyday Life*, ed. Andrew Light and Jonathan M. Smith (New York: Columbia University Press, 2005), 40, 41.

The idea that there is a "hermetic realm of aesthetic experience that has no practical application or motive,"[14] coupled with a focus on autonomous or singular objects that elicit this novel experience, serves to render the relation between object and subject on the spectator model empty, even sterile. On both sides of the relation, humanity is stripped away: the object is insulated from ordinary human values and emotions; it induces an "exalted state" that likewise distances or disengages us from these same values and emotions,[15] and what is precisely forgone is any possible deep link between the aesthetic and human life that may have existed prior to such methodological alienation. The aesthetic is stripped of whatever direct connection it may have had to human concerns, interests, activities, and values; and aesthetics as a discipline becomes an insular study of a peculiar sort of phenomenon, of our unique reactions to it, and of the internal values by which we judge its merits. It is no wonder, then, that in order to uphold this conception of the aesthetic, fine art must be strongly distinguished from craft, popular arts, entertainment, domestic objects and activities, and even most natural and human environments, those that directly involve the messy business of our daily lives and encounters.

Everyday Aesthetics, in its attempt to broaden the scope of the aesthetic, can be read as attempting simultaneously to re-enfranchise philosophical aesthetics as an important part of philosophy at large: only by setting our aesthetic responses on a continuum with cognitive judgements, moral and practical decisions, and quotidian choices and activities, they claim, can aesthetics become an integral part of understanding our defining concerns as human. Saito

14 Crispin Sartwell, "Aesthetics of the Everyday," *The Oxford Handbook of Aesthetics*, ed. Jerrold Levinson (New York: Oxford University Press, 2003), 765.
15 Ibid.

claims that "exploring everyday aesthetics remedies a deficiency in the mainstream art-based philosophical aesthetics by being truthful to the diverse dimensions of our aesthetic life, which is not confined to the artworld and other art-like objects and activities."[16] Rather than being a study of a rarified object or non-natural kind, holding unique internal values that can be assessed only through a singular form of experience, Everyday Aesthetics is precisely interested in "excavating and examining what may appear to be obvious and taken for granted"[17] and placing it front and centre in a new kind of aesthetic theory.

2. THE EXPANSION OF AESTHETICS

Against this background of critique, in recent years a number of aestheticians have sought to broaden the scope of the aesthetic, and what they have in common is this turn from art to everyday objects and experiences. Let me begin with a few representative examples. Yuriko Saito, for instance, calls attention to the aesthetic character of the experience of a baseball game, including as it does "the noisy cheers of the fans, the hot sun beating down on our neck, and the smell of hotdogs," all of which are as significant a part of our overall aesthetic responses as the movement of the players and the competition of the game itself.[18] Sherri Irvin considers "particular moments and local experience" as having an aesthetic quality, such as "the various colours of the dirt and tyre tracks" of a road, and the smell and feel of her cat as she strokes it.[19] For her,

16 Saito, *Everyday Aesthetics*, 243.
17 Ibid., 5.
18 Ibid., 19.
19 Irvin, "Pervasiveness of the Aesthetic," 30–31.

the reason for turning to the everyday is in part quite simple: "We deserve better than to have our ordinary pleasures ... dismissed as insignificant, and our ability to appreciate them accordingly diminished."[20] Crispin Sartwell includes body adornment, knick-knacks, lawns and gardens, cookery, web design, and television as among the things that have an "aesthetic dimension" that is "common to nearly all people" but which would not normally be seen as art.[21] And Thomas Leddy highlights an entire class of qualities neglected from the aesthetic literature, such as "neat," "messy," "clean," "dirty," and so on, which, he argues, are as much aesthetic qualities as those normally attributed to the fine arts but which more often describe everyday objects and activities.[22]

What many of these thinkers also have in common is a desire to link our aesthetic experiences of the everyday with moral experiences and judgements or with ethics in some broad construal of the term. Saito, for instance, argues that "what at first may appear to be trivial, negligible and inconsequential responses that we make on a daily basis ... often lead to serious moral, social, political and environmental consequences,"[23] and devotes a chapter of her work to "moral-aesthetic" judgements that are aesthetic insofar as they are derived from perceptual experience but which have profound moral implications.[24] Sherri Irvin claims that the "aesthetic aspects of everyday life take on obvious moral relevance insofar as they affect my tendency to do or pursue what is morally good." For example, by attending to the aesthetic character of our lives we may "reduce our tendency to cause harm in attempts

20 Ibid., 40.

21 Sartwell, "Aesthetics of the Everyday," 763.

22 Leddy, "Everyday Surface Aesthetic Qualities," 259.

23 Saito, *Everyday Aesthetics*, 6.

24 Ibid., 208. Her detailed discussion of moral-aesthetic judgements can be found in chapter 5 of her work.

to satisfy our needs."[25] Both Saito and Irvin recognize an environmental ethic, among others, at work in our aesthetic choices and pleasures. Roger Scruton more broadly suggests that when we attend to the everyday we "situate the object in the current of human life, endowing it with a moral or social significance."[26] Arnold Berleant makes a claim for a "social aesthetic" forged on the everyday that gives a "sense of being in place, of a dissolution of barriers and boundaries."[27] And Arto Haapala, who focuses on the existential significance of the familiar, claims directly that "[w]hen we are talking about everydayness, its aesthetics, in this sense, it is difficult to draw any strict line between the ethical and the aesthetic aspects of life"[28] because, as with Berleant and Scruton, our aesthetic responses to the world cannot be divorced from the meaning these objects and experiences have for our lives. By shedding the link between fine art and the aesthetic, and between the strange and the familiar, Everyday Aesthetics finds it natural to turn to the ethical dimensions of aesthetic experience, as this experience is now of apiece with our daily lives and the decisions and activities characteristic of them.

These two broad moves—a critique of aesthetics and a call for its expansion—are both motivated by an interest in paying greater philosophical attention to our quotidian experiences and our interactions with everyday objects. However, aside from these prima facie similarities, recent work in Everyday Aesthetics is as varied as in any other philosophical discipline, and diverges noticeably from the theory of design that I have been building throughout this project.

25 Irvin, "Pervasiveness of the Aesthetic," 41, 42.

26 Roger Scruton, "In Search of the Aesthetic," *British Journal of Aesthetics* 47, no. 3 (2007): 246.

27 Arnold Berleant, "Ideas for a Social Aesthetic," in Light and Smith, *Aesthetics of Everyday Life*, 33.

28 Haapala, "Aesthetics of the Everyday," 52.

In what follows I will focus on the work of two recent theorists of the everyday, using Yuriko Saito to examine some of the specifically aesthetic claims of the movement, and Arto Haapala to consider the ways that the aesthetic and the ethical have been seen to intersect. In both cases, I will highlight structural weaknesses in their claims, and demonstrate that these weaknesses are the result of a failure to ground their work in rigorous aesthetic philosophy. While their critique of aesthetics has merit, they err in dismissing the tradition so completely that they are left without a foundation to support the advances they seek to achieve for the discipline. Ultimately, I will claim that Everyday Aesthetics is unable to ground its claims of the significance of our quotidian experiences because it has lost sight of the unique role that the aesthetic plays in our lives.

i. Saito: Activity, Pleasure, Indeterminacy

Yuriko Saito's work *Everyday Aesthetics* is a recent full-length treatment of this emerging field. Among the ways in which she seeks to expand philosophical aesthetics, there are three claims that merit specific attention. The first is her inclusion within the scope of aesthetic experience *action* rather than mere observation. Aesthetics on the art-centred approach privileges, as the movement claims, our disengaged contemplation of the aesthetic object to better appreciate its singular features. With the everyday, instead, Saito seeks to include responses that "do not presuppose or lead to such spectator-like experiences but rather prompt us towards actions, such as cleaning, discarding, purchasing" and all manner of "everyday decisions and actions, without any accompanying contemplative appreciation."[29] This is a seemingly simple but in fact quite

29 Saito, *Everyday Aesthetics*, 10–11.

dramatic turn: heretofore aesthetic experience has been described as purely responsive—to the perceptual properties of the art object, or even to the beauty of nature. But philosophical aesthetics has not adequately considered the idea that some aesthetic experiences are themselves activities, and this is what Saito wishes to highlight.

She makes good use of the traditional Japanese tea ceremony, where what is aesthetically relevant includes "the timing of refilling water in the stone basin and sprinkling water on the plants in the garden, choosing implements and decorations to provide a cool feeling in the summer and warmth in the winter, sometimes brushing off and some other times leaving snow accumulated on trees, rocks and basins,"[30] all aesthetic activities that are merely preparatory for the making and drinking of tea that is the ceremony itself. But even while the tea ceremony is a highly aestheticized custom, Saito's attention to activity rather than mere response can clearly be seen in more mundane and quotidian circumstances. The aesthetics of natural beauty traditionally dwells on our responses to, for instance, flowers, mountains, seashells, and so on, without factoring in the activities that deliver that beauty to us, or perhaps even constitute it, such as walking on the mountain path among the trees, or strolling the beach in the sun and stooping to collect the shells from the water's edge. We do not merely stand still to regard that mountain (although sometimes we do), but we undertake the walk itself as an activity that is—and is meant to be—an aesthetic experience.

More prosaically still, Saito notes that our "usual reaction to dilapidated buildings, rusted cars or dirty linens is to deplore their appearance, prompting us to repair, clean or discard them."[31] Cleaning and repairing, like preparing for guests at a tea ceremony,

30 Ibid., 236.
31 Ibid., 51.

are for Saito themselves aesthetic activities rather than chores to be completed in order to achieve some later aesthetic result. The emphasis, one could say, is on *beautifying* as an experience that has an aesthetic dimension rather than on *beauty* as a quality laid out for us and merely waiting for our appreciative response. Sherri Irvin also attends to the aesthetic elements of activities, including in her list of the everyday not only stroking the cat but also scratching her head "with a mechanical pencil that allows me to part my hair and reach exactly the right spot on my scalp" and jiggling her wedding band "around in my right palm to enjoy its weight before sliding it back on."[32] These are not instances of beautifying in the sense of making beautiful something that was previously ugly or dirty but instead, perhaps, examples of the activity of *aestheticizing* in the sense of *making aesthetic* through action what would previously have been beneath her notice: hair, a pencil, a wedding band, like a teacup, or water on a plant's leaves.

The turn from object to activity opens up the range of what constitutes the aesthetic, to include cleaning, walking, stroking, scratching—all quotidian actions that can legitimately make a claim to having an aesthetic character, or being part of an aesthetic experience, and that do not need, or are not directed toward, a particular object as their goal. This means of broadening the aesthetic is in part relevant to my conception of design because our appreciation of designed artifacts is not limited to their appearance alone. Saito notes that "we experience a chair not only by inspecting its shape and colour, but also by touching its fabric, sitting in it, leaning against it, and moving it, to get the feel for its texture, comfort and stability."[33] With designed objects, as we have seen, our

32 Irvin, "Pervasiveness of the Aesthetic," 31.
33 Saito, *Everyday Aesthetics*, 20.

appreciation depends importantly upon our *use* of them: two chairs may look substantially the same, but the one that deserves our particular approbation will be more comfortable, or more stable, than the other, and we can discover this only by actively using the chair rather than by attending solely to its perceptual features. Our aesthetic experience of design must involve an element of activity that is missing from a spectator approach to the fine arts, but that is common to the aesthetics of the everyday. However, the activity involved in design must be more narrowly construed than the experiences Saito and Irvin describe. In considering a broom, I am not interested in the aesthetic elements of the activity of sweeping per se but in the contribution this use of the broom makes to our appraisal of it as a designed object. Our judgements of design will include and in part depend upon our activities and use of objects, but the aesthetics of design is not limited to the activity alone. I will return to this more circumscribed sense of activity below.

Closely related to this focus on activity, Saito's second claim is that aesthetic experiences of the everyday should not be limited to the "distal" senses of sight and sound but include the "proximal" senses of smell, touch, taste, and feel.[34] Notice that her earlier example of the baseball game required that we feel the sun, hear the crowd, and smell the hotdogs; our appreciation of a chair includes the feel of its texture and its stability beneath us. Irvin, when she strokes her cat, enjoys both the texture of its fur and its smell, "like trapped sunshine or roasted nuts," as well, one would expect, as the sound of its purring appreciation.[35] The art-centred approach to aesthetics is seen to disregard the proximal senses as irrelevant

34 My use of the terms "distal" and "proximal" comes not from Saito's work but from Glenn Parsons's and Allen Carlson's discussion of her claims in *Functional Beauty* (New York: Oxford University Press, 2008), 176–177.

35 Irvin, "Pervasiveness of the Aesthetic," 31.

to our appreciation: most of the fine arts are either seen or heard (and sometimes both); this privileging of the distal senses may in part be due to their traditional role in cognition and intellectual activity, making them "higher" senses than taste, smell, and touch, which are more narrowly associated with bodily pleasures. Saito allows that "[v]isual images and sounds can be arranged according to some rational scheme, hence they are amenable to objective analysis." In contrast, of the proximal senses, she notes that they are considered "too visceral, animalistic and crude to allow intellectual analysis"[36] and thus are too often disregarded as being *un*aesthetic.

Saito's concern is that by privileging a group of objects experienced only by these higher senses, "we neglect a large portion of the aesthetic dimension of our daily affairs,"[37] at great cost to the discipline of aesthetics itself. However, it is not only in everyday experiences that this neglect is apparent. In my appreciation of the mountains, as a form of natural beauty, not only did I need to actively walk in them, but the senses engaged in my experience included smell—of the freshly snapped pine branches of a recent avalanche on my path; and hearing—of the distant rumble of continuous avalanches in a nearby valley. Both senses brought a *frisson* of danger to the walk that day that contributed to my respect for the power and majesty of the mountains that I would not have had, had I experienced them through sight alone. Similarly, my aesthetic appreciation of, say, Jana Sterbak's meat sculpture *Vanitas: Flesh Dress for an Albino Anorectic* would perforce include the range of smells as it decomposed. The proximal senses are not as neglected in other areas of aesthetics as Saito seems to suggest. Nevertheless,

36 Saito, *Everyday Aesthetics*, 22.
37 Ibid.

what Everyday Aesthetics wishes to highlight by attention to the proximal senses is that we are not only rational or intellectual creatures but physical and sensuous beings as well, and aesthetic experience, as a form of perceptual pleasure, is impoverished if it is theorized on a model that neglects one half of what we are.

Focus on the proximal senses is relevant to design, too, because while we need to actively use designed artifacts to appreciate and appraise them, this engagement will involve more than sight and sound, as we saw with Saito's example of the chair, above. Our appreciation of a floral display cannot be complete without the aroma of the flowers, and even our appreciation of (or distaste for) the air fresheners that dangle from cars' rearview mirrors—as designed objects—requires smell as perhaps the primary sense with which we appraise them. Saito claims that the aesthetic value of a knife, for instance, "consists not only of its visual qualities but also of its feeling in my hand … [and] how smoothly and effortlessly I can cut an object." The "sensuous aspects converge and work together to facilitate the ease of use,"[38] and our full aesthetic experience of the knife requires us to hold it and cut with it; we cannot fully determine its design excellence if we do not perform these actions and engage at least some of our proximal senses when we do.

It might be objected that this need not be the case, that design, once it is prized as an aesthetic object, finds its place in exhibitions in museums and galleries, and in these venues we need merely look at the designed objects to properly appreciate them. But in these instances, designed objects are treated as honorary works of art, put in display cases to be contemplated in the way of art, and our experience of such objects in these settings is thereby

38 Ibid., 27.

impoverished. Saito recognizes the frustration encountered in such museum exhibits: they "do not achieve the collapse of the separation between art and everyday life" because "we are prevented from experiencing [these objects] in our everyday use" by sitting on them, cutting with them, wearing them, and so on.[39] I would add that, in order to merit inclusion in such exhibits—or in order to win prizes at design competitions—the objects had to have first been touched, smelled, handled, sat in, and used in the way they were intended to be, before judges or curators could make decisions about their success as designs in the first place. While design may have achieved quasi-art status in some cases and to some degree, design is first and foremost part of our everyday lives, and our appreciation of it will come through its use in familiar and quotidian settings, with the aid of all of our senses.

However, while broadening the aesthetic to include experiences of the proximal senses may to some degree encourage the philosophical discipline to attend more holistically to human experiences and the breadth of human perceptions, there is also a danger in this move: it threatens to collapse aesthetic experience into bodily pleasure in general, a distinction that I have argued it is important to maintain. If, as Saito and Irvin claim, aesthetic pleasure can arise through any of our senses, then the pleasures of "exercising, taking a bath, drinking lemonade or engaging in sexual activity"[40] would all count as (everyday) aesthetic experiences, which we should be reluctant to admit. For Parsons and Carlson, in their work *Functional Beauty*, this is a "*reductio ad absurdum*"[41] of the concept of the aesthetic: drinking lemonade may be pleasurable, but is it in any way beautiful or aesthetically great, meaningful or

39 Ibid, 20 n. 28.
40 Parsons and Carlson, *Functional Beauty*, 178.
41 Ibid., 180.

profound? They point to the "long-standing conceptual distinction between aesthetic and bodily pleasure," a "part of our common linguistic practice since ancient times,"[42] as speaking in favour of our continued recognition of it in philosophical practice. But pointing to a traditional practice of philosophical aesthetics is not itself an argument in favour of maintaining that practice, most pointedly in the context of a movement that seeks to expand the discipline as it has been historically understood. Parsons and Carlson, in the face of this challenge, fall back on supporting the distal over the proximal senses in general as the source of aesthetic experience. But this stance confuses the senses involved in an experience with the pleasures that *result from* that same experience; it is possible to include the proximal senses in an account of aesthetic experience while maintaining that the pleasures so afforded are different from gustatory, sensual, bodily pleasures of a more generic sort. Saito and Irvin both fall prey to this confusion. Saito, for instance, describes the "typical experience" of an apple as beginning with looking at its "perfect round shape and delicate colours," feeling its "substantial weight and smooth skin" in our hands, and concluding with "the crunching sound when we first bite into it ... and the sweet juice" flowing onto our tongues.[43] But is this an aesthetic experience or a subjective hedonic (gustatory) response from someone who simply enjoys eating an apple? Or, perhaps, is it a bit of both that have not been distinguished? In what sense is her description that of a "typical" experience of an apple? Do we all eat with the kind of attention she describes? Equally, one could ask whether Irvin's satisfying head scratch with a pencil is any more than a pleasurable bodily sensation, the satisfaction of an itch, perhaps, or a form of

42 Ibid., 185.
43 Saito, *Everyday Aesthetics*, 20.

fidgeting while working at her desk. Nothing in her description indicates that this activity is particularly aesthetic.

If Everyday Aesthetics is to gain recognition as a legitimate part of the philosophical discipline, and if it is to convince that discipline to turn its attention from the fine arts to an exploration of broader human aesthetic experience, it will need to maintain a robust conception of what the *aesthetic* amounts to, as distinct from the delicious, the comfortable, the sexy, and the physically pleasurable in general. In a recent review of Irvin's and Saito's work, Christopher Dowling echoes my concern, noting that in these accounts "there is a serious danger of ... trivializing what counts as the aesthetic" by "equivocating between 'aesthetic value' and 'pleasure.'"[44] This concern cuts to the heart of the problem of what the aesthetic—as experience, as object, and as kind of pleasure—really involves. And it is a problem Everyday Aesthetics will have to address. I will return to this below; for the moment I would simply like to highlight the need for maintaining a strong distinction between bodily and aesthetic pleasures—as those between the Kantian notions of the pleasant and the beautiful—while allowing for the use of our proximal senses in our experience of the latter. Attention to the everyday need not lead to a collapse of the two, but in order to keep them distinct we may have to exclude some local and particular experiences from the range of the aesthetic.

Saito's third claim is in part a consequence of the first two: everyday aesthetic experiences can be distinguished from those of art because of their lack of a determinate frame. Through active engagement and the use of all of our senses, the objects of our experiences bleed through any determinate boundaries and become

44 Christopher Dowling, "The Aesthetics of Daily Life," *British Journal of Aesthetics* 50, no. 3 (2010): 226.

less focused than those of art, although perhaps the richer because of this. Our experience of a baseball game is not only of the game but of the crowds and sun and smells and so on; our appreciation of a knife includes its feel and look as much as the motions of slicing and chopping when we use it. The absence of conceptual or conventional agreement about the legitimate boundaries of an object in the case of the everyday renders a non-art object "'frameless,' making us a creator of it as an aesthetic object." The "aesthetic price we pay for the frameless character of non-art objects … can be compensated by exercising our imagination and creativity in constituting the aesthetic object as we see fit."[45] For Saito, the lack of determining boundaries in everyday activities and quotidian things is freeing in a way that traditional aesthetics does not allow for: what counts as an aesthetic object will not be directed or determined by arts professionals but will be constituted by the experience—and the experiencing subject herself. "As a result, we are free to rely on our own imagination, judgement, and aesthetic taste as the guide."[46] This move effectively dismisses the metaphysical isolation of art as a sui generis kind whose boundaries are determined by the intentional acts of its creator; instead of being a spectator to this product of "genius" we become active participants in the creation of that which gives us aesthetic pleasure. And this makes the relation between subject and object more inclusive, more intimate, and more alive. Framelessness is vital to Everyday Aesthetics because without the dissolution of boundaries a baseball game or a good head scratch would have no purchase as complete aesthetic experiences.

45 Saito, *Everyday Aesthetics*, 19.
46 Ibid.

But this move also comes at a cost, which Parsons and Carlson, in a related discussion, call the "problem of indeterminacy."[47] While we may have freedom to constitute the objects of our aesthetic appreciation, we at the same time render "a normative dimension for such appreciation elusive: it becomes difficult to see how aesthetic responses to the everyday might be critiqued as more or less appropriate, or how any meaningful critical discourse might be developed in regard to it."[48] Framelessness and indeterminacy bring with them the problems of subjectivity and aesthetic relativism. It might be that for Saito part of the aesthetic pleasure of a baseball game includes the smell of hotdogs, but what if for me these detract from my experience of the game or go unnoticed altogether? How can she and I engage in a meaningful discussion about the aesthetics of our experience if we cannot agree on what counts as an experience of the game in the first place? If we imaginatively constitute the object of our appraisal, then that appraisal, on Parsons's and Carlson's view, can have neither objective purchase nor make a claim for legitimate philosophical analysis. Just what are we analyzing, when the parameters shift according to the imaginations and preferences of the individuals engaged in the experience? For Parsons and Carlson this emphasis on individuality and relativity imposes upon Everyday Aesthetics a "fundamental limitation": "If conflicting aesthetic judgements of everyday things are not better or worse, if they cannot be disputed or adjudicated, it would seem that discourse concerning the aesthetic value of those things can allow little place for criticism, constructive dialogue, or education,"[49] which they see philosophical aesthetics as essentially engaged in. And it does seem that, by focusing

47 Parsons and Carlson, *Functional Beauty*, 54.
48 Ibid., 55.
49 Ibid., 56.

on particular and personal experiences of strolling, eating, and so on, Everyday Aesthetics seeks to capture only the pleasures these experiences provide, leaving behind all critical appraisal or judgement. Dowling, again, echoes this concern. His fear is that "'aesthetic' talk" in the domain of the everyday will devolve into "the mere evincing of subjective responses ... with no indication that the speaker expects anything of her audience beyond mere recognition." And with such a devolution "we are in danger of losing the sharp and significant focus on those responses that legitimately engage critical attention and interest"—we are in danger of asking "what all the [aesthetic] fuss" is about.[50]

A complete loss of the significance of the notion of the aesthetic needn't be the result of work on the everyday, however, and Parsons and Carlson in particular overstate their concerns. The indeterminacy of the aesthetic does not entail that we attend to only those pleasurable parts of our experiences and dismiss the rest as irrelevant even if in fact this has been the trend. Saito and I may disagree about the *merit* of the smell of hotdogs, but certainly we would agree (or through discussion she could make me see) that the smell assaulting our senses makes up part of the broad experience of our going to the game on that (sunny) day. Parsons and Carlson collapse the indeterminacy of the boundaries of the experience into a radical subjectivity of the pleasures we derive from it. Certainly the problem of indeterminacy adds a layer of complexity to our understanding of what constitutes an object of aesthetic appreciation, and of the factors that are relevant to our appraisal of it, or the pleasure it accords. But this complexity is not any more an insurmountable problem for Everyday Aesthetics than it is for the art-centred approach, in the face of contemporary

50 Dowling, "Aesthetics of Daily Life," 229–230.

innovations in the arts themselves. John Cage's *4'33"* is the first example that comes to mind of an art object that explodes determinate boundaries, as do Christo's extended performative pieces such as *Running Fence* in California or *The Gates* in Central Park. The intentional framelessness of Cage's or Christo's pieces does not exclude them from the realm of aesthetic objects nor render it impossible to assess them for their relative merits. Saito's point is that philosophical aesthetics needs to broaden its scope to include factors that we bring with us to our aesthetic experiences. And while these factors do include an element of indeterminacy, this does not on its own lead us to an inchoate aesthetic relativism. Yet Parsons and Carlson are indeed correct to point to a weakness in current discussions of the everyday: too much of the attention of these theorists is on the pleasures of our quotidian experiences to the almost total neglect of how these pleasures can be subject to dispassionate analysis and critique.

The framelessness that is part of Everyday Aesthetics stems from its attention to active experiencing, and suffers some of its same weaknesses, although it too is relevant for a consideration of design. Design on the one hand escapes the brunt of Parsons's and Carlson's critique because each designed object is bounded and determined, and, while we need to use it to appreciate it, this use is also more determinate than the broad notion of experience Saito relies upon. On the other hand, the inclusion of active use and of our proximal senses in our experience of design means that it too will bleed through its boundaries and take on a more unfocused character. In Saito's appreciation of the knife, for example, she includes the weight and feel of it in her hand as well as the way it cuts through an object. When I use a knife, my experience also includes, perhaps, the glint of the blade, the colour of the handle, and the satisfaction in the sound and feel of the knife as it meets the wood of the butcher's block. In our assessment of a designed object, part of our task is to first delineate the features that are relevant to its excellence from those that are not. Does it matter that a chair's material is soft and pliant? How much? And would it be a lesser chair if it were made of hard plastic or rough fibres? Does the physical beauty of a knife detract from or contribute to its functional excellence? And how much of the pleasure we take in the object is relevant to its aesthetic merit? The indeterminacy of Everyday Aesthetics allows for such nominally "external" factors to contribute to our assessment of an object by, for example, allowing us to contextualize it as part of the diachronic aspect of our daily lives. Adding complexity to our normative discussions of beauty or excellence does not render those discussions inutile or even impose a "fundamental limitation" on their relevance to aesthetic appreciation. It merely demands that we broaden the scope of what we understand aesthetically relevant factors to be in our philosophical analysis.

Let me draw these three claims together now and consider the project of Everyday Aesthetics more generally. As I've noted, there are similarities between Saito's work and my own intuitions about design: judgements of design require active engagement with the object, they involve the proximal as well as the distal senses, and consequently design also "bleeds through" its frame in ways that many art objects do not. This close focus on the diachronic—localized, specific, personal—nature of quotidian experiences and objects is what makes our interactions with design unique, and what distinguishes our responses to design from other forms of aesthetic judgement. It is in these three directions that we can push our theory of beauty for it to become a comprehensive model for understanding design as an everyday phenomenon. A nuanced interpretation of dependent beauty that stresses these diachronic factors will perhaps round out our normative account of design excellence. Saito's work is helpful in articulating the ways in which the everyday constitutes a departure from traditional theorizing, which perhaps makes more explicit the elements of design that diverge from the aesthetic norm. However, it is *how* we incorporate these features in our theory that is key. If we consider the movement's claims on their own merit as together comprising a novel aesthetic theory, important weaknesses begin to emerge that undermine the advances that have been made. These weaknesses prevent me from adopting wholesale this emergent theory as a framework for understanding design.

To begin, let us consider a metaphysical question. We can ask, for instance, what the target of the movement really is: *all* quotidian experiences and objects or only those that are pleasurable? The onus is on Everyday Aesthetics to explain what fidgeting, cleaning, and serving tea have in common that singles these activities out as aesthetic phenomena that also distinguishes them from, perhaps, drinking lemonade, engaging in sexual intercourse, or folding the laundry. Everyday Aesthetics is so far silent on this score, and this silence indicates a lack of ontological commitment on its proponents' part. What comprises the everyday is so broad and so inclusive as to threaten to become virtually meaningless. Without setting up its target clearly and carefully there is no object for this movement to "shoot at"—without demarcating the scope of theoretical concern, there is nothing apparent to provide an aesthetic theory *of*, unless it be an aestheticization of absolutely everything, which Everyday Aestheticists surely do not intend. There is a lesson in this: without at least some metaphysical framework in place, there is nothing to subject to our theoretical gaze, and without this, no aesthetic theory, however radical, can even begin.

Similarly, we can ask what the aesthetic nature of our response to these objects and experiences amounts to: does it necessarily involve pleasure? If so, what kind? Does it engage our judgement? Again, if so, what kind? As the critics of the movement have pointed out, Saito works with a loose sense of the "aesthetic" that has no clear articulation, and seems to run together subjective hedonic responses to objects with those that can withstand critical assessment. But a fully developed theory of our interactions with the everyday must describe which aspect of these interactions is particularly aesthetic, what the aesthetic amounts to in these cases, and how our aesthetic responses can be distinguished from other kinds of normative reactions to the world. For example, Saito notes Leddy's use of an expanded vocabulary of aesthetic concepts such as neat, messy, clean, and dirty but gives no indication of how these concepts are to be deployed. On the one hand, she writes as though dilapidated buildings objectively possess qualities that make them ugly or unaesthetic, which suggests some universal agreement in our response to them, or some form of aesthetic realism. On the other hand, she emphasizes the role that individual feelings play in our quotidian experiences, which suggests that what is aesthetic is simply that which brings us pleasure, of some undetermined kind. This equivocation on Saito's part indicates that, along with a failure to provide an ontology of what constitutes the object of her theory, there is a similar failure to explore the particularly aesthetic nature of our interactions with it. But, as I have attempted to demonstrate in the project thus far, these comprise the two axes of any well-grounded aesthetic theory; without addressing either of them it is unclear, as Dowling has pointed out, what all the aesthetic fuss is about here.

At heart, we can see that these core problems stem from a lack of any theoretical structure or clear methodology to guide the movement—that is, a lack of any synchronic framework within which these theorists can defend their particular claims. Yet without such a strong grounding, Everyday Aesthetics devolves into a series of broad gestures that fail to cohere and fail to amount to a substantial theory that can stand up to analysis and critique. By beginning with—and focusing entirely on—the local, specific, and personal nature of our everyday experiences, Saito in particular fails to address the more general and conceptual metaphysical and epistemological issues that form the basis of any philosophical enquiry. We can see the relevance of her claims for design only because we have come the long way round, as it were, and have first established a strong theoretical foundation which can absorb, assess, and even defend her attempts at innovation.

Everyday Aesthetics' lack of synchronic structure, I believe, arises from its criticism—and almost total dismissal—of the traditions of the aesthetic discipline. Let me return to this critique for a moment. It has two central claims: first, that aesthetics has come to be associated with the philosophy of fine art almost exclusively, and consequently that such an association has led to the physical and metaphysical isolation of the aesthetic from our lives and defining concerns as human. However, the former claim need not entail the latter, and neither is sufficient for a rejection of the aesthetic tradition. With the first claim, I am clearly sympathetic; indeed the driving force of this project has been an attempt to argue for the inclusion of design within the discipline. Philosophical aesthetics *has* come to be dominated by theories of fine art, especially in the twentieth century. In this Everyday Aesthetics is surely correct. And this tendency has indeed led to a view that our experiences of fine art on the spectator model are paradigmatic of aesthetic experience in general. But, as I have shown with design, there is still plenty of room to manoeuvre: we can expand our understanding of what an aesthetic object is by a close study of the central claims of aesthetic ontology itself. Design, we have seen, while it shares features of both art and craft, can be defined as importantly distinct from both. And, while its uniqueness arises from a juxtaposition with art, to acknowledge the primary interests of the discipline is not to theorize design on the *model* of fine art but to bring design's peculiar features into sharper relief. We can also claim that our experience of (or response to) this object differs significantly from that of fine art by, again, closely investigating the nature of aesthetic experience as it has been historically understood. Indeed, contemporary work that has occupied itself with notions of beauty, popular culture, craft, natural environments, and experimental art-forms that push traditional boundaries has sought—within the confines of aesthetic theory—to broaden the scope of its concerns. Again, a consideration of how we are expected to respond to other aesthetic phenomena helps us to articulate the particular form of response that is relevant to design. A wholesale rejection of work in the discipline to date would impoverish rather than assist our theoretical goals because we would be starting with no conception of the aesthetic at all.

Saito is quite right to turn her attention to important diachronic aspects of our definition of and response to aesthetic objects. This sensitivity to the historically and culturally specific has been too often overlooked by the discipline. She is also right to claim with Irvin that areas of our lives outside of museum walls have rich aesthetic texture that demand attention. But insofar as Saito is engaged in aesthetic theory, she must make these moves philosophically coherent and intelligible within the methodological structure of the discipline. And by doing so, she could contribute to its advance. If aesthetics has stagnated because of a preoccupation with fine art, this is good reason to push for reform and innovation in the field but it is not good reason to reject the field altogether.

Everyday Aesthetics' critique concludes that a preoccupation with fine art has led directly to the alienation of the aesthetic from our lives such that it is no longer seen to have any significance for human needs and concerns. Saito's work seems to seek the complete "collapse of the separation between art and everyday life" as the main route to rectifying this imbalance and legitimizing our attention to the everyday, although it is unclear what such a collapse would mean. The focus on fine art by the discipline does not actually entail profound alienation, nor a failure of the discipline as a whole. As I argued in chapter 1, outside of the more radical claims of Clive Bell, even fine art must have a human function else it would be without philosophical interest altogether. Indeed, many of the claims made on behalf of art's uniqueness and profundity were intended to secure for art an autonomous—and significant—place in human experience. Everyday Aesthetics makes the point that too few of us have these experiences of the fine arts for them to make a significant difference for our lives, but this is a practical argument about access, not a conceptual one about the nature of those experiences when we do have them. The movement could very well argue instead that many other aspects of our lives have a similar autonomous and aesthetic texture to which the discipline ought to attend. This would place the mundane and familiar on a continuum, with fine art, perhaps, at its other extreme. In this way Everyday Aesthetics could continue to support the aesthetic as an important autonomous dimension of human existence because the movement would remain grounded in a field that takes this import as having long been assured. Instead, the repudiation of the discipline has left Everyday Aesthetics seeking some other way to make good its claims that the quotidian is philosophically significant, and to do this it has turned to moral theory, or to ethics broadly construed. By attempting to collapse art and daily life, Everyday Aesthetics is suggesting that our aesthetic experiences and judgements are of a piece with our moral, practical, and political judgements as well. And this is to give up on the idea of aesthetic autonomy and the different forms of normativity altogether.

By rejecting one synchronic framework within which to substantiate its claims, Everyday Aesthetics merely replaces it with another—one outside of aesthetic theory. And this reinforces my point that it cannot do without a theoretical framework of some form or another. Yet this move concedes to, rather than resists, the purported alienation that arises from a focus on art. The theorists of the everyday seem to have accepted that any attempt to claim for the quotidian an autonomous aesthetic significance is determined to fail, and hence any defense of aesthetic experience as a rich—yet separate—aspect of human lives is not worth undertaking. This turn away from aesthetic theory is the most damaging to the movement, for it undermines its explicit goals. It also leaves its work particularly vulnerable, for a reliance on an alternative normative framework requires just as clear an articulation and analysis of *that* framework as a reliance on aesthetic theory does. And the movement for the most part equally fails to provide this alternative grounding. Let me turn now to this other normative framework, beginning with a brief mention of Saito's conception of the import of the everyday before considering Haapala's work, which is somewhat more thorough. In both cases, though, we will see that the movement leaves the aesthetic behind in ways that lead to even greater confusion as to the ultimate aims of their theory.

ii. Haapala: The Strange, the Familiar, and the Sense of Place

As I noted at the beginning of the chapter, Saito and Irvin suggest that there is a strong moral element to our aesthetic experiences and judgements. Saito in particular considers five kinds of what she calls moral-aesthetic concerns that include judgements of propriety in one's appearance, of condemnation for environmental "eyesores" and degradation, and of consideration and respect in designing for special needs.[51] These sorts of judgements, she claims, are not simply moral judgements "*regarding* artifacts"[52] but moral-aesthetic judgements because they are "derived from our sensuous (often bodily) experiences … [and not] independent of or outside of our perceptual experience"[53] itself. We make straightforward moral judgements regarding artifacts, irrespective of their appearance, as when we condemn a brand of sneakers because of a company's "poor record regarding child labour and working conditions in its overseas factories,"[54] whatever the sneakers look like or however comfortable they may be. By contrast, the moral qualities that are relevant for Saito "are evidenced by the sensuous aspects of the object"[55] and therefore cannot be clearly divorced from our aesthetic engagement with it. For Saito, "our positive aesthetic appreciation somehow implies our endorsement of these objects/phenomena"[56] and of their continued existence, thus giving all our aesthetic judgements and pleasures an irreducibly moral character.

51 Saito, *Everyday Aesthetics*, 213–220.
52 Ibid., 207.
53 Ibid., 208.
54 Ibid., 206–207.
55 Ibid., 216.
56 Ibid., 141.

But this approach has important inconsistencies. By and large these moral-aesthetic judgements depend upon an "anthropomorphic characterization" whereby we attribute to an artifact such moral qualities as respect, consideration, humility, and so forth,[57] which is a judgement of the actions or intentions of its maker more than of the object itself. For instance, of graffiti and vandalism Saito notes that "we are justified in making a negative aesthetic judgement based upon our negative moral judgement on the act that produced it."[58] Such a formulation makes our aesthetic judgements dependent upon our moral commitments about what is inappropriate or disrespectful, for instance, which are straightforward moral judgements of human actions rather than of artifacts—even though these actions are made visible by the qualities of the objects themselves. But moral judgements—indeed all judgements—depend upon perceptions of objects and actions: this perceptual component is not *thereby* aesthetic merely because it deals with the visual qualities that phenomena possess. Saito here again relies upon an ill-defined notion of what the aesthetic means for her theory.

Further, it seems that for Saito our moral commitments actually precede and determine the kinds of aesthetic experiences we will have. Of smokestacks "belching black smoke," Saito notes that they will "repulse the environmentalists among us" but that they have also been "welcomed and celebrated as a symbol of progress by many."[59] And she acknowledges that whether they constitute "an eyesore and pollution or a proud symbol of economic prosperity *cannot be settled by* analyzing [the smoke's] colour, movement and volume."[60] Thus our moral judgements of these objects

57 Ibid., 209.
58 Ibid., 215.
59 Ibid., 217.
60 Ibid., 218 (italics mine).

do not emerge from our aesthetic experiences as she would like, but rather determine them, and this renders her position similar to that of a long line of aestheticians who have concerned themselves with the moral, political, and social implications of the arts, and with the ethical aspects of our responses to them, irrespective of their beauty or excellence. In both cases, the moral aspects of our judgements remain external to our aesthetic appraisals, which are, in turn, dependent upon them. Saito's approach does not compellingly provide the aesthetics of the everyday with a unique and important role in our moral lives; we would be environmentalists, for example, no matter the colour of the smoke, and our environmental commitments would themselves determine what we find beautiful or ugly rather than the other way around. The weakness in her account stems from the fact that we can evaluate the same object in different ways: when we consider its moral, social, political, or personal significance, this consideration *can* remain independent of our purely aesthetic responses to the same phenomenon. What I sought to make clear in chapter 2 is that our normative judgements have different logical forms, of which the aesthetic is a specific and singular kind. Saito has not dissolved the difference between these various normative reactions and judgements because she has not examined the individual features that make them unique. In order to claim that aesthetic judgements are quasi-moral—and, indeed, then, that moral judgements are quasi-aesthetic—Saito must first provide us with a compelling and novel account of normativity that challenges the ways in which philosophy has long understood these terms. And this she does not do. Let me turn to a different approach to the ethical aspect of the everyday that pays closer attention to the alternative synchronic framework on which it relies.

Arto Haapala's work in "On the Aesthetics of the Everyday: Familiarity, Strangeness and the Meaning of Place" sketches out a way in which the ethical, broadly construed, is directly imbedded in our everyday lives. Haapala can best be understood as addressing meta-theoretical questions about the import of the everyday rather than contributing directly to our aesthetic understanding of mundane objects and quotidian experiences. This is both his strength and his weakness, for while he links the everyday to the broader philosophical goal of human self-understanding, he does this at the expense of its specifically aesthetic character; Haapala's claims also in the end render the aesthetic aspect of the everyday secondary to our ethical-existential commitments, and he labours to maintain the aesthetic within his theoretical compass. Nevertheless, his approach better articulates the connection between the everyday and human lives and concerns.

I mentioned at the beginning of this chapter that, for Haapala, traditional aesthetics has been focused on what he calls "strangeness," where art, as the paradigmatic aesthetic object, is "something special and not ordinary."[61] Strangeness for Haapala is not the completely alien but refers to the unfamiliar and new, to things "we are not used to seeing and hearing."[62] Artworks, understood as original and profound, embody this idea; their status as unique stems from their being precisely unlike the quotidian and familiar. Even with contemporary forms that make use of everyday objects and subject matters, like Andy Warhol's *Brillo Boxes*, or more generally, photography and film, "in the context of art the everyday loses its everydayness: it becomes something extraordinary,"[63] which, one might say, is precisely its point. Saito has also

61 Haapala, "Aesthetics of the Everyday," 40.
62 Ibid., 43.
63 Ibid., 51.

recognized the "strangeness" of art on the traditional approach: "art, whatever its designation, no matter how inclusive that notion becomes, and even when its intent is to blur the distinction from life, is necessarily characterized as an *exception to* or *commentary on* everyday objects and affairs."[64] Strangeness for Haapala also refers to our responses to objects: when we face the unfamiliar, we "pay special attention to it," we observe it, try to categorize or understand it, and we become sensitive to its "aesthetic potentiality" because "our senses are more alert in a strange milieu" than at home. In our attention to the strange, we adopt an "outsider's gaze" or a "visitor's curiosity," and this stance is also "very much in the forefront of aesthetics,"[65] as we have seen with the spectator model I outlined above. Putting works in galleries and museums, causing us to take "time out" to experience them, is also forcing us to see with new eyes, as it were: a urinal on a gallery wall demands a response from us that one in a latrine does not; china and brooches under glass in a museum call our attention to them in ways that the same pieces in cupboards and dresser drawers would rarely do.

In contrast to an aesthetic of strangeness, Haapala is interested in theorizing the everyday as an aesthetic of the familiar, but by this he does not mean merely paying attention to objects that are quotidian, mundane, and known. He writes, "I shall not consider aesthetic objects that attract our attention and stand out in our normal daily routines"; he instead seeks to consider "exactly the opposite—what is the aesthetic relevance of the everyday per se?"[66] To approach this deeper relevance, Haapala's existential account ties familiarity to the notion of place, in the sense that living somewhere or "settling

64 Saito, *Everyday Aesthetics*, 40.
65 Haapala, "Aesthetics of the Everyday," 44.
66 Ibid., 40.

down" involves making an environment *jemeinig*, or "one's own."[67] He adopts this term from Heidegger and argues that "placing ourselves within an environment" is the process of "home-building" where "home" is "a place where everything is familiar."[68] Even a work of art can become familiar in this sense if, for instance, a van Gogh has for years hung above the fireplace, or the Coliseum is something one walks past on the way to work each day, just as the most quotidian objects, like phone booths or transit buses, become strange if we are visiting a foreign city and seeing them through the eyes of an outsider.[69] Home-building is not merely a matter of making things familiar and exerting our control over them, however; *Jemeinigkeit* is the "way of being" of human existence itself. When we "place" ourselves in an environment and make it familiar, "we start to construe connections that are significant for us," and so the notion of place becomes related to those of attachment and belonging.[70] For Haapala, following Heidegger, "It would be impossible to live in a constant state of strangeness, of not creating any significant ties, of not getting rooted to any degree"[71] because home-building is part of what it means to be human.[72] We cannot live without having a sense of belonging to some place, whether physical or figurative, and we forge this sense of belonging in part through a process of *familiarization* whereby we create attachments to our surroundings. Haapala writes that "[i]t is the process of settling down that finally makes the surroundings familiar to me, and at the same time makes the surroundings my place."[73] The familiar in this regard can be contrasted with the strange, not in

67 Ibid., 45.
68 Ibid., 46.
69 Ibid., 44.
70 Ibid., 46.
71 Ibid., 49.
72 W. G. Sebald's novel *Austerlitz* is an exemplary literary foray into the breakdown that occurs from an attempt to deliberately inhabit the strange (New York: Modern Library, 2001).
73 Haapala, "Aesthetics of the Everyday," 47.

the sense of the everyday versus the unusual, but instead as that to which we are attached and to which we belong, compared to being in a state of homelessness and alienation. And for Haapala, too, the relation between object and subject on the spectator model, as one of strangeness, is also one of (controlled) alienation.

Haapala's sketch of the familiar makes two further significant claims. First, our relation to our surroundings and our sense of place "constitutes what we are"; this is what he means by *Jemeinigkeit* being the way of our existence. "How we exist determines our identities," and how we exist is in a web of relations of attachment and belonging whereby we create a sense of home.[74] But we create these relations through a process of interpretation that is not "necessarily, not even primarily a conscious and deliberate search for meanings."[75] Interpretation in the hermeneutic sense of Heidegger and Gadamer is an ongoing activity that is constitutive of what it means to be human; it is a creation of connections through living and working in an environment—"a matter of action" rather than intellection, and hence one that "takes place on the level of praxis rather than theory."[76] Insofar as we are engaged in our daily practices and activities, we are "placing" ourselves and forging a sense of belonging, and these activities constitute interpretation in the broad sense of making meaning rather than rationally deciphering a meaning or significance that is already there.

Second, this activity of interpretation and familiarization includes our "relations to nonhuman entities and events"[77] as much as it does to the human ties we forge through our connections as sisters, neighbours, teachers, and so on when we make a place for

74 Ibid., 47.
75 Ibid., 46.
76 Ibid., 47.
77 Ibid.

ourselves through our intersubjective commitments within a community. What gives us a sense of belonging is not only other people but the very things with which we surround ourselves and interact. Design, in particular, makes up the bulk of these nonhuman entities. The majority of Haapala's examples are of designed objects: our homes and offices with all of their furnishings, the buildings in our neighbourhoods along with the cars and phone booths and details of our local streetscapes, the tools we use in our work and daily chores, and so on. Certainly the environs that become familiar "do not have to be man-made":[78] we can feel a sense of belonging to a natural environment—and it can become familiar in Haapala's sense. But in an increasingly urbanized and commodified world, our environs are most often artificial and manufactured, with the natural setting for these serving more as a backdrop for our activities and lives than as something to which we directly connect or in which we feel most directly at home. Haapala's account gives to the familiar an existential import that can be understood as broadly ethical and that differs considerably from the significance normally attributed to our rarified experiences of fine art, or to art's more direct social or political implications. The everyday is deeply important for human self-understanding even while, and precisely because, it escapes our notice as being always before our eyes. Here the moral aspect of the everyday is internal to our conception of its familiarity, rather than an external judgement we make about objects that determines our aesthetic pleasures as we saw with Saito's claims.

However, while Haapala speaks to the import of the everyday, it must be asked what all this has to do with *aesthetics* as a discipline. In what way is Haapala's work not a general philosophical anthropology, a contribution to existential phenomenology, or

78 Ibid., 43.

even a theory of human identity? And if it is any or all of these, what *also* makes it of particularly aesthetic interest? One possible response is to suggest that, with a focus on praxis, the interpretive activity of familiarization is itself an aesthetic act, one that is more fundamental than the aesthetic character of the particular activities of the everyday and their attendant pleasures that Saito and Irvin focused on. But Haapala specifically rejects this option. He claims he is not interested in "the aesthetics of living or the aestheticization of everyday life"[79] and so will not provide an account of creative self-fashioning on a Nietzschean or Foucaldian model, although such an account would situate aesthetics at the core of human lives and concerns. Haapala hints at a second possible response when he notes that his interpretive relations to objects and other people "constitute me as a cultural entity."[80] Here, rather than focusing on the aesthetic activity of self-making, one could suggest that humans are aesthetic *objects* insofar as their identity is the product of an interpretive act, or is determined by their cultural and aesthetic surroundings. With either case—our lives as interpretive activities, or selves as interpreted products—one could argue for the interpenetration of the aesthetic and the (broadly) ethical, but Haapala drops this second option as well, and seeks instead to make a case for the particularly aesthetic nature of the everyday, much as Saito and Irvin did, although in this case Haapala seeks to contextualize the aesthetic within the existential framework he has laid out, with dubious results.

Haapala is aware of the difficulty of showing how his project is specifically an aesthetic one, and of the problems of isolating the aesthetic element of the everyday within the philosophical

79 Ibid., 40.
80 Ibid., 47.

structure he has provided. Because strangeness, for him, is the basis for most aesthetic experience, he notes that "in a state of familiarity ... we tend to lose this kind of sensitivity." "By definition there is less distancing, less possibility of appreciation"[81] with the everyday simply because, as familiar, it is meant to pass beneath our direct notice. And he invokes Heidegger's analysis of the tool, *das Zeug*, to highlight this point. A tool exists between the user and its purpose, and "as long as it functions properly there is no need to pay attention to it."[82] It is only when the tool malfunctions that we start to see it as an object, inspect it, and consider it as separate from ourselves. Until and unless that happens, tools—and our familiar surroundings in general—"disappear into their function" as background, as things we are used to, or as things we use to achieve our everyday purposes.[83] To bring these things to aesthetic attention seems to contradict the point of Haapala's focus on the everyday, as to do so would appear to render them "strange." Nevertheless, Haapala gestures in the direction of an aesthetics of the familiar. "Place," he claims, "has its own aesthetics" that is "stamped by our existential structures," making it more subjective than traditional aesthetic theorizing.[84] He finds that the familiarity of the everyday can give us "pleasure through a kind of comforting stability" in objects and activities that are routine and safe, that make us feel "homey and in control."[85] We can "from time to time sit down and set aside the needs and demands of the everyday and enjoy the familiar scene"[86]—of the fields in which we work, or the café on the corner. And we "enjoy

81 Ibid., 50.
82 Ibid., 49.
83 Ibid.
84 Ibid., 50.
85 Ibid., 50, 52.
86 Ibid., 51.

scenes familiar to us because we know them well and because we are deeply rooted in them."[87] Our pleasure comes not from what makes these things strange or new, but from their utterly ordinary and quotidian familiarity. Beyond these gestures however, Haapala can only define the aesthetic aspect of the everyday in broadly negative terms, as an aesthetics of "the lacking," or of the "quiet fascination of the absence of the visual, auditory and any other demands from the surroundings."[88] What he calls to our attention is, ironically, that which commands no attention at all.

This proposal seems to reduce the aesthetic to some kind of quiet pleasure we feel when things are in their place and we are in control; a gentle sense that "all is right with the world" and we know where we belong in it. But these comments hardly amount to an aesthetics of the everyday as a distinct and significant part of his broader philosophical goals. They first seem to belie Haapala's aim of situating the aesthetic within an ethical framework: feelings of comfort and stability may have a kind of moral character, but it is not clear how these feelings are evidence for the claims he makes about familiarization as having an ethical import, or for the philosophical relevance of the everyday for human lives. We may simply take pleasure in what is comfortable, without this pleasure having any deeper existential or even philosophical significance. Second, it is not clear how such pleasures are specifically *aesthetic*: surely a hot bath or a cozy seat by the fire provide comfort and a sense of security in the way he intimates, and these feelings accompany, or are presupposed in, a large number of our quotidian bodily or sensuous enjoyments. In calling these familiar and quiet experiences specifically aesthetic Haapala is in danger of collapsing bodily and aesthetic pleasures much as Saito and Irvin did, and he will

87 Ibid.
88 Ibid., 52.

have to provide some kind of determination of the boundaries of what is aesthetic—as opposed to merely perceptual or sensory—experience, which he also fails to do. Haapala's conception of the aesthetic dimension of the everyday seems oddly reductive: even if our familiar pleasures are not direct bodily sensations, they seem to be metaphors for these same feelings: the comfort and security we feel in our homes or neighbourhoods is not unlike the more direct comfort of a soft chair or the warmth of a bath. While Haapala has provided us with a philosophical framework within which to situate the ethical and existential components of the everyday, he nevertheless neglects the question of what makes these components of particular aesthetic interest.

What is arresting about Haapala's theoretical goal is the central place he makes for the everyday in human existence at a more fundamental level than Saito's theory provides. Other work that focuses on the creative aspects of our existence (like that by Nietzsche or Foucault), or on human lives as creative products (Danto, perhaps, and Margolis), have drawn on analogies with the fine arts as practices or products to make their claims. Haapala's conception is original in that it uses the everyday to make a similar point. But the difficulty in focusing on the everyday is in making the case for this project to be specifically an aesthetic one. Drawing parallels from art to human existence neatly avoids this problem because it trades on what has long been considered to be of aesthetic importance. Because the everyday is so new to aesthetics—if indeed we can yet claim that it *is* part of aesthetics—the link is weaker in Haapala's case than in others. Unlike Saito, who attempted to claim for the everyday an aesthetic dimension, Haapala takes this link for granted as having been successful, and assumes the problems of an everyday aesthetic have already been resolved, when in most cases they have not yet even been addressed. One could suggest that the obstacle here is purely superficial, and a matter of disciplinary categorization more than anything else. Haapala may have more in common with postmodern thinkers on culture and technology (Heidegger, Benjamin, Baudrillard) than with aestheticians per se, and he could plausibly make his philosophical claims for the ethical import of the everyday without specific reference to aesthetics at all. He did not want to go this route, however, and remains committed to establishing the aesthetic relevance of the everyday for human lives and concerns. Yet, while he argues for the importance of the familiar, he does so at the expense of its aesthetic character, and this underscores the way in which he has substituted one theoretical framework for another. Haapala is more thorough than Saito in articulating and defending the ethical-existential theory on which he relies to demonstrate the significance of the everyday. And indeed the quotidian and the familiar may well have deep import for human lives and concerns: as part of our moral experiences, as contributing to our cultural and personal identities, as providing a sense of belonging in the spaces we call home. But all of these claims take us a long way from establishing any *aesthetic* significance for the everyday, which was the putative goal of the movement at its inception.

What I have sought to show in this analysis of Everyday Aesthetics is that, while it provides a compelling critique of the current preoccupations of the discipline, and a strong call for an expansion of its concerns into the realm of the familiar and mundane as opposed to the exotic and transcendent, it has so far failed in its attempts to explicitly formulate an alternative aesthetic theory. Its relevance for an aesthetic of design is thereby diminished: we can pay heed to the peculiar characteristics of everyday experience Saito has highlighted and incorporate them more fully into the theory of design beauty presently on the table, but we cannot accept the tacit switch to moral/ethical theory to ground these characteristics without leaving behind the aesthetic aspects of design altogether. And this I am unwilling to do.

3. DESIGN AND THE EVERYDAY

The question arises as to whether a purely aesthetic theory of the everyday is possible, or whether quotidian objects and experiences simply resist analysis in broadly traditional ways. Certainly the features Saito highlighted seem to render cultural practices and artifacts, such as ballgames and chairs, unrecognizable as "normal" aesthetic objects, and our interactions with, or responses to, them very unlike the way we have been expected to approach and appreciate other aesthetic phenomena. Nevertheless, I would like to conclude this chapter with a suggestion: the theory of design I have constructed can itself stand as a contribution to an aesthetic of the everyday, albeit one that is perhaps more cautious than these theorists might wish. Cautious it may be, but I would also like to suggest that it is more fully developed than what this movement has so far offered, and thus better able to withstand critical analysis. I ended chapter 3 by claiming that to understand design we must focus on its everydayness. The opposite is perhaps equally true: we can best begin an aesthetics of the everyday if we focus on design. Briefly, I will indicate the ways in which an aesthetics of design can meet the needs of the movement, and will defend my work against some anticipated objections.

To begin with, while design is clearly *part* of the everyday, it admittedly does not encompass all that the movement wished to include in its theoretical scope. Yet casting their net as wide as they have has led to ontological confusion: the colours of dirt on a road, or the feel of the sun are equally part of natural beauty and not specific to the everyday; cleaning, chopping, and repairing are clearly quotidian but not clearly objects of any kind. With design as I have defined it, we have a set of objects that have everyday uses, and that can be distinguished from art, craft, and nature by their functional qualities: quiddity and immanence are central to design from its very inception. A narrower circumscription of the target phenomenon that limits it to a set of identifiable objects allows us at least to claim that design is a central portion of our everyday lives, and to construct an aesthetic of the immanent and the familiar on its basis. Once accomplished, this aesthetic may be expanded beyond a narrow set of objects to include other quotidian experiences, but to begin so broadly leaves us without a clear picture of what the movement is aiming for. Design not only achieves this clarity but, built into the definition of design, we can already see in nascent form the ideas of framelessness, familiarity, and active use that the movement made central to its claims. From the outset, design must be understood in part diachronically, and as resisting ahistorical definition in necessary and sufficient terms.

Everyday Aesthetics may be critical of my approach as one that continues to be dominated by the model of fine art, defining design only in negative terms against this central paradigm. I would respond that, first, definitions of fine art are not clear-cut or unproblematic, as I have attempted to show. This model cannot be as dominant as they suggest, if the properties that make art an aesthetic object remain so inconclusive. Fine art has been variously defined in terms of its formal properties as an object, and in terms of the expressive activities that produce it, and these two approaches have not yet been reconciled by any means. Attention to the fine arts may be an empirical trend, but what makes them pivotal to the discipline is not yet a conceptual certainty. Second,

I have endeavoured to argue that what differentiates design from art (and craft) does not thereby render it inferior to these other phenomena; design is not diminished by the comparisons I have made. Because fine art has become so central to the discipline, to define design with no reference to it is to suggest that design has somehow arisen ex nihilo as an aesthetic object, with no relation to the field. Yet the very fact that design is an aesthetic object means that to capture our theoretical attention it must share *some* qualities that other aesthetic phenomena possess. Finally, central to my depiction of design has been its functional, mute, and quotidian character, and this character marks it out not only as unique, but as intimately connected to our everyday lives and concerns. Design, then, can itself provide a model for what an ontology of the everyday must accomplish, as one axis of a fully developed aesthetic theory.

Second, a focus on beauty has allowed me to define and delineate the specific kind of pleasures our quotidian experiences provide, and to distinguish these from other forms of pleasures and judgements that are not relevant to an aesthetic theory of the everyday, which the movement, we have seen, has been unable to do. By arguing that aesthetic judgements have a unique logical structure, and their attendant pleasures a particular feel, I have shown that judgements of the dependent beauty of design require a category of their own, with features that judgements of nature, art, and craft do not and cannot share. The functional beauty of design marks out its everyday character, which can be experienced only through active use as demanding singular and specific attention.

It may be objected that my emphasis on Kantian theory restrains me to a spectator model for design that the movement sought to reject: all judgements of beauty are, after all, disinterested and merely reflective, and perhaps too propositional for the holistic approach these theorists sought to take. Yet this objection turns on how we understand the operation of judgement, and how we interpret Kant's theory of it. When interacting with design, we are not dispassionate critics, sizing up the merits and demerits of a particular object with the intention of pronouncing on its aesthetic excellence, as though we were judges at a competition or curators of a show: disinterest does not refer to a stance we take towards the object but simply to a freedom from immediate desire for it. And while, as we have seen, the Kantian model is complex in its analysis of the mental processes involved in a judgement of beauty, there is nothing in this analysis to suggest a long period of ratiocination before we make a positive approbation. Reflective judgements are conceptually complex, but need not be temporally prolonged: "X is beautiful," even on Kant's view, is an immediate—in the sense of unmediated—response to the world. And if "X is beautiful" still seems too propositional, we can ask the movement's advocates what other kind of response to the aesthetic they have in mind, unless it is to be some inchoate pleasure that is ultimately untheorizable. With dependent beauty in particular, I have sought to demonstrate that these judgements can only arise from an active engagement with the object, one that requires various diachronic factors that include familiarity and localized conceptual knowledge. In this way, my conception of design has attempted to develop the second axis of a robust aesthetic theory, and do so in a way that highlights its particularly quotidian nature.

Finally, though, it may be argued particularly in reference to Haapala's work that even if my approach is not directly alienating on a spectator model, I nevertheless can only call attention to the everydayness of design by first making it strange and singling it out for specific theoretical consideration, and this makes our relation to design one that is alienating. Does my theory not achieve its goals only by rendering design *unfamiliar* and thus by depriving it of the very import that Everyday Aesthetics sought to capture? Am I not, by making design an aesthetic object, taking it out of its quotidian context and altering its status in some way? If what is important about the everyday is that it generally passes beneath our notice, it seems that I have shed light on it only by disregarding what makes it important in the first place. This, I would counter, is as much a problem for Saito and Irvin as it is for my aesthetic of design, a problem that Thomas Leddy has well articulated:

> It would seem that we need to make some sort of distinction between the aesthetics of everyday life ordinarily experienced and the aesthetics of ordinary life extraordinarily experienced. However, any attempt to increase the aesthetic intensity of our everyday life-experiences will tend to push those experiences in the direction of the extraordinary. One can only conclude that there is a tension with the very concept of the aesthetics of ordinary life.[89]

Saito senses this tension when she writes, "I do not think we need to exoticize" the content of the everyday,[90] but her method of responding to this challenge is to focus on "eyesores," or the dilapidated, the messy, and the dirty, as those things that prompt the everyday (aesthetic) actions and decisions of cleaning, repairing, discarding, and so on. Yet Saito's response is one that Haapala has

89 Thomas Leddy, "The Nature of Everyday Aesthetics," in Light and Smith, *Aesthetics of Everyday Life*, 18. And Dowling acknowledges this tension when he writes that "[i]f aspects of the ordinary that are found to be appreciable are *thereby* lifted (in this respect) into the realm of the extraordinary, it would seem that (contrasting other domains) there can be no such thing as correct or appropriate appreciation of the everyday *qua* everyday" ("Aesthetics of Daily Life," 233).

90 Saito, *Everyday Aesthetics*, 42.

already seen to be insufficient: following Heidegger's discussion of *das Zeug*, if such quotidian things come to our attention only when they break down or wear out, this is precisely what makes them strange for us. While Saito seeks to theorize the ordinary, she may be doing so by first making it extraordinary. Irvin's preoccupation with the local and particular faces the same problem, although more implicitly: by attending to the aesthetic pleasures of otherwise unconscious acts like fidgeting and so on, Irvin makes them self-conscious, and once we begin to reflect upon what had heretofore been beneath our notice (once we realize that we scratch our heads or jiggle our rings when we're thinking), they are no longer familiar and unconscious acts precisely because we have made them the objects of our gaze. The weakest aspect of Haapala's work, in his gestures towards an aesthetics of the familiar and the comfortable, is weak in part because he was aware of this tension and tried to find a way to aestheticize the ordinary without first making it extraordinary.

If there is a way in which my conception of design escapes this dilemma, it is by softening the notion of the strange, and its juxtaposition with the familiar. We can agree with Haapala that when things like tools work, they tend to disappear into their functions as background to our activities. But it is not only when they break down that they come to our attention: we also notice things when they work extremely well, when they perform their functions with an ease or grace that calls for our appreciation. And this appreciation is the kind of aesthetic judgement that is particular to design. Design excellence is extraordinary in the sense that some objects are *better than* the norm, but this does not make them strange or remove them from the everyday any more than it makes them honorary works of art: they remain the chairs, knives, and coffee-pots that we use everyday. It is just that at certain times they come to demand our aesthetic as opposed to cognitive, practical, or moral attention. What my conception of design as dependent beauty demonstrates is that we can appreciate an object only by maintaining it within its quotidian context: its beauty comes to light only through everyday use, and only when it succeeds in performing its function to a degree that merits our approbation. Indeed, by juxtaposing design with art as that which is neither profound nor original, my theory is perhaps best placed to examine the aesthetic aspect of these objects without first rendering them uncommon or unfamiliar. We can acknowledge the polarity between the strange and the familiar—as between the profound and the ordinary—as a heuristic device rather than as the strong conceptual distinction Haapala had wished it to be: its purpose has been to lead us towards an alternative method of theorizing the aesthetics of design, and, once that goal is achieved, it can be left behind. That is, it may not be that the aspects of the everyday that are most important are important *because* they are familiar and ordinary and thus escape our attention, but that we fail to grasp their importance simply because we generally fail to notice them. Design is important not because it fades into the background or falls under the radar of our conscious activities: we have simply failed to notice its importance because of its very mundane quiddity, and the task of an aesthetics of design—as with a fully developed theory of the everyday—is to bring these quotidian elements of our lives to philosophical attention.

Again what I wish to highlight in an analysis of Everyday Aesthetics is that by ignoring or dismissing the aesthetic tradition (with all of its faults), these theorists could not develop a coherent theory of the familiar or of our responses to it. They were left without a clear sense of what makes the everyday aesthetically unique, or why its aesthetic character may matter to our lives on its own terms. They were forced to turn to other forms of normative theory to legitimize their calls for paying philosophical attention to those aspects of human existence that generally fall beneath our notice. In contrast to the efforts of this movement, my goal has been to bring design—as part of the everyday—directly to the attention of philosophical aesthetics and argue for its inclusion as an object suitable for consideration by the discipline. And this has meant subjecting it to the same rigorous analysis that historically has been directed to fine art, natural beauty, and the like. Through this analysis I have sought to provide an aesthetic theory of design that can stand on its own as part of the discipline, but also to demonstrate that such a theory can serve as a model—although surely not the only one—for a robust aesthetics of everyday life. What has remained implicit in this work has been a defense of the aesthetic as an autonomous and significant facet of human experience, one that is reflected in design as much as in any other aesthetic phenomenon, one that needs no further support from other philosophical areas. Implicit, too, has been a sense that a theory of design can itself provide a challenge to the traditional ways in which the field has approached its subject matter. Unlike the movement of Everyday Aesthetics, however, this critique arises from within the framework of the discipline itself. It is time to make these commitments explicit, and I will do so as I close out this work.

Conclusion: The Significance of Design

I will close here by making a couple of meta-theoretical observations about the significance of design that emerge from the various elements of the project thus far. It has been clear throughout this work that I rely upon the long tradition of aesthetic theory to make a case for design, and that I situate my claims directly within its general purview. One of the reasons for this is a commitment to the aesthetic as an equally important—if distinguishable—part of human lives and concerns. This importance has been neglected by philosophy as a whole, in large part for the reasons given by theorists of the everyday: if aesthetics has become identified with theories of fine art, it is more vulnerable to being dismissed as a highly specialized field preoccupied with a phenomenon that has no direct bearing on the lives of a great many of us. Design, because of its ubiquity and its embeddedness in our daily lives, can serve to illustrate this importance, and a theory of design can represent the need for a realignment of aesthetics as a central part of our philosophical endeavours. This reliance upon the aesthetic tradition, however, must not be mistaken for a wholesale adoption of it as though it were without some need of revision. Indeed, a carefully constructed theory of design is uniquely situated to challenge some of the more entrenched positions in the field, and to provide proposed solutions to some of its more intractable problems. Unlike the broad criticism of aesthetics that served as a point of departure for the Everyday movement, however, the theory of design I have presented here itself stands as a form of immanent critique. And it is with this that I would like to begin. We saw in chapters 1 and 2 that I laid out the ontological and normative problems in terms of somewhat stark dichotomies between object and activity on the one hand, and between objective and subjective approaches to beauty or aesthetic experience on the other. In both cases design offers an alternative to these dichotomous strategies and aids in their resolution.

Our ontology of design highlights the inadequacies of ahistorical and essentialist definitions of the aesthetic object. A focus on the qualities of the object alone led to formalism, which suffers the problem of counter-examples: design, craft, natural beauty—indeed, all objects—have form of some kind and cannot be distinguished on this basis. Theories that focused on expression as a singular originating activity also failed because this activity could neither be adequately described, nor picked out by the audience when faced only with a completed product. With design, we can see the need for a consideration of both object and activity, but in importantly different ways. First, while all designed objects are functional, they are not unique in this, and a definition of design cannot end here. However, highlighting this functional quality serves a theoretical need: design cannot be understood outside of the context of its use, and this requires cultural and historically specific knowledge on our part when we approach it. Our quotidian interactions with design are written into its ontological structure: it cannot stand outside of history.

Further, because this function is not unique or "significant" in the way that form was characterized by Bell in particular, our definition of design does not presuppose that it is primarily an aesthetic object or assume that it has some aesthetic import. Its aesthetic interest arises instead in our responses to it. As a mere candidate for aesthetic appreciation, design exemplifies the way that anything at all can be experienced aesthetically, that these experiences can be more common and intimate than those of art, and moreover that an ontology of the object and a normative theory of our response to it are distinct and importantly separable things.

Second, when we turn to the activity of design making, we find that objects with no discernible author can be candidates for aesthetic appraisal, a notion that heretofore had been reserved for natural beauty. Unlike the unique and singular in nature, however, design is characterized by a lack of originality or by its multiplicity and replicability. Not tying design to an identifiable author allows for its maker to be spread across a number of individuals, in different locations, that incorporate mechanized production on a large scale. And this breaks a long-standing identification of the author with an activity that must be in some sense personal, original, and profound. Here again, aesthetic theory has equivocated between what makes something a work of art, and what makes it aesthetically important, and design breaks this connection. With design we do not need to find a way to "read into" a work the particular emotions or thoughts of its author, nor try to theorize how this activity has been made manifest. That an object has been made is important, but how it has been is largely irrelevant to its candidacy as an object of appreciation. Design in this way stands in a relation between object and activity, as its definition relies on neither exclusively but incorporates elements of both.

When we turn to our appraisal of design, we are faced with an object that is not already purported to be significant or profound, original or expressive but that is immanent, mute, and functional. No aesthetic qualities or forms of evaluation underwrite its characterization, which allows our normative theory an element of freedom from presuppositions that many theories of art appreciation do not share. But in theories of beauty, too, there has been a tendency to work on one or the other side of a disjunction: either beauty is a quality an object possesses, leading to a form of aesthetic realism with attendant metaphysical and epistemological problems, or beauty is a kind of response to or pleasure in the object, which results in an indefensible aesthetic subjectivisim. For design, I have sought a way out of this impasse by locating beauty in the faculty of aesthetic judgement itself. Judgements of beauty have an objective aspect in that they make a claim to rightness and require justification, but they do not rely upon a realist account of aesthetic value as part of the furniture of the world, and they allow for disagreement and differences of taste. Judgements of beauty likewise have a subjective aspect in that they are keyed to felt pleasure as part of what makes them legitimately our own but because this pleasure is tempered by rational determination, it does not dissolve into an inchoate sensation that then relies on some external expert to defend our notions of beauty or taste.

Eva Schaper provided the model for an aesthetic based upon judgement, deftly arguing that beauty is irreducibly normative—hence not a fact but a value, which by lying on a continuum between gustatory and moral judgements shares important facets of each: felt pleasure on the one hand, and reasoned justification on the other. Such a model allows us to extend the notion of the aesthetic beyond the fine arts to other kinds of experience, including, crucially, design. With the adoption of Kantian theory, I have been able to argue that anything at all can be beautiful, provided we have the right experience at the right time and make a judgement of the appropriate kind, but I have also been able to show how judgements of design in particular differ from those of natural beauty, fine art, and even craft. If beauty or aesthetic excellence is located in our judgements, we can begin with an ontology of our object that is free of normative considerations: even mundane and mute objects can be candidates for appraisal, provided we understand that appraisal correctly. The real distinction between design, art, craft, and natural beauty will come, then, in the different ways that we respond to these objects rather than in some set of qualities that make them unique. And an appropriately complex theory of the aesthetic that makes beauty internal to judgement can account for the differing intuitions that created the impasse in the first place.

The Kantian model is rich enough to allow for a further refinement in our understanding of aesthetic judgements: while all aesthetic responses have a number of qualities in common—disinterest, freedom from concepts, a play of the rational faculties—we can yet distinguish between pure or free judgements of nature and the dependent beauty that is particular to art and, further, to design. While our appreciation of art is tied to the aesthetic ideas that ground its metaphorical meaning, with design we instead respond to the way an object performs its function with excellence and style. And this response requires an element of conceptual knowledge that is not present in other kinds of aesthetic judgements, that still respects their general form, and that also points to the diachronic or localized nature of our interactions with everyday objects. By beginning with Kant we have been able to provide a general theory of aesthetic judgement that resolves the tensions present in other normative accounts of beauty, but that also applies equally—if differently—to the broadest possible range of phenomena. One of the benefits of an account that locates beauty in our responses to the world is that it does not privilege one kind of object over another as meriting our aesthetic attention.

If anything at all can be beautiful, we can also claim that the aesthetic is more closely interwoven with our day-to-day lives than theories that focus on fine art can suggest. And this leads me to the second area of significance for design that has been implicit in this project. While a focus on design has allowed me to tackle, and attempt to resolve, a number of problems in the field, it has also highlighted the importance of the aesthetic for human lives and concerns. The Everyday movement worried that our lives were seen to lack aesthetic texture because an identification of the aesthetic with fine art had led to an alienation of the discipline. The movement's response was to reject tradition, and begin anew to infuse everyday life with aesthetic import. However, the idea that we live in some kind of aesthetic vacuum can gain hold only if we also believe that aesthetic judgement applies only to specific areas or objects—like fine art, or music or literature. The movement is premised upon this belief: it tacitly accepted the alienated view of the aesthetic that also formed the basis of its critique of the field, and because of this, it was unable to provide a compelling alternative aesthetic theory and was forced to turn to an ethical account instead. A robust account of design, by contrast, with a broader view of both the way that aesthetic judgement operates and the objects to which it applies, is better situated to claim that quotidian life indeed does have aesthetic texture.

But more than providing an alternative model for a theory of the everyday, this account of design defends the aesthetic as being deeply implicated in what it means to be human. Having demonstrated that our daily activities and the mundane objects with which we surround ourselves involve judgements of a specifically aesthetic nature—having shown that beauty is indeed one of our priorities—this project also defends the discipline of aesthetics as having greater philosophical import than many would like to believe. We do not seek out aesthetic experiences only in museums or on Sunday walks in the park; and we are not only spectators, admirers, and critics of aesthetic phenomena. Unlike in the case of fine art, we are consumers, purchasers, decorators, users, and inhabitants of designed environments—all of us. Once considerations of utility, practicality, morality, and so on are satisfied—or, at times, in spite of these considerations—there remains an aesthetic element to our choices of this coffee-pot over that one, to our alignment of the sofa with the window just so, to the colour of our kitchen walls, and to the route we take when we walk to work in the morning. It is the task of my field to investigate this aesthetic element of human existence in general, and if it has not done so in recent years because of a preoccupation with the arts, a theory of design can help recall it to its broader purpose.

This purpose, as Roger Scruton has noted, is to try to "isolate a mental act or state of mind that is in some way deeply implicated in our lives as rational beings"; only by doing so can aesthetics justify itself as a central part of the philosophical enterprise.[1] Of course my account of design does not explicitly undertake this investigation so much as call for it to be undertaken, yet we can see that some of the groundwork for it is already in place. If we return to Kantian theory for a moment, we will recall that judgement in general is identical with human awareness, and aesthetic judgement represents one particular kind. Kant's claims about beauty were intended to contribute to a final exposition of what constitutes rational agency, an exposition that could not be completed without a consideration of the faculty of judgement in its reflective capacity. That is, alongside but not inferior to judgements of fact, of the

1 Roger Scruton, "In Search of the Aesthetic," *British Journal of Aesthetics* 47, no. 3 (2007): 238.

good, of the necessary and the pragmatic, lie judgements of beauty, and together they form a picture of what it means to be a human being in the world. This account of design, having wrested beauty from the narrow domain of the fine arts and having restored it to a place in our daily lives and concerns, in fact contributes to this broader goal of human self-understanding. Design is at times mundane and unexceptional and often overlooked. We do not always approach our cars, toothbrushes, or cubicles with admiration. We do not always make moral or cognitive judgements about our environs and their objects either; an aesthetic response is but one form of response, yet this form contributes equally to what makes us human. And this a theory of design has also sought to demonstrate.

BIBLIOGRAPHY

Abrams, M. H. "Kant and the Theology of Art." *Notre Dame English Journal* 13 (1981): 75–106.

Abrams, M. H. "Art-as-Such: The Sociology of Modern Aesthetics." *Doing Things with Texts: Essays in Criticism and Critical Theory*. New York: Norton, 1991: 135–158.

Adorno, Theodor. *The Culture Industry: Selected Essays on Mass Culture*. New York: Routledge, 1991.

Allen, R. T. "Mounce and Collingwood on Art and Craft." *British Journal of Aesthetics* 33, no. 2 (1993): 173–175.

Allison, Henry E. *Kant's Theory of Taste: A Reading of the Critique of Aesthetic Judgement*. Cambridge: Cambridge University Press, 2001.

Arnheim, Rudolf. "From Function to Expression." *Journal of Aesthetics and Art Criticism* 23, no. 1 (1964): 29–41.

Arnheim, Rudolf. "Beauty as Suitability." *Journal of Aesthetics and Art Criticism* 54, no. 3 (1996): 251–253.

Atkinson, Paul. "Man in a Briefcase: The Social Construction of the Laptop Computer and the Emergence of a Type Form." *Journal of Design History* 18, no. 2 (2005): 191–205.

Bate, Walter Jackson. *From Classic to Romantic: Premises of Taste in Eighteenth-Century England*. New York: Harper and Brothers, 1946.

Baudrillard, Jean. *The System of Objects*. James Benedict, trans. New York: Verso Books, 2005.

Bayley, Stephen and Terence Conran. *Design: Intelligence Made Visible*. London: Firefly Books, 2007.

Bell, Clive. *Art*. New York: Capricorn Books, 1958.

Bender, John. "General but Defeasible Reasons in Aesthetic Evaluation: The Particularist/Generalist Dispute." *British Journal of Aesthetics* 53, no. 4 (1995): 379–392.

Berleant, Arnold. "Ideas for a Social Aesthetic." *The Aesthetics of Everyday Life.* Andrew Light and Jonathan M. Smith, eds. New York: Columbia University Press, 2005: 23–38.

Blocker, Harry. "Kant's Theory of the Relation of Imagination and Understanding in Aesthetic Judgements of Taste." *British Journal of Aesthetics* 5 (1965): 37–45.

Borgmann, Albert. "The Depth of Design." *Discovering Design: Explorations in Design Studies.* Richard Buchanan and Victor Margolin, eds. Chicago: University of Chicago Press, 1995: 13–22.

Buchanan, Richard. "Wicked Problems in Design Thinking." *The Idea of Design: A Design Issues Reader.* Victor Margolin and Richard Buchanan, eds. Cambridge: MIT Press, 1995: 3–20.

Buchanan, Richard. "Rhetoric, Humanism and Design." Discovering Design: *Explorations in Design Studies.* Richard Buchanan and Victor Margolin, eds. Chicago: University of Chicago Press, 1995: 23–67.

Buchanan, Richard, and Victor Margolin, eds. *The Idea of Design: A Design Issues Reader.* Cambridge: MIT Press, 1995.

Buchanan, Richard, and Victor Margolin. *Discovering Design: Explorations in Design Studies.* Chicago: University of Chicago Press, 1995.

Budd, Malcolm. "Delight in the Natural World: Kant on the Aesthetic Appreciation of Nature, Part I: Natural Beauty." *British Journal of Aesthetics* 38, no. 1 (1998): 1–18.

Budd, Malcolm. "The Pure Judgement of Taste as an Aesthetic Reflective Judgement." *British Journal of Aesthetics* 41, no. 3 (2001): 247–260.

Burns, Steven. "Commentary on Forsey's, 'From Bauhaus to Birkenstocks.'" Canadian Philosophical Association, Annual Congress, Toronto, 2006.

Burke, Edmund. *A Philosophical Enquiry into the Origin of Our Ideas of the Sublime and Beautiful. Eighteenth Century Aesthetics.* Dabney Townsend, ed. Amityville, NY: Baywood, 1998: 249–278.

Carlson, Allen. "Appreciating Art and Appreciating Nature." *Landscape, Natural Beauty and the Arts.* Salim Kemal and Ivan Gaskell, eds. New York: Cambridge University Press, 1993: 199–227.

Carlson, Allen. *Aesthetics and the Environment: The Appreciation of Nature, Art and Architecture.* New York: Routledge, 2000.

Carroll, Nöel. *The Philosophy of Horror.* New York: Routledge, 1990.

Carroll, Nöel. "The Ontology of Mass Art." *British Journal of Aesthetics* 55, no. 2 (1997): 187–199.

Carter, Curtis L. "Industrial Design: On Its Characteristics and Relationships to the Visual Fine Arts." *Leonardo* 14, no. 4 (1981): 283–289.

Cohen, Ted. "Three Problems in Kant's Aesthetics." *British Journal of Aesthetics* 42, no. 1 (2002): 1–12.

Collingwood, R. G. *The Principles of Art.* Oxford: Oxford University Press, 1958.

Crawford, Donald. *Kant's Aesthetic Theory*. Madison: University of Wisconsin Press, 1974.

Crowther, Paul. "The Claims of Perfection: A Revisionary Defence of Kant's Theory of Dependent Beauty." *International Philosophical Quarterly* 26 (1986): 61–74.

Crowther, Paul. "The Significance of Kant's Pure Aesthetic Judgement." *British Journal of Aesthetics* 36, no. 2 (1996): 109–121.

Csikszentmihalyi, Mihaly. "Design and Order in Everyday Life." *The Idea of Design: A Design Issues Reader*. Victor Margolin and Richard Buchanan, eds. Cambridge: MIT Press, 1995: 118–126.

Danto, Arthur. *The Transfiguration of the Commonplace*. Cambridge: Harvard University Press, 1981.

Danto, Arthur. "The Philosophical Disenfranchisement of Art." *The Philosophical Disenfranchisement of Art*. New York: Columbia University Press, 1986: 1–21.

Danto, Arthur. "The End of Art." *The Philosophical Disenfranchisement of Art*. New York: Columbia University Press, 1986: 81–116.

Danto, Arthur. "Indiscernibility and Perception: A Reply to Joseph Margolis." *British Journal of Aesthetics* 39, no. 4 (1999): 321–329.

Darwall, Stephen, Allan Gibbard, and Peter Railton, eds. *Moral Discourse and Practice*. New York: Oxford University Press, 1997.

Davies, Stephen. "Aesthetic Judgements, Artworks and Functional Beauty." *Philosophical Quarterly* 36, no. 23 (2006): 224–241.

De Clerq, Rafael. "The Aesthetic Peculiarities of Multifunctional Artefacts." *British Journal of Aesthetics* 45, no. 4 (2005): 412–425.

Dewey, John. *Art as Experience*. New York: Capricorn Books, 1958.

Dilworth, John. "Artworks versus Designs." *British Journal of Aesthetics* 41, no. 2 (2001): 163–177.

Dowling, Christopher. "The Aesthetics of Daily Life." *British Journal of Aesthetics* 50, no. 3 (2010): 225–242.

Ducasse, Curt J. "The Art of Personal Beauty." *The Philosophy of the Visual Arts*. Philip Alperson, ed. New York: Oxford University Press, 1992: 619–624.

Dutton, Denis. "Kant and the Conditions of Artistic Beauty." *British Journal of Aesthetics* 34, no. 3 (1994): 226–241.

Eaton, Marcia Muelder. "Kantian and Contextual Beauty." *Journal of Aesthetics and Art Criticism* 57, no. 1 (1999): 11–15.

Fethe, Charles. "Craft and Art: A Phenomenological Distinction." *British Journal of Aesthetics* 17 (1977): 129–137.

Fethe, Charles. "Hand and Eye: The Role of Craft in R. G. Collingwood's Aesthetic Theory." *British Journal of Aesthetics* 22 (1982): 37–51.

Flusser, V. *The Shape of Things: A Philosophy of Design*. London: Reaktion Books, 1999.

Forsey, Jane. "Art and Identity: Expanding Narrative Theory." *Philosophy Today* 47, no. 2 (Summer 2003): 176–191.

Forsey, Jane. "The Disenfranchisement of Philosophical Aesthetics." *Journal of the History of Ideas* 64, no. 4 (2003): 581–597.

Forsey, Jane. "Art and Identity: Expanding Narrative Theory." *Philosophy Today* 47, no. 2 (2003): 176–191.

Forsey, Jane. "Metaphor and Symbol in the Interpretation of Art." *Symposium: Canadian Journal of Continental Philosophy* 8, no. 3 (2004): 573–586.

Forsey, Jane. "Is a Coherent Theory of the Sublime Possible?" *Journal of Aesthetics and Art Criticism* 65, no. 4 (2007): 381–390.

Gadamer, Hans-Georg. *Truth and Method.* 2nd ed. Translation revised by Joel Weinsheimer and Donald G. Marshall. New York: Crossroad, 1986.

Galle, Per. "Philosophy of Design: An Editorial Introduction." *Design Studies* 23 (2002): 211–218.

Gaut, Berys. "The Ethical Criticism of Art." *The Philosophy of Literature: Contemporary and Classic Readings*. Eileen John and Dominic McIver Lopes, eds. Oxford: Blackwell, 2004: 355–363.`

Gilman, S. *Making the Body Beautiful: A Cultural History of Aesthetic Surgery.* Princeton, NJ: Princeton University Press, 1999.

Glynn, Simon. "Ways of Knowing: The Creative Process and the Design of Technology." *Journal of Applied Philosophy* 10, no. 2 (1993): 155–163.

Goodman, Nelson. *Languages of Art.* Indianapolis: Hackett, 1976.

Gracyk, Theodore. "Kant's Shifting Debt to British Aesthetics." *British Journal of Aesthetics* 26, no. 3 (1986): 204–217.

Gracyk, Theodore. *Rhythm and Noise: An Aesthetics of Rock.* Durham, NC: Duke University Press, 1996.

Greenough, Horatio. "Form and Function." *The Philosophy of the Visual Arts.* Philip Alperson, ed. New York: Oxford University Press, 1992: 364–367.

Guyer, Paul. *Kant and the Claims of Taste.* 2nd ed. Cambridge: Cambridge University Press, 1997.

Guyer, Paul. "Dependent Beauty Revisited: A Reply to Wicks." *Journal of Aesthetics and Art Criticism* 57, no. 3 (1999): 357–361.

Guyer, Paul. "Free and Dependent Beauty: A Modest Proposal." *British Journal of Aesthetics* 42, no. 4 (2002): 357–366.

Guyer, Paul. "The Cognitive Element in Aesthetic Experience: Reply to Matravers." *British Journal of Aesthetics* 43, no. 4 (2003): 412–418.

Haapala, Arto. "On the Aesthetics of the Everyday: Familiarity, Strangeness, and the Meaning of Place." *The Aesthetics of Everyday Life.* Andrew Light and Jonathan M. Smith, eds. New York: Columbia University Press, 2005: 39–55.

Heidegger, Martin. *Being and Time.* Joan Stambaugh, trans. Albany: SUNY Press, 1996.

Heskett, John. *Toothpicks and Logos: Design in Everyday Life*. New York: Oxford University Press, 2002.

Heskett, John. *Design: A Very Short Introduction*. New York: Oxford University Press, 2002.

Higgins, Kathleen. "Sweet Kitsch." *The Philosophy of the Visual Arts*. Philip Alperson, ed. New York: Oxford University Press, 1992: 568–581.

Hirsch, E. D., Jr. "What Isn't Literature?" *The Philosophy of Literature: Contemporary and Classical Readings*. Eileen John and Dominic McIver Lopes, eds. London: Blackwell, 2004: 46–51.

Hogarth, William. *An Analysis of Beauty, Written with a View of Fixing the Fluctuating Ideas of Taste*. *Eighteenth Century Aesthetics*. Dabney Townsend, ed. Amityville, NY: Baywood, 1999: 209–226.

Houkes, Wybo, and Pieter Vermaas. "Actions vs. Functions: A Plea for an Alternative Metaphysics of Artifacts." *Monist* 87, no. 1 (2004): 52–71.

Hume, David. *An Enquiry Concerning Human Understanding*. Indianapolis: Hackett, 1993.

Hume, David. "Of the Standard of Taste." *Eighteenth Century Aesthetics*. Dabney Townsend, ed. Amityville, NY: Baywood, 1999: 230–247.

Irvin, Sherri. "The Pervasiveness of the Aesthetic in Ordinary Experience." *British Journal of Aesthetics* 48, no. 1 (2008): 29–44.

Kant, Immanuel. *Foundations of the Metaphysics of Morals*. Lewis White Beck, trans. New York: Bobbs-Merrill, 1959.

Kant, Immanuel. *Critique of Pure Reason*. Norman Kemp Smith, trans. London: St. Martin's Press, 1965.

Kant, Immanuel. *Critique of Judgement*. J. H. Bernard, trans. New York: Hafner, 1972.

Kant, Immanuel. *Kritik der Urteilskraft*. Willhelm Weischedel, ed. Frankfurt am Main: Suhrkamp, 1974.

Kavanagh, Robert. "Collingwood: Aesthetics and a Theory of Craft." *International Studies in Philosophy* 23, no. 3 (1991): 13–26.

Kemal, Salim. *Kant and Fine Art*. Oxford: Clarendon Press, 1986.

Kemal, Salim. *Kant's Aesthetic Theory*. London: St. Martin's Press, 1992.

Kirwan, James. "The Usefulness of Kant's Distinction between Free and Dependent Beauty." *Journal of the Faculty of Letters* (University of Tokyo) 25 (2000): 49–60.

Kivy, Peter. *The Corded Shell: Reflections on Musical Expression*. Princeton, NJ: Princeton University Press, 1980.

Kivy, Peter. *Philosophies of the Arts: An Essay in Differences*. New Haven: Yale University Press, 1997.

Korsmeyer, Carolyn, ed. *The Taste Culture Reader: Experiencing Food and Drink*. New York: Palgrave, 2005.

Krippendorff, Klaus. "On the Essential Contexts of Artifacts or on the Proposition That 'Design is Making Sense (of Things).'" *The Idea of Design: A Design Issues Reader.* Victor Margolin and Richard Buchanan, eds. Cambridge: MIT Press, 1995: 156–184.

Kristeller, Paul Oskar. "The Modern System of the Arts: A Study in the History of Aesthetics (I)." *Journal of the History of Ideas* 12, no. 4 (1951): 135–158.

Kristeller, Paul Oskar. "The Modern System of the Arts: A Study in the History of Aesthetics (II)." *Journal of the History of Ideas* 13, no. 1 (1952): 17–46.

Kuehn, Glenn. "How Can Food Be Art?" *The Aesthetics of Everyday Life.* Andrew Light and Jonathan M. Smith, eds. New York: Columbia University Press, 2005: 194–212.

Kupfer, Joseph H. *Experience as Art: Aesthetics in Everyday Life.* Albany: State University of New York Press, 1983.

Langer, Suzanne. *Feeling and Form.* London: Routledge, 1953.

Leddy, Thomas. "Everyday Surface Aesthetic Qualities: 'Neat,' 'Messy,' 'Clean,' 'Dirty.'" *Journal of Aesthetics and Art Criticism* 53, no. 3 (1995): 259–68.

Leddy, Thomas. "Sparkle and Shine." *British Journal of Aesthetics* 37, no. 3 (1997): 259–73.

Leddy, Thomas. "The Nature of Everyday Aesthetics." *The Aesthetics of Everyday Life.* Andrew Light and Jonathan M. Smith, eds. New York: Columbia University Press, 2005: 3–22.

Lees-Maffei, Grace, and Lina Sandino. "Dangerous Liasons: Relationships between Design, Craft and Art." *Journal of Design History* 17, no. 3 (2004): 207–219.

Light, Andrew, and Jonathan M. Smith, eds. *The Aesthetics of Everyday Life.* New York: Columbia University Press, 2005.

Locke, John. *An Essay Concerning Human Understanding.* Oxford: Clarendon Press, 1975.

Lorand, Ruth. "Free and Dependent Beauty: A Puzzling Issue." *British Journal of Aesthetics* 29, no. 1 (1989): 32–40.

Lorand, Ruth. "On 'Free and Dependent Beauty'—a Rejoinder." *British Journal of Aesthetics* 32, no. 3 (1992): 250–253.

Lorand, Ruth. "The Purity of Aesthetic Value." *Journal of Aesthetics and Art Criticism* 50, no. 1 (1992): 13–21.

Lorand, Ruth. "In Defense of Beauty." *American Society for Aesthetics Newsletter* 26, no. 3 (2006): 1–3.

Lord, Catherine. "A Note on Ruth Lorand's 'Free and Dependent Beauty: A Puzzling Issue.'" *British Journal of Aesthetics* 31, no. 2 (1991): 167–168.

Mackie, J. L. *Ethics: Inventing Right and Wrong.* Harmondsworth: Penguin, 1977.

Maldonado, Tomás. "The Idea of Comfort." *The Idea of Design: A Design Issues Reader.* Victor Margolin and Richard Buchanan, eds. Cambridge: MIT Press, 1995: 248–256.

Mallaband, Philip. "Understanding Kant's Distinction between Free and Dependent Beauty." *Philosophical Quarterly* 52, no. 206 (2002): 66–81.

Manzini, Ezio. "Prometheus of the Everyday: The Ecology of the Artificial and the Designer's Responsibility." *Discovering Design: Explorations in Design Studies*. Richard Buchanan and Victor Margolin, eds. Chicago: University of Chicago Press, 1995: 219–243.

Margolin, Victor, ed. *Design Discourse: History, Theory, Criticism*. Chicago: University of Chicago Press, 1984.

Margolin, Victor. "The Product Milieu and Social Action." *Discovering Design: Explorations in Design Studies*. Richard Buchanan and Victor Margolin, eds. Chicago: University of Chicago Press, 1995: 121–145.

Margolin, Victor. "A World of History of Design and the History of the World." *Journal of Design History* 18, no. 3 (2005): 235–243.

Margolis, Joseph. *What, after All, Is a Work of Art?* University Park: Pennsylvania State University Press, 2009.

Markowitz, Sally J. "The Distinction between Art and Craft." *Journal of Aesthetic Education* 28, no. 1 (1994): 55–70.

Matravers, Derek. "Aesthetic Concepts and Aesthetic Experiences." *British Journal of Aesthetics* 36, no. 3 (1996): 265–277.

Matravers, Derek. "The Aesthetic Experience." *British Journal of Aesthetics* 43, no. 2 (2003): 158–174.

McAdoo, Nick. "Kant and the Problem of Dependent Beauty." *Kant-Studien* 93, no. 4 (2002): 444–452.

McCracken, Janet. "The Domestic Perspective." *Aesthetics in Perspective*. Kathleen M. Higgins, ed. Belmont, CA: Wadsworth, 1996: 634–638.

McCracken, Janet. *Taste and the Household: The Domestic Aesthetics and Moral Reasoning*. Albany: State University of New York Press, 2001.

McDowell, John. "Aesthetic Value, Objectivity, and the Fabric of the World." *Pleasure Preference and Value: Studies in Philosophical Aesthetics*. Eva Schaper, ed. New York: Cambridge University Press, 1987: 1–16.

McDowell, John. "Values and Secondary Qualities." *Moral Discourse and Practice*. Stephen Darwall, Allan Gibbard, and Peter Railton, eds. New York: Oxford University Press, 1997: 201–214.

McDowell, John. "Are Moral Requirements Hypothetical Imperatives?" *Mind, Value and Reality*. Cambridge: Harvard University Press, 1998: 77–94.

McNaughton, David. *Moral Vision: An Introduction to Ethics*. London: Blackwell, 1988.

Miall, David S. "Kant's Critique of Judgement: A Biased Aesthetics." *British Journal of Aesthetics* 20, no. 2 (1980): 135–145.

Mitcham, Carl. "Ethics into Design." *Discovering Design: Explorations in Design Studies*. Richard Buchanan and Victor Margolin, eds. Chicago: University of Chicago Press, 1995: 173–189.

Morello, Augusto. "Discovering Design Means [Re-]Discovering Users and Products." *Discovering Design: Explorations in Design Studies.* Richard Buchanan and Victor Margolin, eds. Chicago: University of Chicago Press, 1995: 69–76.

Morris, William. *Selected Writings and Designs.* Asa Briggs, ed. London: Penguin, 1962.

Mothersill, Mary. *Beauty Restored.* New York: Oxford University Press, 1984.

Mounce, H. O. "Art and Craft." *British Journal of Aesthetics* 31, no. 3 (1991): 230–241.

Naylor, Gillian. *The Arts and Crafts Movement: A Study of Its Sources Ideals and Influence on Design Theory.* Cambridge: MIT Press, 1971.

Norman, Donald A. *The Design of Everyday Things.* New York: Basic Books, 1988.

Norman, Donald A. *Emotional Design: Why We Love (or Hate) Everyday Things.* New York: Basic Books, 2004.

Nussbaum, Martha C. *Love's Knowledge: Essays on Philosophy and Literature.* New York: Oxford University Press, 1990.

Nuyen, A. T. "The Kantian Theory of Metaphor." *Philosophy and Rhetoric* 22 (1989): 95–109.

Papanek, Victor. *Design for the Real World: Human Ecology and Social Change.* New York: Pantheon, 1971.

Parsons, Glenn. "Natural Functions and the Aesthetic Appreciation of Inorganic Nature." *British Journal of Aesthetics* 44, no. 1 (2004): 44–56.

Parsons, Glenn, and Allen Carlson. *Functional Beauty.* New York: Oxford University Press, 2008.

Pevsner, Nikolaus. *Pioneers of Modern Design: From William Morris to Walter Gropius.* New York: Penguin, 1960.

Pillow, Kirk. "Jupiter's Eagle and the Despot's Handmill: Two Views on Metaphor in Kant." *Journal of Aesthetics and Art Criticism* 59, no. 2 (2001): 193–209.

Pye, David. *The Nature and Aesthetics of Design.* New York: Van Nostrand Reinhold, 1978.

Rams, Dieter. "Omit the Unimportant." *Design Discourse: History, Theory, Criticism.* Victor Margolin, ed. Chicago: Chicago University Press, 1984: 111–114.

Rockmore, Tom. "Interpretation as Historical, Constructivism, and History." *Metaphilosophy* 31, 1–2 (2000): 184–199.

Rosenstein, Leon. "The Aesthetic of the Antique." *Journal of Aesthetics and Art Criticism* 45, no. 4 (1987): 393–402.

Ross, Stephen David, ed. *Art and its Significance.* Albany: State University of New York Press, 1994.

Ross, W. D. *The Right and the Good.* Oxford: Clarendon Press, 1930.

Saito, Yuriko. "Everyday Aesthetics." *Philosophy and Literature* 25, no. 1 (2001): 87–95.

Saito, Yuriko. *Everyday Aesthetics*. New York: Oxford University Press, 2007.

Sandino, Linda. "Here Today, Gone Tomorrow: Transient Materiality in Contemporary Cultural Artefacts." *Journal of Design History* 17, no. 3 (2004): 283–293.

Sandrisser, Barbara. "On Elegance in Japan." *Aesthetics in Perspective*. Kathleen M. Higgins, ed. Belmont, CA: Wadsworth, 1996: 628–633.

Sartwell, Crispin. "Aesthetics of the Everyday." *Oxford Handbook of Aesthetics*. Jerrold Levinson, ed. New York: Oxford University Press, 2003: 761–770.

Savile, Anthony. "Architecture, Formalism and the Sense of Self." *Virtue and Taste: Essays on Politics, Ethics and Aesthetics*. Dudley Knowles and John Skorupski, eds. Oxford: Blackwell, 1993: 124–143.

Scarre, Geoffrey. "Kant on Free and Dependent Beauty." *British Journal of Aesthetics* 21 (1981): 351–362.

Schaper, Eva. "Free and Dependent Beauty." *Studies in Kant's Aesthetics*. Edinburgh: Edinburgh University Press, 1979: 78–98.

Schaper, Eva. "The Pleasures of Taste." *Pleasure, Preference and Value*. Eva Schaper, ed. New York: Cambridge University Press, 1987: 39–56.

Schaper, Eva, ed. *Pleasure, Preference and Value*. New York: Cambridge University Press, 1987.

Scott, Robert Gillam. *Design Fundamentals*. New York: McGraw-Hill, 1951.

Scruton, Roger. "The Aesthetic Endeavour Today." *Philosophy* 71 (1996): 331–350.

Scruton, Roger. "Modern Philosophy and the Neglect of Aesthetics." *Philosopher on Dover Beach*. South Bend, IN: St. Augustine's Press, 1998: 98–112.

Scruton, Roger. "In Search of the Aesthetic." *British Journal of Aesthetics* 47, no. 3 (2007): 232–250.

Sebald, W. G. *Austerlitz*. New York: Modern Library, 2001.

Selle, Gert. "Untimely Opinions (an Attempt to Reflect on Design)." *The Idea of Design: A Design Issues Reader*. Victor Margolin and Richard Buchanan, eds. Cambridge: MIT Press, 1995: 238–247.

Sibley, Frank. "Aesthetic Concepts." *Philosophical Review* 68, no. 4 (1959): 421–450.

Sibley, Frank. "Aesthetic and Nonaesthetic." *Philosophical Review* 74, no. 2 (1965): 135–159.

Slade, Giles. *Made to Break: Technology and Obsolescence in America*. Cambridge: Harvard University Press, 2006.

Smith, Norman Kemp. *Commentary to Kant's "Critique of Pure Reason."* Amherst, NY: Humanity Books, 1923.

Spark, Penny. *An Introduction to Design and Culture in the 20th Century*. London: Allen and Unwin, 1986.

Stecker, Robert. "Free Beauty, Dependent Beauty, and Art." *Journal of Aesthetic Education* 21, no. 1 (1987): 89–99.

Stecker, Robert. "Lorand and Kant on Free and Dependent Beauty." *British Journal of Aesthetics* 30, no. 1 (1990): 71–74.

Sturken, Marita, and Lisa Cartwright. *Practices of Looking: An Introduction to Visual Culture*. New York: Oxford University Press, 2001.

Thomasson, Amie L. "The Ontology of Art and Knowledge in Aesthetics." *Journal of Aesthetics and Art Criticism* 63, no. 3 (2005): 221–229.

Tolstoy, Leo. *What Is Art? Art and Its Significance*. Stephen David Ross, ed. Albany: State University of New York Press, 1994: 177–181.

Townsend, Dabney, ed. *Eighteenth Century Aesthetics*. Amityville, NY: Baywood, 1999.

Townsend, Dabney. "Cohen on Kant's Aesthetic Judgements." *British Journal of Aesthetics* 43, no. 1 (2003): 75–79.

Trott, Elizabeth. "Permanence, Change and Standards of Excellence in Design." *Design Studies* 23 (2002), 321–331.

Trott, Elizabeth. "Revealing Being through Good Design." *Maritain Studies* 19 (2003): 62–70.

Truax, John. "The Philosophy of Craft: An Idea Whose Time Has Come." *Philosophy of Education: Proceedings of the Annual Meeting of the Philosophy of Education Society* 41 (1985): 141–151.

Tyler, Ann C. "Shaping Belief: The Role of Audience in Visual Communication." *The Idea of Design: A Design Issues Reader*. Victor Margolin and Richard Buchanan, eds. Cambridge: MIT Press, 1995: 104–112.

Verbeek, Peter-Paul. *What Things Do: Philosophical Reflections on Technology, Agency and Design*. University Park: Pennsylvania State University Press, 2005.

Verhaegh, Marcus. "The Truth of the Beautiful in the Critique of Judgement." *British Journal of Aesthetics* 41, no. 4 (2001): 371–394.

Weitz, Morris. "The Role of Theory in Aesthetics." *Aesthetics: Classic Readings Form the Western Tradition*. 2nd ed. Dabney Townsend, ed. Belmont, CA: Wadsworth, 2001: 298–306.

Wicks, Robert. "Dependent Beauty as the Appreciation of Teleological Style." *Journal of Aesthetics and Art Criticism* 55, no. 4 (1997): 387–400.

Wicks, Robert. "Can Tattooed Faces Be Beautiful? Limits on the Restriction of Forms in Dependent Beauty." *Journal of Aesthetics and Art Criticism* 57, no. 3 (1999): 361–363.

Wilde, Oscar. "Preface." *The Picture of Dorian Gray. The Norton Anthology of English Literature*. 2 vols. New York: Norton, 1968: II, 1403.

Wittgenstein, Ludwig. *Philosophical Investigations*. G. E. M. Anscombe, ed. London: Wiley-Blackwell, 1991.

Zaccai, Gianfranco. "Art and Technology: Aesthetics Redefined." *Discovering Design: Explorations in Design Studies*. Richard Buchanan and Victor Margolin, eds. Chicago: University of Chicago Press, 1995: 3–12.

Zangwill, Nick. "Kant on Pleasure in the Agreeable." *Journal of Aesthetics and Art Criticism* 53, no. 2 (1995): 167–176.

Zangwill, Nick. "The Beautiful, the Dainty and the Dumpy." *British Journal of Aesthetics* 35, no. 4 (1995): 317–329.

Zangwill, Nick-. "Aesthetic/Sensory Dependence." *British Journal of Aesthetics* 38, no. 1 (1998): 66–81.

Zangwill, Nick. "Feasible Aesthetic Formalism." *Noûs* 33, no. 4 (1999): 610–629.

Zangwill, Nick. "Skin Deep or in the Eye of the Beholder? The Metaphysics of Aesthetic and Sensory Properties." *Philosophy and Phenomenological Research* 61, no. 3 (2000): 595–618.

Zangwill, Nick. *The Metaphysics of Beauty*. Ithaca: Cornell University Press, 2001.

Zangwill, Nick. "Are There Counterexamples to Aesthetic Theories of Art?" *Journal of Aesthetics and Art Criticism* 60, no. 2 (2002): 111–118.

Zangwill, Nick. "In Defense of Extreme Formalism about Inorganic Nature: Reply to Parsons." *British Journal of Aesthetics* 45, no. 2 (2005): 185–191.

Zangwill, Nick. "Aesthetic Judgement." *Stanford Encyclopedia of Philosophy*. Edward N. Zalta, ed. Fall 2010 edition. http://plato.stanford.edu/archives/fall2010/entries/aesthetic-judgment/.

Zemach, Eddy. "Thirteen Ways of Looking at the Ethics-Aesthetics Parallelism." *Journal of Aesthetics and Art Criticism* 29, no. 3 (1971): 391–398.

Zemach, Eddy. *Real Beauty*. University Park: Pennsylvania State University Press, 1997.

Zuidervaart, Lambert. "The Artefactuality of Autonomous Art: Kant and Adorno." *The Reasons of Art*. Peter J. McCormick, ed. Ottawa: University of Ottawa Press, 1985: 252–262.

INDEX